SUSPENDED SENTENCE

SUSPENDED SENTENCE

When my son is arrested for possession
of a stolen firearm and drug charges,
I start to realize that he isn't the only
one who has recovery work to do

A MEMOIR

JANICE MORGAN

SHE WRITES PRESS

Published October 2019
Printed in the United States of America
Print ISBN: 978-1-63152-644-2
E-ISBN: 978-1-63152-645-9
Library of Congress Control Number: 2019912711

For information, address:
She Writes Press
1569 Solano Ave #546
Berkeley, CA 94707

Interior design by Tabitha Lahr
Interior sketches by James Secor

She Writes Press is a division of SparkPoint Studio, LLC.

AUTHOR'S NOTE

The characters in this story are based on real people and events; however most actual names of individuals as well as names of local towns and places have been changed to protect privacy. Much of the story has been reconstructed from journal notes I wrote during the time events were actually occurring, while the backstory was composed later from fragments of my remembered experience.

CONTENTS

In memory of my parents,
and my brother

And for my son

*Out beyond ideas of wrongdoing
and rightdoing, there is a field.*

I'll meet you there.

—Rumi

CHAPTER 1: THE BOY

A t this time of year, the sunlight falls at a lower slant into the living room in broad swaths of gold. When that happens, the sun sends shadows of the tulip poplar leaves outside to dance inside on the brightness of the wood floor. These are always a signal of time passing: changing leaves, crickets singing at night in the tall grasses, dry wood smoke—memories.

The shifting light sends me back to my photo album, searching for the three photos of my son at eleven years old. I think back to that summer afternoon in '99.

Somewhere during those first couple of years of being a divorced single parent, I remember thinking, "Look at your son. He's going to change soon, become a whole different person. He'll suddenly grow tall, his face will change, his voice will deepen, hair will grow. In no time at all, you'll barely recognize him." I was thinking of other friends' kids, young persons I had known for years and then didn't see for a while before suddenly catching sight of them at the bank or at an event in town. They'd be standing with their parents as tall, totally transformed teenagers, persons who held only a faint resemblance to the children I had so easily recognized before through their years of steadily inching upward. Then, seemingly overnight, the slowly munching caterpillar turned into this new, winged creature who was returning my gaze from new heights. It would happen to my son, too. By age eighteen, the unimaginable would have taken place. That's why I would sometimes steal a watchful look at him at dinner, noticing his child's cheeks, round and pink from the sun, his throat encircled by a macramé necklace, the skin so fine it looked like a girl's, his eyes—those long lashes. Well, the lashes might stay, but the rest, it was going to change for sure. I just didn't know how yet.

I page through the album to look at other photos from this time in Dylan's life. There are photos of him negotiating curves and waves on the BMX track. Then, after the race, standing tall with his trophies. There are photos of Dylan taking summer trips with his dad somewhere in a deep forest, Dylan crossing a log high above a creek. Photos of Dylan in his new clothes from Grandpa and Grandma, practicing tricks with a brightly colored yo-yo before showing them to a crowd. These were all photo ops; he was performing. But it was around that same time that I felt it was important to capture my son at a "before" moment, when he was still a child. I wanted to hold on to those moments. One day, rather than choosing a particular event to record like a photojournalist, I tried something different.

I kept my camera undercover. Then, as my son twirled around in our living room at a time when we weren't doing anything in particular, I quickly took three candid shots. For once, he's not flashing a goofy smile or taking up his "look at me" bravura pose. Instead, his gaze is averted. He's looking at something else across the room, maybe something that's not even there. The photos catch him somewhere in mid-daydream flight. In the third shot, he's looking down pensively, his head tilted, almost as if in question. It must have been summer. He's wearing a t-shirt that's a bit big on him, and his hair is moist from sweat on his forehead. Probably he's just come in from outside. I remember the heat of his compact body, his torpedo rushes of energy and emotion, the stories he would tell.

These are the three photos I stare at now, trying to go back in time. I wonder what he was seeing then. I study his face, so different from the face of the young man he is now. Isn't there a hint of loneliness I didn't notice at the time? Something I missed? And there I was all the while, so confident he was an open book, telling me everything. Of course, he did tell me most of what he knew when he was eleven years old. I believed then that he and I were going to traverse the realm of teen years together. We would cross the threshold into his adulthood side by side like other parents and their kids: ball games, trips, vacations, diplomas, proms, plans. Now, though, I wonder about all the things he didn't tell me. Would I have been open to hear them if he had? There would have been much he couldn't even put into words yet. Just as neither of us knew how, exactly, the terrain would change ahead of us. That boy is gone now, but I want so much to be able to go back and find him: to see him again, talk to him. Even just for those hours and days. And I wonder what I could have done differently.

CHAPTER 2: BOMBSHELL

When I hung up the phone, I knew I had to get my hands on today's newspaper. I pulled on my jacket and walked up to the local Walgreens. As soon as I got there, I could see where they were, right next to the checkout counter. I glanced at the date, June 16, 2011, and the large front-page photo. A young blonde was placing a rhinestone tiara on the local county fair queen. Nope, that wasn't what I was looking for, but the date was right and I knew there would be another story inside. Allison Marie had just called to tell me so. Rather than just dive on the paper and rifle through the pages, I thought it would be better to maintain some everyday nonchalance. I drifted into the cosmetics racks, scanning rainbow rows of nail polish. I decided on one and made my way casually to the counter, remembering—as if at the last moment—to pick up a newspaper to add to my total. I tucked the bag under my arm and strode home quickly to read the bad news in private.

Spreading out the newspaper to its full size, I immediately found the article I was looking for. It was on the front page after all, just lower down. "CPD charge man with cultivation," the title read, with a color photo of flourishing marijuana plants being grown in a large indoor planter box. The story continued on the next page, along with a mug shot of the young man in question, his last name under the shot along with his age, twenty-three. He had been arrested a few days earlier on a tip from an acquaintance that he'd been waving a gun around while drinking at their apartment. Then he'd fired it upwards on a whim when friends dropped him off in his apartment's parking lot. He was later charged with wanton endangerment and possessing a stolen firearm. Several days later, the police came with a warrant to search his apartment for another gun they suspected he had but didn't find. However, they did discover the illegal plants growing behind one of the walls. This story would be only vaguely curious to me if I had just happened to stumble across it, if someone else were the subject of the story. But this was excruciating. The guy in the mug shot was my son.

Of course, since the night he was arrested, I had already learned all the information conveyed by the paper. When I found out about the firearm, I was horrified. My son with a gun! No one in my family used firearms. When Blaine, the apartment manager, told me about the police coming to search the apartment, he said I might want to be there, so I was, waiting in the dark parking lot while several officers tromped upstairs and spent considerable time rummaging around. When they finally came down, each one had an armload of planter boxes and leafy plants to be loaded into a truck. Yep, it was a clandestine marijuana installation, that's what they called it. The rest I could read in the newspaper or find out in court.

Way beyond the cold facts, what the phone call from Allison Marie drove home for me (and what the newspaper article made crystal clear) was that my son and my family were all out there in the wind now, exposed. My son was a criminal. He was in jail on felony charges. He'd had infractions before, but nothing this bad. By extension, we were all scandalous social outcasts—or so I felt. This was not supposed to happen to mild-mannered, liberal-arts-college-professor parents, even if they were divorced like I was. Especially not if you were a college professor living in a small, conservative town in west Kentucky that takes pride in strong family values and community spirit. By all rights, my kid should have straight A's, be on the honor roll, and maybe even be one of those young princes in a tuxedo dancing with the tiara-crowned princesses. But no, here it was in black and white. My son had definitely set himself into the renegade category of society, and now with this latest episode, it was all out there, with me plunged knee-deep right into the mess as his mom.

Closing the newspaper pages, my cheeks were burning. I felt scorched by the shame of it. I heard Rev. Allison Marie's voice over the phone again: "It's always that way in a small town. And everybody's going to be talking about it." She had spoken to me for a long while in her calm, reassuring voice. She was the co-vicar, along with her husband Rev. Patrick, at the local Episcopalian church, St. Alban the Martyr, and she wanted me to know others had gone through this and survived. I would make it; I had support, she said. But today I wasn't so sure. How could I sustain such a massive breach of my security? Any cover I ever had was blown. The wildcat was out of the bag, the unruly horse miles away from the barn. This was no minor infraction, nothing you could patch up quickly and move on. Fortunately, it was summer, so I didn't have to prepare classes. But was there no cave I could hide in for a while? Mammoth Caves weren't too far away, and I had never visited them. Or how about a quick trip to the West Coast to visit Uncle Albert, just until the storm blew over? Of course, even as I was fantasizing about this, I knew I'd have to stay right here in Croftburg; there would be a lot to do to follow this through. But just allowing myself to think of a possible escape far, far away helped me get through the day. Allison Marie had told me to come over if I felt like it. We could sit on their deck in the evening sometime and chat, an offer I was sure to take up soon.

Meanwhile, the reactions from others didn't prove to be nearly as painful as I feared. During the week, only a few of my colleagues ever mentioned it. They would wait for a private moment, then let me know they had read the article, waiting for me to respond, to see what my reaction was or if I had a story. I would sigh, shrug, and shake my head. That was my only official statement for the moment. I felt their concern; they respected my silence. One or two told me in hushed tones about a court case that their cousin, a nephew, or their daughter had to face—but their tales weren't anything as serious as this. Not three felony charges all at once! No, I kept the lid down tight on the firestorm inside.

CHAPTER 3: TIME OUT

The next day dawned cool and sunny. Normally, I would have noticed the beauty of such a morning, but recent events had disabled all my beauty sensors. For a while now, I'd noticed this pattern. Whenever I woke up after a life-altering incident, there would be a split-second of benign, sheltering fog, then—like a thunder clap—the new reality would strike me.

You've just broken up with your boyfriend!

Your marriage is over!

Your son is in jail!

That's when I'd realize that I must have actually fallen asleep, finally, the night before . . . but now I was awake. A deep dread would set in. My stomach would start to churn like the back end of a garbage truck. Still, I'd go downstairs and prepare breakfast mechanically. It's not that I was actually hungry, but I had to keep a ritualized schedule for myself, go through the motions. Pretend it was going to be some kind of a normal day. Most of all, drink strong coffee and get my bearings.

Mid-June already. More than high time to get the garden in. I'd been putting it off now for a few weeks. First there had been the press of final exams to make up and grade, then the trip to Boston. Then, just when I should have been easing into a more relaxed summer work pattern . . . nope, I fell into full catastrophe mode. I was sad, angry, confused. *My son just ruined his life! How will he ever get through college now? How will he have a career?* Well, I couldn't just sit and stew about it. Time to head for my community garden plot.

I'm a true garden warrior. Gardening is in my blood because my parents and grandparents were gardeners. Just about everything I know about working with dirt, seed, and plants I learned as a little kid, playing alongside them while they toiled under clear Minnesota skies. My mom was from Blue Earth county, and trust me, people in her generation knew a thing or two about how to grow things in that rich black soil. Before setting off, like them, I have a whole ritual I observe: special clothes, special tools. After donning my old jeans with multiple pockets, armed with my hoe, rake, and spade, I feel like Roland at Roncevaux, mounting his horse with his sword, Durendal, by his side. The steel blade has a special name because it's one of his best friends. That's the way I set off for the garden.

I knew my principal aim was to get the soil in shape. I set down my basket alongside the tools and put on my battered, leather garden gloves. It was going to be a *mano a terra* combat. I gazed at the garden plot, not without some dismay. If I had done this earlier, right after our chief garden organizer had done the tilling, my job would be much easier. Since then, there had been a rain or two, and some grasses and weeds were cropping up. I would have to get rid of those with the hoe, then use it—or maybe even the spade—to break up the heavy clay soil again into smaller chunks. I knew the ideal was to get the soil fine and almost siftable, like flour for making bread. The finer the soil, the easier for tiny roots to grow into. Hum, we'll see about that; at least the clay was reasonably dry by then. That was one good thing. And it wasn't too hot yet. That was another.

From the edge of the plot, I set to work with the pronged hoe, hoping that would be enough to dislodge the small clumps of new grass poking up. As I got into a rhythm of turning the soil, my thoughts and worries churned right alongside. I'd known the whole month of May, right after the final push of the semester was over, that Dylan might have trouble adjusting, might go off-track—only not this far! With him, I'd learned that supposedly quiet, slow times could be downright treacherous. So when he'd say "Everything's cool, Mom," that's when I needed to prick up my ears for trouble coming over the horizon. When he didn't have to worry, that's when I had to do overtime.

Why hadn't Dylan gotten a summer job right away like we talked about? That was the plan, and it seemed easy enough. But no, instead, right after finals, this guy Keith Birchen shows up, a visit by an "old friend" from Cincinnati. I should have smelled that rat from day one. Instead, gullible Mom, I thought at first: "Oh, this will make a nice change. Give Dylan some needed companionship. He's feeling so isolated. Having a friend here will give him a boost." Yeah, it was a boost, all right. A boost that landed him in the county jail.

I felt betrayed. My heart burned with the pain of it. Why did I ever try to persuade Dylan he should come here to continue his undergrad education? Wasn't that just asking for trouble? As long as he was out there, somewhere, I could field the curve balls as they were thrown to me, but I would have my home and my job to return to as refuge. Now, with him right here in town, I had no refuge at all.

I'd persuaded him to come here because I thought this place could help him. Instead of being caught up in fast-paced Cincinnati, he'd be back in the small, friendly town where he grew up. He'd be enrolled at a smaller college that took pride in nurturing students and push/pulling them through the hoops required of an undergraduate degree. And I was a faculty member there, chair of a small department. Yet even here, in this protected spot, and despite his presumed best intentions, there had been incidents. A DUI, for example. And him telling me beforehand that he thought it was unfair that he didn't have a car. OK, so what about when he DID have a car? Two different ones over the years: an ancient white Camry that I gave him for free, and after that a black Camry that we researched, found, and bought together with his dad while Dylan was a student at the University of Cincinnati. And that was a couple of years ago when all he had were simple traffic tickets. Now, back here in Croftburg, he'd gotten another DUI driving *my* car to do an errand, or so he said. I found out later he'd used it to get beer, then drove while he was drinking to de-stress. Sure, he could handle it. *No, you can't! Guess what, NO MORE CARS for you, buddy! Go take a walk!*

And now, having transferred here and managing to get through two semesters, he pulls this stunt. And it wasn't like all the other careless, stupid things he'd done in the past. No, this was a pre-meditated plan—at least the illegal marijuana-growing part was. I should have left him right where he'd been in Cincinnati. He could have continued his downhill trajectory there. If he was so hell-bent on destruction, he could have gotten locked up there instead of here where I live. What an idiot I'd been! Was there no end to this madness?

I was working up a sweat and a rage. Toiling away in the bare garden plot, I could feel the sweat running down into my collar. Every time I came upon a new clump of grass starting to grow, I'd have to claw at it with the hoe; the roots were amazingly tenacious. No wonder I was getting a workout. Soon, I arched back in a full torso stretch and removed my long-sleeved shirt down to the tee underneath. For a moment, I felt a lingering cool breeze on my face and neck. It felt good. Before tying the shirt around my waist, I used it to dry my forehead and the sides of my face, my neck. The sun was climbing higher. I looked at the soil I'd been working on. I was making some progress; the offending clumps of grass were strewn on the sides of the plot like flotsam and jetsam on either side of a boat.

No, more like all my best mom plans from the past now dug up and cast aside. I took a few sips of water, then picked up the hoe again.

And then the whole circus of Keith Birchen's impromptu visit. A blast from the past. And me trying to think it was probably OK. No, it wasn't. It really wasn't. When dealing with my son's bipolar disorder and the potential for disarray it can cause, I always worry. So then I don't know when I *need* to worry and when I don't. Don't know how to handle it. So, for example, before I left town, I met with Dylan at his apartment and he assured me that Keith was leaving in a couple of days. After that, of course, he would look for a summer job. I told him where I was going and when I'd be back. When Dylan introduced his friend to me, Keith smiled, chatted for a bit, and gamely shook my hand, while assuring me, "Don't worry. I'll take care of your boy." How could I be so naïve? But then, how much control did I really have?

My partner John and I then took off on our trip. Was I not entitled to a vacation like every other working person I know back at the office? It seemed that everything was fine. At least until our plane landed in Boston. Then my phone rang.

Dylan's voice on the other end sounded flat. "I'm feeling depressed," he said. "I think I need to go to St. Clair."

This was the psychiatric clinic I had taken him to late last fall, when he'd had a crisis and needed to be checked in to stabilize for a few days. As we talked, I tried to find out more about what was going on, but the only clear message Dylan came out with was, "I don't have any more money." I reminded him about looking for a job. He said it would be OK. He could borrow some cash from Keith to get by. Our connection in the noisy airport wasn't very good, so I told him I'd call him back later and we could talk more.

But later when I called, there was no answer. By then we were at John's brother's house. In this more relaxed atmosphere, I could have gotten a better sense of what was going on. But my son didn't answer, and he didn't call back. Not that day or the day after. It didn't surprise me because there had been many tempests in teapots before, a crisis where the sky was falling and then, just when I was ready to call in the first responders, suddenly everything was fine again. That was a pattern. And so I figured it would be like all the other times; Dylan would muddle through. Besides, he was with a friend who had a car. If Dylan really needed to go to the clinic, they could go. I was concerned, but it seemed too extreme to drop everything and fly back.

Yes, Keith had a car all right. He also had a gun, an illegal one that had been stolen. In addition to a firearm, there was plenty of firewater around—another thing I didn't know. About twenty empty bottles of vodka were all lined up on the floor around the main room of the apartment. I saw all this when I eventually entered it with a key to get Dylan's meds for him after he called from jail. I was surprised they allowed me to do this, but they did. Just looking around at the tumbled decor, the med bottles in disarray on the kitchen cupboard shelf and on the counter, barely a scrap of food in the refrigerator, a picture emerged for me of what must have gone on there. The story behind the scene got filled in by what the apartment manager, Blaine, told me later. He was a vet who went to AA meetings on his motorcycle and lived quietly in the apartment below with his girlfriend and their child. After talking with him, I could only surmise glumly that with all the goings-on upstairs, those two guys could have been apprehended by the authorities at any time during the two weeks Keith was visiting. The truly amazing thing is that they both survived, and neither of them was shot!

My back and arms were getting sore from the constant heaving and turning of the soil. I had to lean back again, pause, catch my breath. I could feel my heart pounding, feel a dry rasp in my throat. Time to reach for the water bottle again. The air was no longer cool; instead, I felt the heat of the sun on my arms, more sweat dripping down. I hated to wear a hat. It just made my head feel hotter, but it kept the sun off. Mostly, I wanted to get this job done. In a short while, I could shift to the rake.

As for Keith, he had left before Dylan got arrested. The two apparently had a fight because Dylan insisted he give him the gun. Dylan told me later he needed the gun because he had to protect his investment in the marijuana, which Keith never found out about. It seemed that paranoia was growing in those planter boxes, too. Nobody knew about the forbidden plants except Dylan, until the police got a search warrant. What they were looking for was another gun that one of his drinking buddies had reported was there somewhere. They never found a second weapon, but they did find the hidden Schedule 1 plant installation. That was the third felony on top of the charge for wanton endangerment and the one for possessing a stolen firearm.

The fact of the matter was—and this hurt me the most—my son had been flat-out dishonest with me. Here I was, being generous, noble, helping him through all the ups and downs, the challenges. Then, instead of just doing what he was supposed to—climbing up the path, getting his college degree, and landing a job for the summer—Dylan pulls this outrageous stunt. How could he do this to me?

Betrayal, pure and simple. He was playing off my generosity, all my good intentions. Instead of openly disagreeing with me, he'd just decided to deceive me, keep me in the dark. No wonder he was slow to look for a job; he'd already decided to use his creativity to make money undercover. It would be much easier, much more fun. He was going to harvest his own pot and sell it in Cincy. Ah, but then, his Big Plan fell apart—and so did mine. Now, instead of being a heroic mom, I'd been cast without my permission in a low-budget B movie, a potboiler. Yeah, that's the part my son offered me. No heroics here, folks, just a quick crime show that won't end well.

The sympathetic landlord talked to me twice—and for a long time, too. Finally, he informed me gently that Dylan's apartment would have to be vacated. "Everything out by the end of the month," he said. "I'm sorry, but that's how it goes."

This whole catastrophe felt like some kind of huge joke being played on me. I thought about the time I took Dylan to the therapist in Parksville, thinking that therapy, along with the right meds, was going to be part of the way toward better awareness and better choices. Of course, isn't that what you're supposed to do if your son has a mood disorder? And it might have worked out that way, too, in about ten more years. However, it just so happened on this particular day that a special copy of *Newsweek* magazine happened to be lying on the coffee table in the waiting room. Its cover photo showed a lush green plant with star-shaped leaves, sporting a frothy spray of flowers on top. And the feature article? It was all about the new legal pot industry in Colorado, how growers were making fortunes by producing both medical marijuana and its cousin, recreational marijuana. The distinction had to do with the particular type of cannabinoids and terpenes present in the resin-covered flowers. Photos showed skilled gardeners carefully tending plants in greenhouses, labeling each one. For sure, Colorado was on the edge of a bold, new experiment. Dylan pounced on the magazine and read avidly, showing me the highlights, until his name was called for the counseling session.

So then later, in jail, Dylan revealed to me that this very article was his impetus to "kick it up a notch" and lay claim to his share of the entrepreneurial venture. If Blaine, the pot-smoking landlord wouldn't go into the business (as a veteran with health issues, he preferred to stay under the radar on that one), then Dylan would. On his own, too. Not legal here in Kentucky? A risk, but well worth taking. Nowadays an enterprising person can learn even the most arcane horticulture right off the internet. Want to grow cannabis in your home? No problemo: here's exactly what you need to do.

Later, Dylan admitted to me that he'd made countless trips to Lowe's on his moped (and probably in my borrowed car, too) to get lumber for planter boxes, red rocks, soil, and plant-boosting nutrients. Of course, there was the challenge of providing high-intensity lighting in a dark closet, so he'd had to wire up some mega-watt lights from the ceiling that would beam on day and night. He'd used his tools to rig up a ventilation system, too—ductwork to carry off any telltale odors from the eventual flowers. What amazed me was so much ingenuity going up through the roof right along with them. Then he'd sent off his order for seeds via the internet. No one would be the wiser after all these plans and precautions. In a few weeks, he planned to harvest a genuine cash crop of pot, enough to sell for a small fortune, enough to buy any car he wanted. Nobody would find out. Not even Keith knew there was a prime plot of weed growing right there behind the locked closet doors, and he'd been visiting for over two weeks.

I was still furious, but there was righteous indignation in my anger, too. I was wronged, but I wasn't going to take it lying down. I was going to survive. I'd find a way out of the B movie somehow. Sitting down on the wood-chip path beside the freshly turned soil, I pulled off my gloves and grabbed my water bottle. Gazing over the plot, I already felt a spark of satisfaction at one small thing I could do. If I couldn't have any positive impact on my son's life, at least I could fix up this garden.

Taking a sturdy rake, I began smoothing out the soil, stopping every now and then to tamp down a resistant clump of clay, watching with satisfaction as it yielded and broke into smaller pieces. In no time, I was raking the soil in broad, long sweeps.

With the end of the hoe, I could make four furrows crosswise in the garden plot. Not too deep, just enough to make a shallow trough. Rummaging in my basket, I located several packages of seeds. Tall zinnias were my favorites for their bright colors and the butterflies they attracted. I poured the contents into my left hand and held them closely; they were light enough to be blown away if I didn't watch out. Dropping them into the furrows, I used my gloved right hand to pulverize and sift those remaining small soil clumps to cover them, just barely, then press lightly. I didn't want to take the chance on rain, because that could take a while and there could be the wrong kind of rain, a pelting type that would carry the seeds away. Better to water them in. I unwound the hose and dragged it over to my plot. After a light shower, the soil and sun could do their magic.

By the time I rolled the hose back up and trundled all my garden tools back home, I was hungry for lunch. I would come back, maybe tomorrow, maybe the next day, with some small plants to put in: zucchini, cantaloupe, peppers, tomatoes, herbs. This afternoon, though, I would have to see about a lawyer. I already had a few ideas about that. I sighed. Ah, what I was really hoping for, after all this hard toiling under the sun, was finally being tired enough to fall into a deep sleep later on. For a whole night. Maybe.

CHAPTER 4: GET TO GIGI'S HOUSE

When did I first know that Dylan was a little different from other kids? I'm not sure. What I do know is that from the time he was a baby, he could be hard to comfort sometimes. I saw moms carrying their tiny babies in snugglies, babies who seemed perfectly content to be carried next to their mothers' bodies. But I could never do that with Dylan. He would get restless. He squirmed, he fussed. At times, he felt more like a tiger cub than a baby. He never stayed long in a playpen, either. And for all his energy and curiosity, there were times during the first two years when he could get hard-core upset—and stay that way for what seemed like a very long time, while his dad and I tried to comfort him. We could not figure out why our efforts weren't working.

Once I remember Dylan was having a particularly bad evening. Both of us were. It was during the summer when he and I were at home alone, and everything had been fine until bedtime, and I put him into his crib. He was a toddler then, young enough that I could still carry him. It was early evening and he was just plain unhappy, tired, inconsolable. His crying filled the air. Who knows? In retrospect, maybe he was just hot and cranky. Or maybe he had a headache and couldn't tell me. I talked to him, I picked him up,

I tried different things, but nothing seemed to calm him. After a while, his being upset made me upset, too. Being patient and calm under duress is not something I'm good at—and I was especially bad at it when facing these challenging times alone. Mike was away on a trip for work. I was too much on the nervous end of things myself to be much use in calming down a child who cried and cried and couldn't tell me why.

If Mike had been there, maybe he might have managed better than me. He was way more inventive than I was in trying out soothing tactics. One strategy he eventually discovered, which could usually do the trick, was taking Dylan into the shower and holding him against his own body with the water falling over both of them. After a while, the combined forces of voice, body, and water somehow relaxed him. But me, I would not have tried to hold such a feisty, strong child in a slippery shower. Even I had enough common sense not to try that. Believe me, that kid's strength was amazing; as a tiny baby, he had to be fairly wrestled into his clothes. As soon as he felt the slightest guiding pressure toward a sleeve hole, that little arm would resist my hand with a Paul Bunyan junior countermove. For him, it was a fun game, which he enjoyed immensely. He could laugh as hard as he cried. That's one of my earliest memories of his temperament.

This particular evening, though, fun games were out of the question. With Mike hundreds of miles away, I turned to the one person I was pretty sure could help us out, an older woman who often took care of Dylan while we were at work. Her real name was Susan, but she went by the name Gigi—short for great grandma, because that's who she was to her own family. Back then, there weren't many daycare places working moms could turn to, so Mike and I put out the call to find a trustworthy caretaker. Gigi answered, and we were so glad we found her. She was exactly what we needed: a steady, grandmotherly figure who knew how to deal with a wide variety of situations. On this exasperating evening, I gave her a call and just hearing her voice gave me some hope of a peaceful resolution. "Come on over," she told me.

First, though, she gave me directions to the house where she was working as a caretaker for an elderly woman. Notes stuffed in my pocket, I carried Dylan outside and strapped him into his car seat in the back. He was still upset, but I told him not to worry, we were going to Gigi's house. Still talking to him, I drove for what seemed like miles and miles on winding roads into the remote depths of the country. How I managed to get there even once I can't say. I just know it was a confusing journey on a hot evening with the windows down, a toddler crying in the back seat, and me trying to navigate back roads I didn't know even existed. There was no GPS back then, no smartphone. Once somebody gave you directions, you just went and made the best of it. Feeling lost was part of getting there.

After a good half hour with dusk advancing rapidly, I finally found the last road Gigi had told me to look for, hoping I would soon come upon the house she had described to me. I felt sure that if Dylan and I could be with her for a while, she would talk and laugh and tell me what to do, and things would be OK again. I remember arriving, finally, just at dusk, the two of us piling into a small wooden house. Gigi greeted us, asking Dylan what was wrong in her wonderful grandma voice. By that time, after the excitement of the drive, feeling the wind on his face, seeing all the trees go by, the endless turns, he was starting to come around. He probably understood something was up when I first told him we were going to see Gigi. She was our in-state grandma because the other grandma lived far away and couldn't always be there whenever we needed her. Still sniffling, he was intrigued by the house, wanted to investigate all the rooms. We explored with him a while, then Gigi led us back to the living room to comfortable chairs, motioning for Dylan to sit in her lap. After a few minutes, he jumped down to check out where the cat might be in the kitchen.

Gigi and I talked about what was going on in our lives. She'd lived in California and had plenty of tales to tell, so I loved listening to her stories. Listening tonight, though, I realized how many concerns she had on her own account. She essentially had a double shift as a caretaker, and her own health was being tested by the long hours. Even people in their sixties had to make a living. And here I was showing up with my child, seeking out her protection and common sense, two more stragglers for her to take care of at an odd time. But she was welcoming, and I was thankful. For a precious hour or so, we could talk and listen, even laugh a bit. It was dark out, but we were all together and safe.

I didn't realize it then, but my little family should have kept Gigi as Dylan's caretaker for as long as we could, for years. I should have paid half my salary to her so she could have steady work. During those early years, Dylan's dad and I, amid all our concerns about career development, our money, our house, our lives, didn't fully realize how much of a godsend she was to us, how much she could help us just by being who she was. The fact is, she had something neither of us could give so freely to our son at that time: her calm, steady presence, her experience coming through many storms, her patience, her laughter. How she maintained her spirit through her own trials and tribulations, I can barely imagine.

Eventually that evening, it was hard to say who among the three of us was more ready for bed. After hugs all around, I gathered Dylan up, and we went outside. We said good-bye; we waved. "See you tomorrow!" Thank God, and thanks to Gigi, I felt we could make it to tomorrow.

Could I have gotten the same calming results with Dylan if I'd given him a cool bath that troublesome evening or just taken him out for a ride? Maybe. I just couldn't think to do those things at the time. All I know is that Gigi was a lighthouse to me when I was a lost boat on a rough sea, as she was in countless other ways later on during the time we knew her. Even after she wasn't Dylan's regular babysitter anymore, we continued to visit her throughout the years, and she remained the same wise, generous person she'd always been, even up to the end when her health gave out, right before she died in 1999. None of us will ever forget her. And I could have learned a lot more from her than I did, if only I'd paid more attention.

CHAPTER 5: LOCKED UP

I felt better after my meeting with Allison Marie and Patrick. The three of us talked about my family disaster on their oak-shaded backyard deck over a glass of wine. Somehow, from that perspective, with their input and experience to bolster me, Dylan's arrest seemed a little more manageable. That is to say, survivable. Mainly, they assured me that I wasn't alone in this. They knew a few others who had been through something similar with their adult kids. Two families had now, or did have, young men in jail. As clergy, Allison Marie would put out the call, and these parishioners would get in touch with me. By the time I left their house, though I still wanted to crawl under a rock and stay there until the storm blew over, I felt that maybe, just maybe, I could get through this.

Back home, when the phone rang, I jumped. Every time. No matter how often I heard it, I couldn't get used to the recorded female voice, even if it did sound so professional, so matter-of-fact. "You have a pre-paid call from . . . (slight pause for the inserted voice) *Dylan*, an inmate at the Doran County Jail. All phone calls are subject to being recorded, except for privileged communications between attorney and client. If you agree to accept this call, press 1." I discovered that once someone lands in jail, there is a whole set of protocols you have to learn about: putting money on phone accounts, setting up commissary, what mail you can send, how you can send it, when you can visit, what you can bring into the visitation booth, etc. Contact visits, where you can sit across from your incarcerated family member to talk and even hug by way of greeting and leave-taking, are not permitted at most jails—not unless a person has been sentenced and placed under the Department of Corrections, and serves in a work program. This was no country club low-security prison like the one Piper Kerman told us about in Danbury, Connecticut. There, you had the opportunity to work different jobs on the compound, let off steam by running on an outdoor track, make friends with an inmate cook, maybe even sneak out what you need to make fake cheesecake on the cheap for somebody's birthday.

None of that happened at the county jail, not if you're being held as part of the "general population." Besides, each jail is its own little fiefdom with its own rules, which can change weekly by jailer fiat. At first, I was a little worried about the recording of conversations, but I soon got over that; what choice did I have, anyway? Besides, I wanted to find out from my son's own voice what he'd been thinking and how he had gotten into this predicament.

Despite my intentions, these inmate phone calls with my son were not encouraging. Of course, at first I was alternately disbelieving (*Why did you do this?*) and furious (*How could you do this to me? I loaned you my car and you used it to get alcohol and get drunk?*). We went over Keith Birchen's May visit, the whole descent-into-the-underworld narrative. For the most part, Dylan was defensive. His rationale was that he wasn't at all content living the way he had been, quietly and on the sidelines. He wanted more, and growing pot was a way to "step it up." As for getting the beer on Friday night, he knew that probably wasn't a good idea but felt he wasn't doing anything unusual compared to what most college kids were doing on that same evening. As for the gun, that had come from Keith and

its purpose was to "protect his investment," the leafy one growing
behind the locked closet doors.

In all this scheming, however, what he didn't realize was that
by drinking the beer, then hitting the bottle of scotch on the table
at the friend's house, he was not going to be in the best position to
make decisions about safety—not his own, not anyone else's. And
then, all drinking aside, I wondered aloud why he had put a gun
in the backpack when he went out. To brandish it at a dramatic
moment and scare everyone around him? To give himself a sense
of power he couldn't get any other way? We didn't have any family
history with guns. Dylan himself admitted to me that he'd been
afraid of the pistol until Keith showed him how to use it. After that,
they'd had great sport practice-shooting off the apartment balcony.
And all that was going on while trusty Mom was waiting for him
to return my calls from Boston. Maybe the weapon was yet another
way to "step it up"—only this one backfired on him big-time.

No doubt, all these questions should have been asked in the
confidential situation of "privileged communications between attorney and client," but as of yet there was no attorney. That's because
it would fall to me to find and pay for one. And I wasn't so sure I
wanted to. Not after what we parents and grandparents had paid
already for Dylan's education and wellbeing. Had I believed my son
was innocent of the charges, I would have found the best lawyer
I could. But he was far from innocent. I didn't want to send the
message to him that Mom and Dad would always be there with our
checkbooks, ready to bail him out. It didn't seem the right thing to
do anymore.

I talked about this with John. I knew John was not in favor of
any bailing out whatsoever; he was aware of Dylan's past infractions.
Neither was Mike, who lived in Cleveland. The initial bond was
high, $10,000. This would later drop, but the truth was, we weren't
eager to get him out. He needed to get stopped in his tracks, think

about what he'd done. Jail was useful for that. And we needed to think, too.

To get another viewpoint on the attorney issue, I decided to check in with my new friend, Sandra. She was our local NAMI chapter leader; the acronym stands for National Alliance on Mental Illness. She and her husband, Robert, had a son whose crazy irresponsibility when he was a teenager turned out later to be due to schizophrenia. He'd had a record of legal problems, including DUIs and illegal drug possession—mainly marijuana but other things, too. She told me they had paid for an attorney once, but when it happened again, they decided to let their son be represented by a public defender. Things worked out; it wasn't the worst choice. Public defenders didn't have much time to spend consoling or consulting with their clients—maybe ten minutes face-to-face with them in a spare room before court appearances. But Sandra said that she and Robert, as parents, weren't prepared to fork over a higher fee for a wayward young adult who didn't learn the first time. Mind you, Sandra was a really kind, tender soul, too, not a rough-edged person like me, trying to be tough-minded.

Nonetheless, I found two private attorneys who offered an initial free consultation. One of them had an office right near the courthouse. When I explained the situation, Mr. Larkin spoke affably enough, asked questions, reviewed the situation, suggested a diversion plan he would argue for, and stated that his fee would be $2,000 per felony, and I could think it over. Well, for three of them, I didn't see any sort of bargain. The second lawyer turned out to be much more entertaining. I could tell she would be a good trial lawyer by the questions she asked and the possible tales she was already starting to spin based on my answers. Given the circumstances, though, I doubted that there would be a trial, or that it would be worth it even if there were one. In my talks later with Mike, what it all came down to was guilt and cost. We'd already hired a lawyer to defend our son in a misdemeanor case involving marijuana in Ohio. This time, we didn't want to pay for a guilty defendant. He would be assigned a public defender.

During this time, I visited Dylan in jail. Whereas my previous experience involved inducting students into an honor society, now (thanks to my son's unfortunate brand of ingenuity) our whole family was being inducted into the criminal justice system. No matter how many times I went for visits, it always felt strange to leave the ordered, respectable world of my college office to find my way to the back-street county jail behind the Justice Building. It was like leading two parallel lives, or having an alternate identity. I had to get there early to sign in, then find a seat among other, assorted family members of inmates. They were of all ages, from grandparents to little kids. Honestly, the only other place I've seen that many rambunctious young children is the elementary school playground—either that or the pediatrician's office. It made me realize how many inmates are parents, not to mention brothers, sisters, spouses, boyfriends, nephews, nieces, or grandkids. When our male inmates' names were read, we were allowed to file into a dull green, booth-lined corridor. We all walked slowly past the men on the other side, each of us looking for that familiar face behind the plate glass. To talk we each picked up an ancient phone receiver hanging on the wall. In no time, there would be a cacophony of sound on all sides, with each visitor watching that face, listening for that one voice they had come to hear.

Dylan looked a little roughed up from the arrest but basically OK. He showed me a cut he'd received on his head from being taken into custody.

"Look at this, Mom. They tazed me and slammed me onto the hood of the police car."

I winced. The apartment manager, Blaine, had told me about that on the phone right after it happened. I could see grazes on Dylan's hands, too, but all the wounds looked clean and healing.

"They had to take me to the hospital to make sure I was OK. Then they brought me here."

"Well, it looks like you're going to survive," I said, then shook my head. It wasn't the first time he'd had to be patched up after an incident. I asked him what it was like in there. He told me he was in a cell with about sixteen other guys. It was essentially one big holding tank, with each prisoner having a different court date and slightly different charges. There was one toilet and one sink for that many, with bunks against the wall. They got to go out into the courtyard and play ball maybe once a day. I couldn't imagine, but I asked him everyday questions to normalize the situation.

"So, how's the food?"

"Horrible quality, small quantity. We're all starving."

"How's your shoulder doing?

"OK, trying to limber it up, take care of it in the crowd."

"You're taking your meds?"

"Yeah, the nurse distributes them and makes sure I swallow."

"Can you work in there? What do you do all day?"

"No, the work program is only for convicted state inmates, Class D felons. They apply and have to wait their turn."

"Can you read books?"

"Sure, I read a lot in here." But he warned me. "No edifying reading materials, Mom. If you send me anything, make it a good thriller."

Sure thing. OK, so now I'd be hunting for edifying good thrillers. Margaret Atwood flashed through my mind, but I knew she'd be too Canadian-dry for his taste. I shrugged and gave him a Mom look.

In any case, I found out later that you can't just pass or send a book from home to an inmate. You have to order it from an outside source and have it sent directly to the jail to that person. If, that is, the local facility allows a book to be sent at all; some don't. Every jail is concerned first and foremost about any contraband drugs that could be slipped between pages or glued into bindings. As in the case of the airplane shoe bomber, if it happened anywhere once, afterward the authorities would suspect all travelers wearing shoes because they might conceal explosives.

Before long, we talked about upcoming court dates. At the time of his arraignment, Dylan found out that his public defender would be Ms. Wesley Pulaski, and she planned to make a plea of not guilty, so that things could be worked out over time. Basically, the court had to decide what to do with him. The court would agree that he wasn't a hardened criminal. He was a first-time offender. Usually, the law is more lenient in that case. We talked about how he could make the best case for himself, show that he is worthy of having a suspended sentence. Chastened, Dylan said he had a plan for his life and shouldn't be put away for this one bad lapse of judgment. He'd been able to accomplish things, like two more semesters of college courses here as well as the ones at the University of Cincinnati. His slate didn't only have black marks on it. We talked about persons who could put in a good word for him: the landlord after he helped out with some repairs, also his marketing and math professors. Dylan knew from Ms. Pulaski, though, that in order for him to get the diversion he wanted and be able to resume his studies, he would have to complete some kind of substance abuse program. "I'll do it," he said.

Soon, our half-hour visit was over. The correctional officer gave the signal, and all the inmates got up and moved away from the booths. The next hearing in court would be important; at least we had some plan. I didn't like what my son did, but I wanted him to know I was on his side.

I didn't mention, though, that I'd decided to write a letter to the judge to personally advocate for him. I thought Judge Marlowe needed more background than he would get otherwise. The truth is that before writing it I felt guilty, like I wasn't doing enough to help. At a NAMI meeting in Louisville a few weeks earlier, I'd attended a workshop led by a young lawyer who was advocating for persons, like her brother, who had mental health issues and had been picked up for vagrancy or petty theft. Usually they were talking about persons with schizophrenia who hear voices and are clearly delusional. In cases like that, the issue of not being in control of one's actions is clear-cut. But other people have mental health problems, too, even if they're not as severe, not as visible. I explained to the judge that my son had been diagnosed with Bipolar II, and though he was fully rational, he was also subject to impulsive actions and bad decisions. I'd learned, too, that he had addiction problems. Those three all went together in the same package, along with the good stuff: talents, interests, accomplishments. "Judge Marlowe, the way I see it, he's an at-risk individual who needs a chance to work his way back toward the possibility of having a good life."

Before the next hearing, under Sandra's counsel, I left a phone message for Ms. Pulaski. I wanted to tell her about some substance abuse program options the family had been researching. But even though I tried to throw in my two cents' worth, I got the distinct impression that our influence would be limited. For one thing, Pulaski was Dylan's defender, not mine. I had to wait and see if she would contact me; and she, in turn, would be mostly attuned to her client and the workings of the court.

Two months later, on Monday August 8, in circuit court, there was finally a major hearing after several preliminary ones. Fortunately, I'd been able to mobilize moral support. Mike and Linda up in Cleveland wouldn't be there, but John would be with me. Sandra from NAMI also offered to come, as did Rev. Patrick from St. Alban's. I was glad we were all together; it felt like a united front even though, to a large extent, we were only observers. Circuit court that day was a full house. We four had to search for a place wide enough on the pews to accommodate our group. It felt like we'd assembled at church, with the altar being the judge's bench. By now, I'd become used to the recurring rituals: for example, everyone standing up as one body when the judge emerged from his chambers and the bailiff pronounced solemnly "All rise."

Sandra had coached me in how to locate the docket online so I could print it out. Dylan's name was on page three, and I knew from previous hearings that he wouldn't appear until later. I scanned the other names. More than one looked vaguely familiar, probably from a previous court appearance. Just as there were regulars at bars and restaurants, there were regulars in court, too. After Judge Marlowe settled in, the audience remained quiet while a flurry of activity took place on the floor. Private attorneys stepped forward to present their cases first, scurrying between clients, passing in and out of doors off-stage on the left to check files or copy documents. Stage right, presided over by the bailiff, was reserved for jailed defendants, who would be brought over in handcuffs. The four of us speculated as to where Dylan was being held. Maybe he was still at the jail. Or maybe he was being held in a locked chamber somewhere down one of those hidden, backstage corridors. We knew he'd be led in when his case was called. Gradually, we got used to the flow of events. It would just take as long as it took to get to Dylan's name. For him, it must have felt like being a tense racehorse locked inside the starting gate right before the Kentucky Derby, only he'd be waiting in that tiny gate for an hour or more before the pistol went off.

Finally, the public defenders took their turn. Armed with seven or eight dossiers each, two of them came out to the crowd to take clients one by one into a private room to discuss their cases. Suspense mounted as the court moved through them one at a time. I kept an eye on Pulaski. At one point, there was a lull in the proceedings, and the defender approached me. We went out into the hall to discuss. She told me the plan was to argue for a diversion, proposing Drug Court for Dylan as a treatment program. He was young, though; this option was usually reserved for someone older who had tried other, less rigorous options. However, he would be a college student with a felony on his record otherwise. A flash of painful recognition passed through me like a sword: *My son! No, how could this be?* I'd felt that before, always the sharp pain. But the defender's steady voice continued: completing Drug Court was a way he could get the felonies expunged from his record, as long as he followed the rules. I nodded, taking this in. I didn't even try to talk. Instead, I imagined a giant eraser cleaning a whiteboard. The image comforted me: *Yes, dear God, a clean slate. Please let this happen for him.* We returned to the courtroom.

As 10:00 drew closer, a side door opened and inmates were finally admitted to the courtroom by the bailiff. I heard sounds of distant doors closing, keys rattling. I shifted to get a glimpse of Dylan's face as he entered the room. He looked stoic and glanced briefly at the crowd, but there wasn't time for him to locate us. He had to take a seat with the others. Only the backs of their heads remained visible as the inmates faced the bench. It was hard to see my one and only child in a line-up like that. Each of them remained handcuffed in court, making it difficult for them to sign their names, which they had to do. Finally, Ms. Wesley Pulaski's turn came up. As a public defender, her clients were these. Dossier by dossier, she moved through them steadily, a calm, organizing force amid the chaos of some of these lives: shoplifting, assault, non-payment of alimony, drug charges. At last, Dylan's case was called, and he was summoned before the bench with Pulaski beside him. Part of the ritual was that he must state his name and address, but I could barely hear his voice since he was facing the judge. As Pulaski presented the idea of a diversion, Judge Marlowe seemed to be only half-listening. I wondered if he would be lenient. After witnessing several similar hearings for other defendants, I wondered if the judge felt overwhelmed sometimes by all the chances the court gave to individuals to take a higher road, change their lives, stay off the docket. By then, he'd shown he was willing to be the Judge of Second Chances, but I knew he had to be wary, too. We'd heard him remark in court on a previous case about how clients can lie.

Pulaski presented the evidence on Dylan's behalf that he and I had discussed and prepared: the letter from the landlord, the note from his marketing professor. The good and the bad had been laid out. I wondered if Judge Marlowe had received my letter. Would it make any difference? Who could make sense of the crazy quilt story of my son's infractions over the last three years? But after Pulaski spoke, the judge stated simply that the court would take this into consideration. Another date of review was set up: Monday, August 22 at 8:30 a.m. The defendants were led out again. Dylan stole a look to find us. Our eyes met, and he gave a nod. I smiled back. Then he was gone.

Well, that's life in the courtroom. Dylan's name had been called, the starter's pistol had gone off, but then we all found out the race would have to be postponed. Back to the paddock for the tense racehorse.

We all filed out and sought refuge outdoors in the open air. John, Sandra, Patrick, and I debriefed, each of us shaking off the nervous energy of the morning—at least I was. Of course, we were all novices at this court-system business, so we learned that this was just one major hearing with more to come. The public defender mentioned Drug Court. What was that? We wondered how it worked, what was involved? It must be tough. Didn't Ms. Pulaski say it wasn't recommended for younger adults because it was so rigorous?

I could tell from John's face and low energy that he was feeling drained—we all were. He thought the judge would come up with a grand pronouncement or a definitive sentence right away; we only at that moment got the picture that the wheels of justice turn slowly. In a case like this, guilt was only part of the issue. The larger question was what to do with the person's life for the future. In Dylan's case: was this guy salvageable? If he had substance-abuse problems, could they be treated? How much of a danger did he pose to society? To himself? What were his chances to get back on a path that would lead to a productive life? With time and cross-deliberation, these questions would be taken up. It took time to arrive at a possible solution. But for a parent, it was hard to be patient, let alone objective.

After the hearing, I felt exhausted, and being with John in the same condition wasn't helping. We'd met six years ago and had been visiting each other ever since. He'd driven across the state to be with me through this crisis, just as he'd done for several years now. When Dylan was a student in Cincinnati right across the Ohio River, we would meet up there. Crises aside, we actually had a lot in common; we were both college professors, for example, and in the same discipline. We were usually able to tune in to each other's broadcast frequencies instantly, effortlessly.

Today was different, though. We were both divorced and had sons, but his three sons put together didn't have ANY of the problems my one son did. Right after our first big court scene, he was clearly baffled by having to deal with this kind of blind uncertainty. I had to recognize that John was from the "other side," where things like this didn't happen. Not that he has ever said this; he wouldn't do that. I acknowledged his feelings as we walked back to our car, but it made me feel even more frayed around the edges than I already was. After a quick lunch, he told me he needed to take a nap to recover; neither of us had slept well the night before. I went back to my office. When we met up again, we discussed our bad moods and agreed to hang in there. We would get through this somehow. When you have a son like mine, you learn to take on strange situations.

Over the summer, there were several other court hearings, spaced out by a week or two. It's true what they say: Lady Justice takes her time with the scales. By the second week in August, Dylan had court dates in both courts, District and Circuit: one for DUI charges, the other for the felony charges. His public defender didn't enter a plea for District; the blood alcohol sample hadn't been analyzed yet, so the case was still pending. The review dates churned by, but nothing definitive was being decided yet. Dylan was getting edgy. I figured he needed guidance and help—but family wasn't always the best source. Fortunately, Patrick agreed to visit and talk with Dylan again to give him a fresh perspective. Patrick had known Dylan since he was a little kid on the soccer team he used to coach, so there was a bond of trust there.

Later in August, while at the Judicial Building, John and I decided to ask about Drug Court. After the public defender first mentioned it, we wanted to know more. A clerk passed us a name, a phone number, and an address. It was close by, so we decided to go there. It was located in an older, brick building at the corner of 10th and Maple, near the clinic, and had been donated by a doctor. A receptionist soon introduced us to Darlene Winchester, Recovery Coordinator. She smiled in greeting, shook our hands, and led us into her domain, a large room with about twenty chairs arranged in a circle. They were empty, but I knew this must be the room where Drug Court group meetings were held. Ms. Winchester was a petite woman with henna-streaked hair, a long, flowing skirt, and ankle boots. She dressed with flair, a latter-day Stevie Nicks. You could tell by the way she walked that she was determined; not much was going to slow her down. She turned around a couple of chairs and asked us to take a seat across from her.

She saw my stress, asked me how I was doing. As I told her about our situation and she responded, I could tell that she was smart, articulate, and perceptive. Face-to-face, I felt I was talking to Julianne Moore—not the steely character from *The Hunger Games*, but the sensitive professor/mom persona she played in *Still Alice*. As she spoke to us and answered our questions, it was clear that Drug Court was her passion. As a social worker, when the judge asked her to head up Drug Court for the circuit court, she knew she wanted to do it, but only if she could have certain things in place: a strong curfew and a long enough time frame to make a difference in someone's life. From her, we heard again that the program was very tough, very directional. Yes, it did take away many of the participants' civil rights to privacy (there were home searches, drug tests, possible review of financial accounts), but all this served a purpose. The goal was to teach people with drug issues new skills and a new way of living, and this process took time and mentorship. Participants ranged in age from twenty to sixty, but the average age was about mid-thirties through forties. They'd tried other things, and now for many of them, this was their "last best chance," at least from a legal-expungement standpoint, to get their lives on track.

Ms. Winchester talked to us about the brain—how the prefrontal cortex, in charge of executive functioning, usually wasn't fully developed in men until about twenty-five years old, or even later. Consequently, impulse control to avoid risky behavior needed to be internalized. She cited another brain research program that showed how brain cells could heal and develop throughout a person's lifetime. Scientists were tracking the growth of new neural tissues as well as new messaging pathways, yielding positive findings on how brain plasticity can support recovery from addiction. It was an incredibly complex problem, involving everything from brain chemistry to social attitudes. Still, there was hope.

As she spoke, I could see she was tough, too, but caring. She characterized herself as having been a young person who "pushed the envelope," who didn't accept limits easily.

"My own son is just like me," she said. "So I know the territory you're going through as a mom."

She looked at me intently. "Your son might not be ready yet. Don't push him. Just ask him about having a felony on his record. How does he feel about that?"

She explained the stakes: in Kentucky, you only have one shot at Drug Court. If you don't successfully complete it, you can't do it again. So a person had to be ready. The recovery coordinator left us with this advice: "Don't worry about your son. Go out and live your life. Let him make his decision." Ah, if only I could!

I felt better after having talked with her. But at the same time I couldn't help but reflect on how different it was for me, now getting this support from the outside world, while my son was still locked up with fifteen other guys in jail, unseen, all residents of some alien universe unknown to me. I was haunted from an earlier time, when Dylan was sixteen years old and in juvenile court. Would my son continue to get into these situations? How could it be that our two lives could be so closely knit, yet worlds apart? Once again I felt that strange mix of emotions: a desperate hope to bring my son over to my side of life and then, just as strong, a desire to fly away and leave this strange, complex, and unasked-for challenge behind.

John could tell I was lost in reverie.

"Let's go for a walk," he said.

We held hands as we debriefed about what we'd just learned from Ms. Winchester. Then we decided to take her advice, the part about "live your life," at least for the evening. We drove out to Cypress Cove to the fish restaurant by the lake. Everything about the trip was enjoyable: the drive through the rolling, open countryside, the small road through the dense woods as we approached, the way the winding turns eventually open onto the lakefront. We ordered our food: hot, crispy fried catfish with a grainy cornmeal coating, crunchy hush puppies, and beignet-like fried onion rings with a side of coleslaw. Though this was not our usual fare, that night we ate it all, topping off our meal with a huge piece of Mississippi mud pie shared between us. Through the windows, we could see the sky and the lake around us slowly turn brilliant colors with the sunset. When we walked down to the marina later, we saw two young families with children coming back from a fishing expedition and a group of four young men strolling in from a boat, carefree and hungry. We watched turtles swim up to the dock as kids threw bread into the water.

At last, on the drive home, we moved through the cooling air, viewed the darkening dome of sky slowly closing the day overhead. The first stars would soon appear. I'd experienced all this before and hoped to again; the ordinary beauty of it was profoundly reassuring, as if to remind me that, even during troubles, it's important to keep a window open on everything still good and right in the world.

CHAPTER 6: SIGNS AND PORTENTS

My family and I didn't know much about bipolar disorder back in the late 1980s and early 90s. It wasn't much talked about. In any case, if such a disorder were diagnosed, it would be done for persons who were in late adolescence or early adulthood. Children didn't have it. That's what the experts said back then. The fact is that we knew Dylan's behavior was unusually intense. Either he was extremely happy and carefree, or else he was extremely irritated. We knew this from the time he was very young. His behavior wasn't a problem every day, just sometimes. But those sometimes could be difficult to handle, requiring enormous stores of patience and problem-solving skill. Mike usually was the one to take over in those situations, just like the time he invented the shower water therapy that somehow helped Dylan get through a terrible pre-sleep melt-down. We eventually figured out that Dylan would be at his worst if he got over-tired or over-stimulated for a long period of time. When we went out in the evening, we learned to avoid letting him fall asleep if he would have to be wakened again to go to bed. His interrupted sleep would surely bring on a red-alert, four-limb-thrashing fit lasting forty minutes or more. We knew, too, that he didn't adapt well to changes in his daily regimen. As he got older, he could tell us more, and that helped. By living alongside my very young son, I could see how acquiring language and a conceptual knowledge of different time frames conferred a marvelous freedom from the particular pain of the moment. "It will be better tomorrow" was such an important mantra for us. But in the long years that brought us to Dylan's adulthood, we found there were times when faith in our mantra strained against all credibility.

Thank goodness we had Gigi's calm wisdom to help us in the beginning. Then, when Dylan was about three years old, we enrolled him in the local Montessori School. We wanted to give him every advantage. The teachers were wonderful, the whole learning environment a dream come true. He liked it and did well there—again, except for certain days. I remember one occasion early on when the school director said she needed to speak to us. Dylan had gotten angry and frustrated during an activity. Before anyone even knew what was happening, he had grabbed a pencil and was striking another child in his rage. The director, a teacher herself, was passionate about early childhood development and education. She knew this behavior was something to watch. She told us the teachers had separated Dylan from the other children for a while until he regained his composure; then they could talk to him about it. He told them he got mad and couldn't help what he did. She told us what we already knew: "When he's good, he's very, very good. But when he's bad, he really goes off the deep end." Then she said something else that stuck with me: "He needs to develop a quiet voice inside himself that can calm him down in these situations. Until he does that, you (the parents) can be that voice."

It was comforting to have someone with her teacher's understanding talk with us and share her knowledge. Dylan stayed in Montessori for two years, learned a lot, and made many improvements in his social skills. Fortunately, there weren't any other eruptions as serious as this early one. Sometimes, though, I wondered if we should have continued his care with Gigi instead of putting him in pre-school. Maybe intellectually it was better for him at the school, but what about emotionally? With me having to put so much effort into my career at that stage of my life, I didn't feel I had either the time or the inner resources to be the kind of parent the pre-school teacher indicated we needed to be. I was on board with the philosophy, but the practice eluded me.

Sometimes, Mike and I would have disagreements about how to handle Dylan's tantrums and oppositional behavior at home. Mike wanted strict guidelines and rules that would be implemented quietly and consistently, like in the *How to Raise Your Spirited Child* books we were reading. The principle there was to implement time-outs or "consequences" for bad behavior, but to do this in a calm way, not showing anger. I went along with this but was more reactive. When storm clouds broke, I had to work much harder to go with the program and not get angry myself. In this, I became all too aware of my shortcomings as a calm parental guide. Maybe I would have done better if I'd had to attend trainings and report back to a parents' support group every week. It amazes me that though we're all obliged to train in the simplest of life skills, like practicing to get a drivers' license, anyone can take their chances as a parent—no instruction required. It truly wasn't easy to face a child who was so volatile and so different from myself in many respects, especially one who knew exactly how to push my buttons. Still, with our rules and consequences in place, we were forging ahead somehow. When a particularly bad episode arose, I would worry about my son's future. How could he be two different persons, as his Montessori teachers had said? But the next day, the sun would come up again; I would look at him and see a strong, smart, healthy kid growing up in front of me. We were resilient; everything was fine. As soon as the trouble of the moment lifted its weight from my foot, I was ready to skip away every time.

In first grade, Dylan was fortunate to have a teacher who worked with his "high spirits." Her classroom didn't have rows of chairs. Instead, there were work and play stations, with micro-environments for artwork, storytelling, numbers, writing, and music. Often, children worked together at one table. When she found that Dylan often got distracted from his task by being overinvolved with other kids, she separated him for a while so that he could do the work on his own. Then, she'd allow him to rejoin the group when he had finished. At a parent/teacher meeting in the middle of the school year, I remember her telling us that she was encouraging Dylan to focus on his work, even when he was with a group, so that he wouldn't have to be separated. Eventually, towards spring, she reported that he was able to do this, and we were reassured. Meanwhile, he was learning well; his worksheets and drawings came home with high praise. But I doubt we fully appreciated at the time all the skill this teacher deployed to bring our wayward son into the fold.

In second grade, things were different. By this time, we had moved into town, and Dylan entered the city elementary school. It had a great reputation, but the classroom atmosphere was not as easygoing. His teacher, Ms. Scoffield, with twenty years of experience under her belt and structured expectations, found that Dylan was a bit over the top, a bit hyper—yes, we did know that already. In her classroom, that meant he frequently forgot to raise his hand before speaking; he jumped out of his seat to talk or, being irrationally exuberant, didn't stay in his seat because he wanted to move around instead. Worse yet, he sometimes failed to turn his work in on time. She recognized he had some abilities but was not pleased with his lack of self-control. Yes, lack of self-control—that was the crux of it. He could be a tough kid to keep on track. The list of his infractions became longer as the year progressed. His weekly star sheets came home with frowny faces marked in red, even though the quality of his work was still high. I found a note Mike had written one day when the dreaded star sheet came home one Friday. Dylan had turned from smiles to tears when Dad asked for the folder he'd brought home, saying he felt "he couldn't be good." He knew there would be more frowns on the page, more infractions to account for. The problems were behavioral, the teacher emphasized. She thought he probably had ADHD, and had we ever thought of having him checked out by a psychologist for that? Maybe he could take Ritalin to stay calmer.

Mike and I discussed this, but we weren't too eager to have our child take a medication all the time, especially if it wasn't easy to determine whether he actually had a condition like ADHD or not. We knew this was a huge topic in the magazines of the time; it made the headlines. Lots of boys, in particular, were diagnosed, and many were taking the medication. We were dubious about all this—it seemed more like a fad than something to be worried about. And even if he DID have something like ADHD, weren't there other, less medicated ways to deal with the situation? By then, we had found that keeping Dylan on a regular schedule of waking and sleeping, letting him get lots of outdoor exercise so he could blow off steam, and keeping him away from too much stimulation could keep him on a more even keel.

As proof of that, we'd noticed how having the grandparents visit and take charge with loads of new toys and constant fun attention would have a high impact on all of us after they left. Instead of making Dylan happier, he'd be driven over the edge of his energy level, not to mention his expectation level. It was hard when we tried to explain this to my doting parents. "Look, we need to keep him calm, within bounds. He just needs a few things, not a lot. There's too much of a contrast after he comes back home and has to follow the rules again." They didn't get it; it was their civil right to spoil their grandson, they said. We parents were being too severe and should lighten up.

Instead of Ritalin, Mike and I decided to seek out a counselor. We were less worried about Dylan's behavior at school than we were about blow-ups at home with us. That's where the real frustrations were coming out, especially after a long day of Dylan trying to meet classroom expectations, or conversely, being with doting grandparents who granted his every wish. Mike asked around and found Kevin Oakland, who worked well with children. He was easygoing, had a good rapport with kids, gave us advice, and talked with Dylan. As the year went on, the blow-ups became less frequent. Despite the second-grade teacher's comments, our perception was that our son was actually doing better now, not worse. From what she said, though, it was clear that the expectations were getting higher for what he was supposed to be able to do. And the penalties for lacking self-management skills would only get stiffer down the road, she warned us. We were determined to work through the difficulties as best we could. We just wished the teacher would ease up a little and see the glass half-full like we did. But one truth we found out as parents is this: by the time you learn how to handle your child in one phase, they've moved into a new one, and you have to figure things out all over again.

CHAPTER 7: CIRCUIT BREAKERS

By late August, John had gone back to his own home and responsibilities across the state. Dylan was glad about the prospect of a diversion to avoid being sentenced for charges. It's just that he didn't want to do this here in town where he'd been living the past year. Instead, he wanted his possible diversion transferred to Cincinnati, where he would follow court orders, take substance abuse–recovery classes, and resume his college work. According to him, the defender didn't say that this was impossible; she listened and took this alternative seriously. Not so the family. To us, Dylan's going back to Cincinnati could only spell trouble. Drug Court in town sounded like a far better option: easier to get around without a car, easier to keep appointments and go to AA meetings. More family support, too—fewer dubious pals like Keith Birchen. Eventually, he could re-enroll for classes at the college.

Dylan didn't agree at all. Not to mention, he had other advisors. Over the phone, he told me that a couple of guys sharing the same cell had told him that Drug Court was really strict: endless drug tests, rules, meetings to attend. One had even been in it once, then got kicked out.

"They tell me it's extremely unlikely that I'd make it through," he told me. "They say as soon as you mess up even slightly, you're out."

I wondered about that.

"Well, maybe that means it's a good program with high standards," I said. Dylan didn't see it that way.

Classes were starting up again, so I had a lot on my mind. One Saturday morning, while drinking my coffee, I flipped ruefully through the collected mail I hadn't gotten to yet, some of it forwarded for Dylan with ominous addresses like Kentucky Motor Vehicles, Progressive Auto Insurance, etc. All bad news, I was sure. Lately John and I had had long, drawn-out discussions about Dylan and all the unexpected expenses I'd been incurring. There would be many more, too. With the second DUI, there would be court fees and fines, the cost of substance-abuse counseling sessions, and more jail time, which would also be charged to Dylan (read, "to the family"), since he hadn't been sentenced yet.

John told me, "Fine. Tally up what Dylan owes. You don't pay it; he does. I've heard in Traffic Court how the judge asks the defendants about a payment scheme, usually $100 a month. If they can't handle that, the defendant can ask for something different, but that's the going rate."

"Yes, I should have had Dylan pay at least half of his first fine last fall," I admitted.

John knew I tended to make excuses for my son. I'd say things like "He's a student; he doesn't have enough money." Or, "With his mental health issues, I'm afraid to put too much pressure on him."

"No, he should have paid for ALL of it," John said. "Next time in court, I'm going to put duct tape over your mouth so you can't say you're going to help with fines."

I made a face but realized the truth of what he said. I did help—too much—the first time around. I've always been on the side of wanting to smooth things out, not increase the load on an easily stressed-out person. But then, what had he learned about managing money, despite all the parental lessons? What would he ever learn if I kept paying like I had?

This morning, however, one of the envelopes attracted my attention enough to open it; it was from the college. Inside, a monetary miracle awaited me. I liked the blue tint and wavy lines imbedded in the paper: the refund check for fall tuition. I was amazed and thankful it had been processed so quickly—thanks to the registrar who responded to my plea. Still, I had to shake my head. Once again, John was right; there was no way Dylan was going to get out of his legal difficulties in time to resume coursework at the college for fall semester. John had thought I was crazy to pay any tuition money this summer, even though Dylan had been tentatively scheduled for classes since last spring. My hopes had gone up after all that talk about a diversion and Drug Court, but now they were down again. All was uncertain.

At that moment, the phone rang; it was John. I confessed to him my avoidance mechanisms coming out—all that unopened bad news set aside—then . . . hurrah! The good news of the refund check.

"Hope you have a reality check in there, too," he said.

"Yeah, I need one of those at least twice a day," I laughed. All too soon, I realized I had only ten more minutes to get ready and out the door because it was visitation day. There was business to discuss at the jail.

For one thing, I needed to have Dylan sign the check over to me, because even though I'd paid, the tuition refund was made out to him. However, the correctional officer on duty in the lobby informed me that if any money came for Dylan in the form of a check, the jail would take half of it for his expenses. Well, at least he warned me. I decided to wait until a court date; I could pass the check in a folder to the public defender for Dylan to sign then, and Ms. Pulaski would return it to me. I wondered what state Dylan would be in today, if he would open up and talk or be in a funk. It didn't matter; I had to be there. I had to be the steady lighthouse.

As it turned out, Dylan was talkative. He nodded as I passed by the booth window. Taking a seat, I picked up the phone receiver. First, I commented on his new buzz haircut and asked how he was doing. He let me know: he was hungry and would like to be able to buy more food at the commissary. According to him, the meals were really small in there, like what a kid would eat at elementary school lunch. He'd had money earlier in his wallet but that was long gone. Out of the $20 I'd paid to commissary each week, only $10 remained for anything he wanted to buy: cans of tuna, peanut butter, shampoo, toothpaste. Can you believe this jail siphons off 50% of every bit of money family or loved ones pay into commissary? And most family paying for this are not people with plump bank accounts or loose cash lying around. In jail, the corporate kiosk selling peanut butter charges $4.50—at least $2 more than at a supermarket—so $10 doesn't go far at all.

I asked him if his meds were still holding out; didn't he have to get them renewed?

"No, I'm doing OK. I don't want to take them while I'm in here," he said.

"Why not? Don't they help?"

"I don't like the way they make me feel," he said. "As if I'm more detached from my emotions, as if I'm detached from the world. That's not me."

This wasn't the first time he'd said this.

"Well, keep an eye on how things go," I said. He knew I didn't like this at all, but he was in one of his brash bulldozer periods. He wouldn't be listening to me about meds. He would just say I didn't understand, and that would be that.

"Hey, Mom, I'm going to need some new clothes. The sweatpants and shirt you bought last time shrunk a size in the wash.

A buddy loaned me this one," he said, pointing to the roomy gray sweatshirt he was wearing. "Please get me pants and a sweatshirt, the XL size, so it'll fit like this."

I realized how cold it must be in there. On the visitor side of the glass, I was wearing light summer clothing, as were all the parents, wives, girlfriends, and little kids around me. The gray guys on the other side were wearing several layers of clothes, as if it were Siberian winter. I assured him I'd find some and bring them over. Suddenly, a new topic came up.

"Someone named Darlene Winchester from Drug Court came to see me," Dylan said. I waited expectantly for Dylan's reaction. Apparently, she'd come to talk the day before, Friday.

"Yeah, Drug Court is probably my best bet. It's not what I want, but I can do the program and take courses at the same time. I can finish in two years probably; that's what she said. Still, that's a long time to be stuck in one place."

I listened, gave him space, hoping he would see the advantages. I felt glad to have this new ally on the diversion front.

Ms. Winchester said that addictions have family histories, so as a member of Drug Court, he'd have to find a place to live on his own, detach himself somewhat from his parents. This resonated with Dylan. She stressed that he would have to be accountable to the group for himself.

"That's what I want," he said. "To be independent."

I nodded, pushing back the memory of having heard this before many times.

"If you're rich, you can go to one of those spa-like treatment centers to get a new lease on life, but me, I'm going to have to take whatever the state offers."

"Yes, that's right," was all I could reply, holding back tears, frustrated by this prince-or-pauper mentality. *Why can't you just be a regular, middle-class guy? Why is that so hard?*

He knew the special advantage of Drug Court: it could help release him from the felony charges—that is, if he could complete the program and then continue to do well later on. Darlene Winchester must have presented the case in the way most likely to grab his attention now. According to Dylan, she spelled out in detail how much more difficult your life can be with a felony charge: it's harder to find a job once you have to check that box asking, "Have you been convicted of a felony?" And it's harder to find housing, too, since many apartment applications have a similar box to mark. Having a felony charge scares people. Then, too, in today's internet world, it's so easy to do a background check on someone and find out exactly this type of information. Your computer can automatically pop them right up for you, like bread out of a toaster. As a felon in our state in the year 2011, you'd also lose your right to vote, to bear arms, and to travel abroad because you wouldn't be issued a passport.

"Ms. Winchester said I could be a half-citizen the rest of my life, if I don't watch out. She said taking charge of my recovery in Drug Court would help me avoid that."

"Yes," I nodded. "Hope you'll be able to sign on."

For a moment, I could imagine the director leaning in to speak to twenty-three-year-old Dylan with her steady gaze: "I have to tell you, having a felony on your record *severely limits* your options."

But soon I heard a rustle around me as people started packing up and saying their goodbyes. The guard motioned everyone away from the booth windows. Our half hour had slipped by. Jumping up, Dylan pointed to his sweatpants. "Please, Mom, big like these," he said into the phone. "And don't forget the commissary."

That was my next stop. Along with other family members pushing cash in envelopes, I put in $40 dollars this week; with the jail taking half, that meant he'd get $20 for extras—like tuna and peanut butter. "Prison is a business," Tupac said, and that was over twenty years ago. Commissary, clothes, phone time—all cost money.

Not to mention the myriad court fees, medical expenses for nurse visits, pharmaceuticals. Most jail products and services were out-sourced, too, so that meant there could be an extra layer of fees you'd be forced to pay on top if you couldn't pay cash. This system made it easier for the jails, but not for families.

And now I've learned for sure it's mostly family members who literally pay for crimes, not the inmates, because inmates don't work for actual wages. *Why the hell not?* It seems to me that allowing inmates to work, earn, learn, and manage their own funds would do them all—and us—a world of good. Let's just say, most incarcerated folks have a ways to go in the personal-responsibility department before they can manage well on the outside. Apparently, citizens and elected officials haven't seen the light on that yet. But here's the truth: while buying stuff is a necessity for all, working at a job to earn wages is rapidly becoming a privilege for the few. And whereas in the Old Testament the sins of the father can be visited on the son, in today's American jail economy, good ol' Mom can pay out the wazoo for the sins of *her* son.

By my next talk with Dylan, the winds had shifted. He stated he was not necessarily leaning in the direction of Drug Court. He hadn't decided against it yet, but he was at the moment not inclined to take that option.

"Well, what else will you do?" I questioned, trying to control my exasperation.

He mentioned a six-month treatment program in nearby Parksville, after which he could be released on probation. What he really didn't like about DC is that it would keep him dependent on family the whole time—that, and the 10:00 p.m. curfew. Then, too, he couldn't take a trip anywhere else, except maybe to Cleveland in northern Ohio for a few days at Christmas to visit his dad. He would essentially have to give up his freedom and be here for two whole years, an eternity.

"Well, it's better than being locked up during that time," I pointed out.

"Yeah, but there must be other options. You know, I don't have access to the internet in here, so I can't look up anything for myself. I have to rely on what I hear from other guys with me, which is limited. Or I have to rely on you and my dad to find things out. What I need, Mom, is more information about other state-run programs I would be eligible for." He asked me to look some up, ones he'd heard about.

Over the next week or so, I searched for state-run recovery centers as an alternative kind of diversion agreement. One big problem with them was the waiting lists; there weren't enough recovery centers for the demand. The one closest to us had a six-month waiting list, with well over a thousand men on it. A center farther away had a three-month waiting list with only fifty-five men waiting. In 2011, these were new in Kentucky, and the demand was high. Some of these programs I had already heard about in court, as they were utilized by other defendants with drug charges. I passed along my information to Dylan, who was otherwise relying on testimonials or hearsay of other inmates. From those sources, he came up with another option: "Well, I hear Lighthouse Ministries offers a good program, and you can be out in nine months," he told me. "The last three months are for vocational training." I looked it up, and found the training included a heavy component of born-again religion. Dylan said he'd heard that, but it wasn't necessarily a deal-breaker if other aspects worked out. Given Dylan's views on religion, I doubted he would be too sincere about being born again. What I suspected is that this alternative program sounded shorter and easier. But it, too, had a waiting list.

Meanwhile, Dylan's dad and his partner, Linda, weighed in on matters. The more we discussed it, the more our collective family members agreed we wanted him to stay here, do Drug Court, and go back to college. Plus he'd be in a smaller place, one with more support and stability. Within two years, he could be well on the way to finishing his degree and have the chance to wipe out his felony charges gradually—though that would take five more years of good behavior on probation. Drug Court did sound rigorous, but isn't that just what he needed to get his head straight? Could he successfully complete it? We didn't know, but much depended on his willingness.

For his part, as one week followed another, Dylan gradually reverted to his first position of wanting to leave the area altogether. To him, it seemed perfectly reasonable to transfer any diversion agreement, be it Drug Court or whatever, to northern Kentucky near Cincinnati, so he could attend UC again. He'd find a way to do it, with or without our support. After a while, Dylan refused to talk anymore about further treatment options. He was concerned about getting this decided before the date when fall quarter started up at UC. We were at a stalemate. Rather than reaching any consensus, the rift between our positions was widening. Sometimes, I wondered if Dylan's digging in his heels like this had something to do with his being off meds. How was that affecting his reasoning now? But I figured it was all part of a larger pattern, my son's stubborn defiance of any authority. The defender, Ms. Pulaski, confirmed that the Drug Court Committee was meeting soon, and Dylan's candidacy would be assessed. She knew about Dylan's other plans. "I guess he has his own ideas," she told me with a smile. I could only shake my head.

The next hearing was scheduled for Monday, September 12. By the time I arrived at court, Sandra was already there. She had graciously agreed to come for moral support. So had Patrick, but he would be coming a little later. While making our way upstairs, we encountered a large crowd sitting in the waiting room. Defendants exchanged brief greetings with attorneys, and families sat quietly together, glancing nervously at the courtroom door to see when it was time for us to file in to take our places on the wooden pews.

Our faces showed the strain. Weeks or months of sleepless nights, guilt-ridden daydreams, the fear and dread of waiting for some kind of a positive outcome to a desperate situation, everyone hoping Judge Marlowe would throw a successful "Hail Mary" pass. We didn't know each other; our paths might never cross outside this room. But on that morning, we'd all be sitting on a courtroom bench, waiting for a decision that would impact our lives.

Once the bailiff opened the courtroom doors, we streamed in, and soon began the familiar rush of activity as attorneys moved about the room among their tense clients. We heard the injunction, "All rise," as the judge entered. By then, I had managed to gain a sense of Judge Marlowe's personality: serious-minded but with a quirky sense of humor. God knows that when you're meting out justice every day, much of it unwelcome news to the assembly, you have to lighten the load with a joke every now and then. Not to mention, a judge bears daily witness to every human frailty and shortcoming. Occasionally, a touch of testiness would crop up in his voice. Yet on this day, all seemed to go smoothly. In fact, the judge appeared to be in a good mood; it helped that today's batch of defendants were either getting or staying on track. When Judge Marlowe read his admonitions to those gaining pre-trial diversions, he would say: "Do you have any questions?" Hearing none forthcoming, he would add: "Good luck to you, sir." One defendant, a middle-aged woman in simple attire, stood before the bench to be acknowledged for having completed her probation successfully. Congratulations were in order, and the judge concluded by telling her cordially, "That's good, you can leave us then, and we hope not to see you here again." The exchange gave me hope; good things could happen. Watching it all, I shifted restlessly in my seat. *Yes, to get out of here and never have to come back again . . .*

At about 9:00, Patrick came in to join us. As the docket continued, the tension mounted. With each preceding case, the notch of the screw in my stomach tightened. The uncertainty of what would take place gnawed at all of us. I could only hope that defender Pulaski would use her calm manner and her rational arguments to steer Dylan toward his own best interest. He didn't even want to talk to us now. "I think you should all back off," he'd told me last Saturday by phone. "The problem is: you and Dad think you can live my life better than I can."

On that one, he was absolutely right. We were sure of it.

After a while, I noticed that Ms. Pulaski hadn't appeared in court at all yet today. She couldn't have been out conferring with clients all this time. Was she away? During a break, I was able to catch Ms. Beaumont's attention; she was the other public defender, the one who always seemed to wear the same bright fuchsia outfit you could easily pick out in a crowd. When I asked about her absent comrade, the news wasn't reassuring: Wesley Pulaski wouldn't be there this week, and Ms. Beaumont was taking her place. "But don't worry," Ms. Beaumont said brightly, seeking to inspire confidence. "Ms. Pulaski has thoroughly briefed me about your son's case. He'll be coming up after the break." I gulped and nodded.

When Court resumed, I noticed a slim woman in black emerge from one of the back doors of the room, behind the judge's bench and off to one side. As she moved down the aisle and toward the exit doors, I recognized her as Darlene Winchester, the tough-minded woman who talked like a social worker and dressed like Stevie Nicks. "That's the director of Drug Court," I said to Sandra next to me. What impressed me most at that moment was her intensity as she passed us: she looked straight ahead, a dark expression on her face. Maybe she had just talked to Dylan and heard him say he didn't want to do Drug Court here in town. If so, that would explain the set of her jaw. I could relate. Tension mounted. I stretched my back, shifted again on the wooden bench.

Finally, the inmates were led through the side door by the

bailiff with a clanking of keys. Dylan glanced over the barrier to catch sight of us before taking a seat. Before long, I heard, "Next, Mr. Stafford." With Dylan standing next to the defender in handcuffs, having given his name and address, Ms. Beaumont stood before the bench and began to speak. Just then, another voice piped up from the prosecution's side of the courtroom.

"If it please the Court, sir, Ms. Winchester just reported that some new information has come up in this case that needs to be considered. We advise meeting together and postponing the hearing until Friday the 16th."

I held my breath.

Judge Marlowe, raising his eyebrows, asked, "Good or bad information?"

The prosecutor shrugged her shoulders.

"Indifferent?" Marlowe said. "We'll see, then. This case will be continued on Friday the 16th."

I collapsed against the hard wood behind my back. Four more sleepless nights!

The three of us filed out of the courtroom and held our own counsel outside in the parking lot. I was just trying to breathe and keep my blood circulating, which seemed to require more effort than usual today. How long could this uncertainty go on? On the other hand, we should have known by now that the courtroom is always full of surprises—or rather delays. I speculated openly about Ms. Winchester's demeanor. We figured that the court hadn't been aware of Dylan's new position and the results of his recent talk with Ms. Winchester of Drug Court, hence the need for further discussion before moving forward. Rev. Patrick volunteered to visit my son that afternoon, since he had special clergy privileges, to see what Dylan knew and thought of the proceedings. We all agreed we would get in touch later. I called John to tell him what little I could report and then had to get back to campus and teach a class, back to my other life and responsibilities.

Right after class at 3:30, I received a phone call from jail. I asked Dylan what had happened in court. He confirmed what we had suspected about Ms. Winchester's talk with him. A few minutes into our conversation, Patrick made his appearance at the jail for a visit, and I could hear Dylan's name being called through a loudspeaker. Later that evening, another call came from Dylan. Unlike me, he didn't seem upset that Ms. Pulaski hadn't been there. In fact, he'd heard that Ms. Beaumont was "better"; she went along with his plans and found them reasonable. Inside, I groaned. Furthermore, it was his belief that the judge was probably making sure that the Circuit Court of Kenton County would take his case so that it could be diverted to northern Kentucky. He seemed to accept the delay, though he also mentioned that his plan was to get to UC by next Wednesday in order to begin the fall quarter.

"But how can you just start the quarter with no place to live, no preparation?"

He didn't have his mind on details like that.

It was another big circuit court day for us on September 16. Sandra, Patrick, and I took up our customary places in the courtroom at 9:00 a.m., a low buzz of activity going on around us, mainly off the side of the judge's bench. Just the typical back-and-forth stitching of fates between the attorneys for the defense and those for the prosecution, I assumed. We chatted nervously and eventually noticed that it had been fifteen, twenty, twenty-five minutes and still no judge. Where was he? By the time Judge Marlowe eventually stepped from his chamber to the bench, his black robe swirling around him, he was a full hour late. Even the bailiff was caught off guard; we only had time to half-rise before sitting back down. The judge told the court that he'd just been involved in a light truck accident, was shaken but obviously glad to be alive. After a bit of banter with the attorneys, he plunged into the docket. No Ms. Pulaski, of course; she was still away, and fuchsia-clad Ms. Beaumont remained the only public defender for the day. Other cases came up, but not the one I came to hear, and I didn't have much time left. By 10:30, I already had to leave because of my upcoming class at the college. Both Sandra and Patrick said they could stay on and promised to fill me in later.

After class, Sandra told me Dylan had been offered Drug Court—right there in Doran County, nowhere else—and Judge Marlowe was stern: take it or leave it. Having heard the judge pronounce in previous first-offender cases, I could imagine clearly what he must have said. Dylan would have to make a plea of guilty in order to get this diversion. The judge always asks whether the defendant understands his rights and that he is giving certain of them up in order to get this diversion. He would also ask, "Are you of sound mind? Do you testify that you are not under the influence of drugs or alcohol?" It's serious because you can't go back and plead not guilty after this; you give up your right to a trial. Then, punctuating the pronouncement several times as the terms are read to the defendant, Marlowe would have asked, in tones and a cadence I would recognize because I had heard this ritual question in court so many times by now: "Mr. Stafford, how do you understand the terms I have just read to you?" Then Dylan would have reiterated in his own words what the judge had explained to him.

"He took the offer," Sandra reported.

Moments later, Patrick called, too. He confirmed everything and told me Dylan would be released soon. My hands were shaking as I got off the phone. Released soon! I would have to sort out my emotions later—part jubilance, part apprehension. Mainly relief. But for now, an adrenaline rush! I had to get to the jail ASAP; Dylan had an appointment at Drug Court at 1:00 that very afternoon, at 10th and Maple. I grabbed my car keys and headed through crowded halls downstairs to the outside and then across town to the jail, where I parked and walked quickly through the doors. Almost simultaneously as I entered the building, I heard the clank of heavy steel doors down the corridor. Suddenly, Dylan was walking toward me in his jeans again. He was free.

We walked outside into the light of day, he for the first time in many weeks, both of us dazed. We hugged briefly and headed for my car. There was no time for speeches or hardly even conversation. I glanced over at him sitting next to me and smiled. In fact, I was speechless but happy. I knew only this for certain: Drug Court was starting up, and Dylan had just a few minutes to get there for the first meeting.

CHAPTER 8: DRUG COURT

The very next day after his release, Dylan was summoned to the city park to help with a 5K Run for Recovery, headed up by Ms. Winchester. Later on, Dylan said the Drug Court director remarked, on first seeing him, that he looked about as cheery as a man on Death Row. By now, we all knew Darlene Winchester wasn't one to hold back what she was thinking. On the following Monday, the new regime started in earnest, as Dylan had to show up for a drug test in the morning, then attend a round of activities in the afternoon. He reported that Judge Marlowe had been tough on him at the 1:00 meeting, but he also got more of an impression of how things would go from seeing the other people in Drug Court and being involved with the group. He was not the only young man there—far from it. There were about thirty people of all ages doing the program. While attending his first meeting, he got a lead on a job in town, which he intended to pursue. Meanwhile, the judge said he could talk to his public defender the next day at 2:00 to explore alternatives if he wasn't sure he wanted to do Drug Court. Dylan wouldn't be expected to sign final papers for DC until the following Monday. Nobody was being coerced. It was a big commitment, and the choice was his.

Drug Court ground rules in a west Kentucky town, circa 2011:

- You must live independently: you can be with another adult but not a parent or family member.
- You must be productive: you must have a job or be a full-time student.
- No drugs or alcohol of any kind can be used. Only prescribed medications are allowed. Random, frequent drug tests ensure compliance. Your residence may be inspected for violations.
- Every morning at 7:30, it is necessary to call in to see if there will be a drug test that morning. If so, this must be completed before 8:30 a.m. at a specific location.
- Curfew every evening at 10:00 p.m. Call in and confirm you are home either by landline or cell phone with GPS.
- Required attendance at these meetings every week: at least four AA meetings, one court meeting with Circuit Judge, and one group meeting for education and counseling. For newcomers or those needing it, you must also have a one-on-one meeting with Ms. Winchester.

For someone coming straight out of jail, or for an addict who seldom adhered to any kind of daily schedule, or for a college kid taking psych meds and/or prone to self-medicating as he deems fit, this regime could be a definite shock to the system. Coping with problems without resorting to any un-prescribed mood-altering substances? Showing up for meetings to discuss openly what you'd normally hide or skip over? Living with one hundred percent accountability? These have to go from being vague concepts for sometime in the future to a regular daily practice—as defined by a court, starting right now. It definitely gets a person's attention.

Drug Court offered a clear structure, but there were plenty of basic problems for individuals to solve: housing, transportation, and finding work. Though families were, in one sense, off the hook in terms of reinforcing total responsibility for behaviors, in another sense, we were still very much on the hook for lending a hand, especially in the finance department. After consultation with Dylan's dad, I told Dylan the family would be willing to help him out with rent as long as he would do his part in Drug Court. Being a full participant was his MAIN job. For spending money, he would have to earn what he could through finding some kind of remunerative work, not from the family. Many of the particulars had to be figured out on the fly. That meant some trial and error.

To comply, the first problem Dylan faced was to find housing. He'd lost his apartment in the legal fray; now he had to find another, which wouldn't be easy after the start of the semester when all the student housing close to campus was already taken. After much searching, we found a house close by that seemed to fit the criteria—almost. It was too big for one person, but it had earlier been subdivided into two apartments, and Dylan was counting on getting a housemate, another young guy at Drug Court named Connor, to occupy the other part and pay rent. After two visits to make sure they each had their own kitchens, bathrooms, and living spaces, Ms. Winchester finally approved the dwelling for both of them. However, she stressed that they would each have to maintain their own domains and be responsible for following the rules. There could be an inspection at any time. A week later, Connor moved in "next door" and his girlfriend moved in, too. Dylan could see the advantages of having a buddy nearby, especially one with a truck who had to attend a lot of the same meetings he did. Now, he had a roof over his head, food, a pal, and freedom. Freedom with plenty of limits.

As for me during this time, work continued to be my refuge. In that space, I never felt alone. My colleagues were smart people, skilled at whatever needed to be done on any given day. My office itself, with its solid shelves of books in rows, its folders bulging with lesson materials, gave me a sense of order and abundance. The omnipresent computer screen with its magic files, all openable with a mere click, stored my professional archives. Meanwhile, the internet could give instant access to encyclopedic knowledge, seeming to offer answers to any question and solutions to any problem (except the pressing ones involving my family). As for teaching in the classroom, I loved the structure, discipline, and play of it—the improvisational aspects of helping students to engage with the strangeness of a different language, seeing what new aspects of the codes, colors, and rhythms of it they could weave into their lives. For me, as well as for them, class activities were adventures, but they were much more contained than the ones we encounter in the chaotic world. No wonder my workplace offered that island of security I often craved. Now that Dylan was a free man in Drug Court, I felt we were each operating within the appropriate jurisdiction we belonged in—at least, for now.

And how was Dylan reacting to all this? One scene stands out for me. On a Saturday afternoon, maybe a few weeks into the new regime, Dylan came over to my place while I happened to be raking leaves in my garden plot. He was basically doing OK, but he wanted to vent his frustrations. Mainly, he felt that Drug Court was running him ragged with one requirement after another. And the endless meetings! There was another one at AA coming up that evening. He barely had time to breathe.

"You'll get used to it. It's just hard at first because it's all new to you," I said.

"Yeah, well, you have no idea. These people are addicts, Mom! ADDICTS! They've been on meth, cocaine, opiates, and who knows what else? And this is who I'm spending time with—a lot of time, too!"

He was already mounted on his moped in the middle of the stony driveway, ready to take off. As if to emphasize his point, he gunned the engine and spun around in a circle, stones flying out from under the wheels in a dramatic spray. In that moment, my son looked like an angry centaur, rearing up on its hind legs, revving its engine with the roar of a thousand killer bees—as if to assert, "Me, an addict? No way!" I guess he was forgetting about the empty bottles of vodka I'd found lined up around his apartment in June, or the flourishing pot garden he'd planted—not to mention a second DUI. Small stuff? Well, the consequences hadn't exactly been small. Before I could say anything at all, he peeled out in a blast of noise. No, I wasn't surprised, but I was worried. How in the world was this going to play out?

When the second DUI charge had been confirmed, no one in the family thought he should be driving this wheeled vehicle, or any other, anytime soon. After his release in September to attend Drug Court, and up until the time he had to appear in district court for the DUI, he had continued to ride the moped around town, arguing that he needed transportation to get to meetings and various odd jobs. In fact, he'd spent quite a bit of time fixing up the inexpensive Chinese Tao-Tao. The scooter had been all black, and he'd decided to paint the fenders a bright yellow, a vivid contrast to the black core body. Dylan was pleased with the effect; not only was it a safety feature to brighten things up, but it was a way of giving the moped a new identity. "Just like I'm doing for myself now," he said.

Though I admired the paint job, I confronted Dylan with the fact that his license had been taken away. He said he knew continuing to drive the moped could be a legal problem, but he seemed sure this would not affect his main charges in the higher court. I wasn't at all convinced. He told me Drug Court knew he was still driving the scooter. "It's OK, as long as I park it behind the building and don't advertise the fact. They know I have to get around." I remembered how, early on, I'd had the idea of hiding the bike from Dylan in a friend's garage, but that plan didn't meet with enthusiasm on the part of the garage owner. Now it was way too late for that. So during most of that autumn, Dylan was inseparable from the moped. Besides, I had to recognize that Dylan was twenty-three years old. When I talked with him about my concerns, he said, "You don't need to worry about me, Mom. I can make my own decisions. I know what the consequences might be and I'm prepared to take them. This is a risk I'm willing to take."

I could only shrug my tense shoulders. "We'll see."

And so it happened that Dylan was literally flying by the seat of his pants down the road. No longer a student for this semester, he had to find work. I thought it would be relatively easy for him to snag a job at a sandwich place or one of the fast-food restaurants all over town. Anything would do. He said no one would hire him with his bad record, but I'm not convinced he tried all fifty-plus possible employers. Did he try even one of them? Instead, Dylan ended up being a chronic gig chaser. Sometimes working with his housemate Connor, sometimes alone, he would clean out garages, do repair work, help out with construction, do whatever odd job came along. He heard about these jobs at AA or through the Drug Court group or from an internet listing. This more or less worked out for him, but not always. And on those occasions, I tended to be the first to find out about it.

One day in late fall, Dylan had a plan to make $80 a day working for a farmer who had a ranch and needed help repairing fence posts. The job was on hold for a while due to heavy rains. Finally, the weather cleared, and the plan was a go. The only problem was the fact that the ranch was a good forty minutes away by car, and Dylan didn't have one. Instead, he found himself on a country road on his moped. As it happened, the scooter gave out about two or three miles from his destination. That is to say, it continued to work, but at a top speed of maybe ten miles per hour. Don't ask how many phone calls I received that day from unknown byways in the country! I'd be sitting in my office, answering e-mails (fortunately, it was a slow day), and yet another update from remote Strandville would come in. Since I couldn't leave my job to pick him up any time soon, I discussed the situation with him on each occasion: call ahead and leave a message; hide the scooter and walk to the ranch; look for the farmer—all to no avail. The man was older and didn't have a cell phone.

This episode turned into something like Sandra Bullock's situation in *Gravity* when she's lost in outer space and has to call in to Mission Control: "I've lost my contact; my capsule has lost power. The plan is failing; tell me what to do now." When Dylan found the ranch, there was no house there, and no one around to ask about the job. The whole day was a wash. Instead of working on fence posts, what he could do was continue on the road, slowly—very slowly, and with a long line of vehicles behind him—into the distant town for a late lunch and a long wait. More phone calls came in: "How can I dock up for rescue out here? How can I get back to Earth?"

I admit in my second career as an X-treme Parent, I sometimes felt like Peter Graves's secret agent character in the old TV show, *Mission: Impossible*. The show always started with Graves playing a small cassette tape and opening an envelope of photographs to find out about his next assignment. Dylan's moped predicament was about to become mine. Already I could hear the inevitable words, "Your mission, should you decide to accept it, is to . . ." Along with the words, I could already hear the hiss of smoke as the tapes started to self-destruct. Oh yes, and just like for Graves, if I failed, all the authorities would disavow my actions.

By the end of the workday, I managed to locate a friend named Gordie who had a truck with a trailer big enough for the docking operation. It was getting dark as we pulled up to a parking lot outside a boat shop in Riverton. I immediately caught sight of Dylan in a tan, one-piece work suit and waved. He walked up to the truck, no doubt glad to see us. In a few minutes, he and Gordie roped the recalcitrant Tao-Tao firmly into the trailer, then all three of us squeezed into the front seat of Gordie's vehicle. We talked hunting and fishing on the way back—well, Gordie did most of the talking. Dylan was clearly mortified by having to be rescued like this. He admitted it wasn't such a great idea to go so far with a scooter that had an unfortunate tendency to conk out every now and then. Tinkering with the engine in town was one thing, but there was a limit to what you could do an hour from home with only minimal tools.

True, on occasion, I felt I still had to jump in and be the rescuer. Though Dylan was out there fending for himself and answering to a judge every week, there were still times, like that one, when I could be on tap for special interventions. Other days, though, I had to sit back and be the "silent witness." This is the art, known to many but not fully mastered by me, of listening with empathy but not feeling like you need to rescue the person—or even do anything at all, other than listen. Every parent has to learn this, no matter who your kid is or how protective you may be. But let me tell you: it's extremely difficult to practice this craft with an at-risk young adult you have every reason to believe will NOT always make the right decision.

Such a test came up, for example, on the evening of the disastrous fencepost trip. After Dylan went to one of his required AA meetings, he called to ask if I would pick him up afterward and take him to Walgreens. Seated next to me in the car, he started opening up about his addiction situation. The meeting had evidently triggered a recognition of how his own drug and alcohol use had been getting worse over the years. He had never talked so openly about this with me before. Usually he would dismiss the topic if I brought it up. Instead, he'd maintain the story that he only used alcohol, for example, on "certain occasions"—to steady himself after a bad day or to counter-balance one of his ever-fluctuating mental states. That's what his mood-balancing meds were supposed to do, but people with bipolar don't always trust their meds, or the meds don't always work, or they just prefer to take their chances with their own form of self-medicating. All the same, I was glad Dylan had finally agreed to make an appointment with Dr. Peltay again to renew his prescriptions.

Well, today had definitely been a bad day for him, only now instead of pouring the booze or smoking pot, he'd been attending an AA meeting—hearing other peoples' stories, thinking about it. He'd always somehow managed to convince himself that marijuana and alcohol helped him along, but he also knew that alcohol had gotten him two DUIs within twelve months. His legal problems were worse, and without a license, his options for improving his situation were less appealing. He was facing the magnitude of it all—that alone was remarkable. And now he was actually saying that a person had to face his own choices, take responsibility for them. Could it be that some kind of self-realization was starting to take hold?

Suddenly, I checked the time. It was getting late. Dylan had limited time to go into the pharmacy, get what he wanted, and get back to his place before curfew at 10:00 p.m. When I dropped him off at his place twenty minutes later, I found myself sighing with relief. But, later at home, a twinge of worry crossed my mind. I hadn't reminded him to call in, but something told me that on this particular evening, he probably needed to be. "Wait a minute: why should I have to?" I thought. *All these micro-worries. I haven't been reminding him, and I shouldn't go so far as to take on his curfew responsibility.*

Well, I found out five days later that Dylan was headed for a sanction: two nights in jail, Wednesday and Thursday, for curfew infraction. Turns out that very Friday evening at Walgreens, something had come up after he got back to his place, and yes, he'd forgotten to call in on time. I couldn't believe it, but I remembered that wave of concern crossing me that evening, like a sixth sense tuning in. At the very next moment, though, I knew I had to set it all aside. Dylan had to take responsibility for what he did or didn't do. Hadn't he told me this himself?

"Don't worry, Mom," he said. "I've got a ride to the jail. And it's OK: I'm still in Drug Court. I just have to take this sanction; that's all."

"That's good."

"Just filling you in. But I was wondering, can you pick me up when I get released? That'll be Friday at 6 p.m. at the jail." He must have sensed my distraction because I didn't reply right away.

"OK, I'll be there Friday."

"6:00, on the dot. I'll probably be outside already."

He didn't know it, but I was practicing being The Rock. That's my code word for setting aside my impulse to fret, grieve, or feel like I have to jump in and try to solve somebody's problem—especially my son's. Instead, I was trying to be the silent witness, making myself as steady as a boulder.

Whatever my initial reaction to his telling me about the jail sanction, I was still processing things hours later. The wonder of it was that every time my son got sent to jail, I felt two overwhelming feelings at once, and they were completely contradictory. On the one hand, I was hugely disappointed that he messed up once again— to the point of almost being ill. But then—and here is the strange part—I also felt a great sense of relief. *He's safe; he's going to be OK.* Though that may not have been completely true, the fact was that, for me, having my son lifted out of the enormous pressures of life and placed in a structured environment was like having someone in a storm being taken to a calm place of shelter. And I didn't always know if that someone needing shelter was Dylan or myself.

During this same time period, however rock steady I may have tried to be, the two of us definitely had a few blowouts. In general, it seemed that our relationship was having as many fits and starts as the Chinese Tao-Tao engine. Not long after Gordie dropped the yellow scooter off at Fred's Small Engine Repair shop south of town, Dylan called me one Saturday afternoon because he thought maybe the power failure had to do with drawing fuel. Maybe if he installed a new fuel pump, that would fix the problem. He said he'd ordered one; it had come in, so would I take him out to the shop?

I wasn't at all enthusiastic. I'd just been about to go for a long walk in the park to decompress, but I reluctantly agreed maybe it was worth a try. Arriving at Fred's in the middle of the afternoon, the scene looked completely different from what it had been during an earlier season. Gone was the canopied summer workshop on the hill among the trees. Instead, small, motorized vehicles of all sorts were parked in every available space close to a large shed near the house. This was moped land in late autumn, and on a Saturday afternoon, Fred and Company were nowhere to be found.

Dylan soon located his scooter and set to work installing the new pump. I wondered how long it would take, and should I come back at a certain time? He told me it would take about fifteen minutes, and he would find out if this took care of the problem or not. I strolled among the small vehicles for a bit, then approached Dylan's scooter where he was working on it, adjusting parts and then spraying some kind of starter fluid on a mesh-covered cylinder, the carburetor. In a while, he asked me to help spray the fluid while he adjusted something else. After repeated attempts to get the engine started, we could both hear it trying but not fully kicking in. The next thing I remember was Dylan glancing up and getting enraged at me for, in his words, "having a dumb grin on my face." I don't remember grinning at all, but from my perspective, I—knowing next to zero about engines and getting machines to work—was just trying to make the best of getting into a job I didn't want to do.

The explosion (a different kind of combustion emanating from a different kind of carburetor) continued with my son launching into a tirade about how selfish a person I was, not willing to take fifteen minutes of my day to help him out, and why was I grinning when he was doing all the work, and it obviously wasn't going well? Was I making fun of him? I was surprised at the intensity of his anger, which seemed way out of proportion to what had actually happened. Resisting the urge to defend myself vigorously from what I considered an unjust attack, I made some kind of neutral remark, then subsequently found out that no matter what I said, it was just going to inject more fuel into the combustion engine, so I'd better lie low and wait for it to sputter out on its own. Time again to be The Rock. Reflection would have to come later. After some more fruitless tinkering with the fuel pump, Dylan decided to abandon the effort. The elusive Fred would have to work on it next week.

The tirade went on, too, for most of the trip back, a whole riff on the selfishness theme. I knew this had its roots back in my son's childhood, him believing that I chose to spend so much time on my career, apparently abandoning him, not having cared for him as much as he needed when he was young, not wanting to spend time with him, not being there for him.

"Life is easy for *you*, Mom. You don't have any problems!" he roared. "Me, I've got nothing but problems, one after the other. As soon as I get one solved, another crops up—or maybe two or three at once! Life is really unfair. Why don't you get that?"

Finally, pulling up in front of his residence, I remember him getting out of the car, still taking a few parting shots, but then—as he spotted someone else coming down the street—toning his voice down and saying something dismissive, like "Well, I'm not even that mad anymore. See ya." I drove off, thinking, "Great, glad *you're* feeling better, buddy. I should have just taken that walk." But, I admit, deep down I was hurt—just as hurt and wronged as he felt he was. He'd been subject to flash anger ever since he was born. It probably reminded me of times I tried to comfort him as a baby, and it didn't always work. Then, later on, there were all those broken-off pencils in his jeans pockets, the hole he kicked into the wall, the torn-up drawings on the floor that were perfectly good ones—he just ripped them up because he got frustrated that they weren't perfect. Just like I wasn't the perfect mom.

To tell the truth, when it came to my son's predicaments, I often didn't know how much credit I could claim for helping, or how much blame I should take when things went badly. I talked about all this with Sandra, but more often with John. That's when John would let his word-bomb drop, the one he had first used earlier in the summer. He suggested I was letting myself get trapped in a codependent relationship.

"Let your son grow up. He needs to figure things out for himself," John said.

Needless to say, the word "codependent" provoked a reaction, especially in an anxious person like me, trying to be The Rock of Gibraltar. Trying to be heroic.

"What?! Me, *codependent*?" I would say as I launched into my Wounded Mom persona. It was just like being zapped into the cartoon story box of a graphic novel, something à la Roz Chast of *The New Yorker*. Just like in her drawings, my hands would be thrown up in shocked indignation, forehead furrowed, frizzled hair sticking straight up, eyebrows jumping clear off my face, mouth wide open in a shout of triple-exclamation-point vexation. "Are you kidding me?!!! Me, have issues? Is it codependent to drive someone in Drug Court to another town once to pee in a cup during my workday so he won't get sanctions, or to arrange a rescue mission out in the boonies, or to help repair a scooter and get yelled at? *My* feelings about all this? Look, I'm a perfectly in-control, professional person. It's the other guy I'm dealing with who's out of control. Can't you see?"

But I was beginning to suspect John was right. All that damp, anxious, wormy self-doubt—that was the flip side of The Rock. Then, too, sometimes I really was the mom character in a wacko cartoon. Seems I had a few contradictions to sort out for myself. This whole mom business was way more complicated than I ever thought it would be.

CHAPTER 9: NAMI I

A few years before my son's arrest, I was telling my friend Maureen about some of the problems that came up while he was a student in Cincinnati.

"Why don't you try going to a NAMI meeting?"

"Oh?" I asked vaguely.

"They meet in a church up in Parksville, about twice a month. I think they have one support group for family and another for persons living with a mental illness. You might get some help."

At the time, I was slightly irritated that Maureen would even bring this up. Her son Daniel had schizophrenia, so of course she was going to join a group like the National Alliance on Mental Illness. Back then, I didn't believe my son's case was that serious. Yes, he had a diagnosis from a psychiatrist. True, he'd had some behavior problems all along, and he'd been on the wrong side of the law with intoxicants a few times. But surely, his life wasn't going to be as severely impacted as Daniel's was. Stumbling around as a young adult was just part of growing up, wasn't it?

After Dylan got arrested, my opinion changed. Only a few weeks before that event, I found out there was a new NAMI group in town. The notice for monthly meetings was posted at the new psychiatrist's office, along with a contact number. "Why don't they have meetings for me?" Dylan had asked when he saw it; the notice was addressed to family members. I finally decided to go. That's where I met Sandra, who was heading it up. Turns out she and her husband, Robert, had gone to the very meetings in Parksville that Maureen had told me about earlier. After attending a NAMI Family-to-Family mentorship program, the couple felt motivated to start a support group here, to raise awareness in our small town.

I wasn't the quickest convert. Half-curious, half-reluctant, I started attending meetings every month, though I often dreaded it. This entailed leaving my comfortable, predictable educational world to go directly into the chaotic, unpredictable, emotional one shared by these parents. I wasn't used to shifting those gears—not openly, not deliberately. And I wasn't sure this was really a tribe I belonged to.

I went first and foremost because I was grateful for the help Sandra had given me in my hour of need. After all, how many people could I count on to go with me to Dylan's court hearings, especially when John couldn't be there and the rest of the family lived 700 miles away? And to listen to all my woes with a son whose irresponsible behavior left me feeling like an emotional basket case and a bad parent? I went because Sandra understood, and so did the other parents there. With them, I could start to shed some guilt and look with a clearer gaze on what was going on.

At this particular November meeting, we sat in a circle. After our usual introductions, Sandra turned the floor over to Rita. It was clear that things had been happening behind the scenes. Everyone wanted to know more about Rita's son, Brett, who had been diagnosed with a severe form of paranoid schizophrenia. He was living in a group home in Owensboro, since there was no such residence for him in our town. He was taking medication now and was doing better, but he still heard voices and was delusional. He had a history of being in and out of Western State psychiatric hospital, but the cost of that was $720 dollars a day (paid by the state), so they kept him in for a maximum of ninety days or less, long enough to be pronounced "stable." Then they released him. Lately, with budgets tight, the stays were shorter—more like a week, sometimes only four days.

Brett was thirty-two years old, and during his adult life he'd been to Western State maybe twenty times, lived in group homes, wandered off, gotten lost, been homeless, been arrested, and put in jail. Eventually, he'd get court-ordered back to the psychiatric hospital, and the whole cycle would start over again. All this with a family who was doing their best to keep track of him. Hearing Brett's story made me wonder: What other form of illness in America would condemn someone to wander around in hopeless circles like an inhabitant of Dante's *Inferno*? When you heard these testimonies, you wondered which one was crazier: the delusional person with a serious brain disorder, or the mental health care system in our country?

"Brett wants to come home for Christmas," Rita said, "but I just can't imagine handling the fallout from that. Just dealing with everyone on top of Brett. No, it wouldn't work." Like Sandra, Rita was remarried and had a daughter as well as a son. "Besides," Rita added, "I remember what happened the last time we tried transporting him between places. Can't take that on again, just can't."

Rita was referring to an earlier occasion, when Brett had been released from Western State hospital to live in an apartment with occasional visits by a case worker. However, he quit taking his meds, and rapidly became delusional again. One night, he became convinced that monsters were attacking him. He smashed his TV and other furniture trying to get rid of them. Both parents agreed he needed to go back to Western State. But what they really wanted was a more long-term solution, something stable for their son. How could someone who already had so much chaos in his head deal with such a disordered pattern of treatment and so many changes of residence? After phone calls to the police, it was decided that Brett's dad would pick him up and take him to Western. But then, in the middle of the drive while they were making a fast-food pit stop, the young man hopped out of the car and fled.

"You remember, we had to call the police to help find him," Rita reminded us.

We remembered. The police soon located him, but it took the intervention of two county judges, the police, the parents, and the negotiations of Sandra and Robert from our NAMI group before the young man could be safely escorted back to the psychiatric hospital. Part of the problem was administrative: in non-criminal cases, judges could only make decisions within their jurisdictions, so crossing a county line involved calling to get another judge's approval. Besides, though the local police were trained to do crisis invention, they couldn't always be available to round up mentally unstable persons and drive them to a treatment facility ninety miles away. Rita shook her head.

"He's been through so much already. We all have. I don't want to ask his dad to pick him up again after what happened before, getting the police involved."

Rita had a lot to juggle, keeping her regular family life going and also supporting Brett. Earlier on, she'd tried to take care of him at home, but with a full-time career and a new marriage, it didn't work out. Now, this year's Christmas would be complicated. What could she do for Brett so that he could celebrate the holiday and not be alone?

Earlier, Rita had shown us a picture of her son, taken maybe ten years previously, when he was an attractive, earnest-looking young man, a photo you might see posted on Facebook. Yet Rita had told us there were times within the past twelve months when she barely recognized him. After wandering away from another group home in Lexington, Brett's hair had grown out wildly, his clothing filthy, with bits of food encrusted on his shirtsleeves. At times, Rita didn't even know where he was. He needed to take his meds, but he didn't understand why he should take them. Our group had learned the term for that, *anosognosia*. It was a Greek-based medical term used for a person who lacked the awareness that he or she was ill, disconnected from reality. People in this condition, due to brain-circuitry dysfunction, were too ill to follow any health regimen. They would be too delusional to benefit from their civil right to make use of mental health services, even those available to them through the expanded coverage of Medicaid under the new Affordable Care Act (2010).

Both Sandra and Rita were devastated by the way illness had changed their sons' lives. They each said it was as if the true self of the person they'd known earlier had been taken away and some stranger put in his place. Even during the relatively good times, when their sons were receiving better care and in fuller possession of their understanding, it wasn't the same.

"Seems like my son is in a state of arrested development. Like he's caught in a time warp when he was fifteen or sixteen years old," Rita would say. "But I've learned to really appreciate the times when he's healthy and knows who I am. He smiles and says he loves me. Then I know my Brett is still in there somewhere."

"I feel the same way about Brad," Sandra said. He was in his early thirties, too, like Brett.

"It doesn't seem to make any difference what his chronological age is, our son still acts the same way he did when he was a teenager," husband Robert confirmed. "He rebels the same way, has the same temper tantrums if he doesn't get what he wants."

"And sometimes I feel so bad about everything he's missing out on," Sandra added. "I look at his younger sister moving on with her life, and I know Brad will never do those things: graduate, get a job, travel, get married, start his own family."

Whenever this theme came up—and it came up often—it sent her to the edge of tears. Robert handed her a box of Kleenex.

"Well, that's sad for us," Robert reminded her, "but Brad—he's happy most of the time as he is, just staying inside his apartment playing his video games." Both parents wished he would want more—a job, a sense of purpose. And they were always concerned about his propensity to use drugs or host drug parties in his apartment. But for now, they were glad their son would agree to get his prescribed shot once a month from Dr. Peltay, allowing him to remain relatively stable. Their plan was to explore other possibilities for him, but he had to be open to trying them, and that was something beyond their control.

"Well," Rita went on, "I've thought about it, and I've made my decision. I'm going to tell everyone at home that we can do all kinds of activities together over the holidays, but I'm going to spend Christmas Day with Brett. I'll drive in the morning to where he is at the group home in Owensboro. I'll take some presents and some food, and that way, he'll have family for at least one day."

You could almost hear a collective sigh around the table, everyone thinking about what that day would be like. More questions for her while the Kleenex box got passed around.

"Wow, Rita, that's amazing," I told her. From what Rita had shared with us, I figured that Brett was well enough now to greatly appreciate his mom being with him at Christmas, even for just one day.

In my first few months of these meetings, after hearing such heartbreaking dilemmas, I often felt undisguised relief at their ending. Sometimes I would stay to talk longer like the other moms did, but more often I'd be the first out the door, emotionally drained and hungry. That's how it was this particular evening. After a hug or two, I took off. Facing harsh reality is something I can only stand for a scant hour, maybe once a month. It was all still new to me, this way of being open about something I tried not to look at, not to see. For a pie-eyed optimist, hearing these stories was like sampling the strongest and strangest brew the tap room offered. I hadn't acquired a taste for the bitters served by this kind of life, this reality. Not yet. But I was working on it.

CHAPTER 10: THE RULE OF TWOS

As Dylan moved through the early months of Drug Court, a number of practical matters had to be dealt with. For one, it was early December and the troublesome moped needed some serious engine repairs. It was clear that Fred had done what he could with the Chinese scooter, but if Dylan were really going to rely on this vehicle for transportation, it would have to be checked out and repaired by an outfit that knew these kinds of engines backwards and forwards. Dylan found such a place in Nashville and came up with a plan for the two of us. We'd rent a truck to transport it there and have it fixed. On the same trip, he decided to put his dirt-jumping Kona bike on Craigslist and sell it, which he did, for $380. Getting the moped fixed was the solution to Problem #1.

Next, he was finding that living with Connor and his girlfriend in the next-door apartment wasn't working out too well. Even though the apartments were separate, they weren't separate enough, and the girlfriend came over to talk endlessly about her problems while Dylan was home and Connor was away at work. "Why doesn't she get a job? Then, at least, she'd have something to do," Dylan said. "When I'm in school again next semester, there's no way I'm going to be able to study with her around yakking." As for Connor, Dylan liked him well enough, remarking, "It's hard to believe, but he's even more impulsive than me. I'm sure he has some mental health issues going on, too." Still, he knew Connor wasn't going to break up with his girlfriend anytime soon; she was part of the living arrangement.

"I've got to find another place," Dylan concluded. "I want to stay on good terms with Connor, but this house-sharing concept is just not going to work." Fortunately, he soon found an available apartment. It was nearing the end of the term, and students who had finished degrees were moving. The location and price of the single apartment were excellent; it was a nice one. The only issues now were giving the landlord notice, telling Connor, and doing the physical work of moving. Dylan didn't seem daunted by any of that. It had to be done. So, moving would be the solution to Problem #2.

Yet another problem loomed in the early months. Dylan's first sponsor at AA wasn't working out. First, the sponsor wasn't available when Dylan wanted to contact him; next, Dylan found out his new guide to sobriety had fallen off the wagon. *Oh no, is this going to be a case of the blind leading the blind?* That's when I started hearing about someone named Arlo. Apparently, Arlo went along with what I started calling the Rule of Twos. Just as Dylan's first residence didn't work out and eventually he had to look for another one, so his first AA sponsor hadn't been the right fit, either. According to Dylan, though, the second volunteer for this job, Arlo, was super-reliable. Arlo had been a radiologist who'd lost his job a few years back because his weekend drinking habit started encroaching on the rest of the week. Now he'd successfully quit drinking altogether, went to AA regularly, and worked for his parents, who owned rental properties in town. Arlo did a lot of carpentry and maintenance work. In the summer, he also did some farming on the side. He was low-key and sympatico. If Dylan called to talk or wanted to ask him about something, he responded. Not only that, but occasionally, he could even give Dylan some paid work to do. Also, Arlo had a truck, which could be extremely useful to a guy who only had a moped—and who had to move his household in the winter. There was a limit to how much Dylan could prevail on Connor to use his black Silverado, especially since he didn't know exactly how Connor would react to his suggestion that they each get separate dwellings. Dylan was highly aware of trying to spread his requests for assistance around, so no one person would feel overwhelmed. So in many ways, Arlo went a long way toward solving Problem #3.

About these changes, Dylan reported that Ms. Winchester of Drug Court wasn't surprised. By now, he was calling her Darlene, as the other DC members did. According to him, Darlene said that if something in your life isn't working, then you should think about it, and either you need to change yourself or you need to change the situation. As for the housemate situation, she said simply, "Well, I'm only amazed that it's lasted this long for you and Connor." She must have heard a few of their complaints. And when Dylan broached the topic with Connor about them each getting their own places, he was surprised to find he accepted the idea without much resistance. Eventually, Dylan signed a new lease, while Connor and his girlfriend found a new place for themselves. The previous landlord received a thirty-day notice, and luckily, no one protested the new arrangements.

As for me, though initially perplexed, I soon came around to the idea that Dylan needed to find a better living situation for himself as a single person. It meant I would be out a month's rent for the change, but I had to admit: relying on Connor to pay his share of rent had been a colossal headache. Even though he had a steady job, he was chronically late in his payments. In fact, the whole topic of finances continued to be a source of concern. I wanted Dylan to be back in school again. I could better justify my financial assistance if I thought it was going toward a clear goal. Dylan's dad felt the same way, but since he was a freelancer, I knew he didn't have the same steady income I had. He wouldn't be able to pay half of Dylan's expenses without taking on real hardship. My dad was gone already, and it took his entire pension to support my mother's expenses as an Alzheimer's patient at a special facility. So, as the main person working full-time for a salary, I was carrying the major part of financial management. Thank goodness Dylan could be covered by my health insurance up to age twenty-six! That was a real lifesaver, even if I had to pay more.

By this time in our lives, Mike and I had developed a strong case of financial PTSD. Anyone with a close family member who has bipolar will understand: spending sprees, bounced checks, bank overdrafts, speeding tickets, court fines, impounded vehicles—these are just some of the Improvised Explosive Devices we'd encountered on the back roads of our son's personal finances over his young adulthood. Not to mention psychiatrist bills, medications, special programs, and therapy. Mike was much more of a frugal money manager than me, but even I had to start putting up a few roadblocks, just to maintain solvency. And though it's not in my nature to be an accountant, I had to turn myself into one. In this new, evolving situation, *somebody* had to monitor the ticker-tape figures zooming around at the speed of light, and that person ended up being me. I was determined to view the present expenditures as an investment, but it was far from certain how any of this would turn out. Somehow, I told myself, amid major scooter repair, a change of lodging, upcoming semester tuition expenses, and health insurance, the bills would get paid.

Mainly, I was just thankful my son was still in Drug Court. That alone was worth solid gold. He hadn't dropped out; he hadn't been kicked out, either. That was truly something to celebrate as year-end holidays approached. By Thanksgiving and then Christmas, as we prepared our feasts, I was feeling supremely jubilant. We all were. I'd even managed to get Dylan to attend a service at St.

Alban's, where Rev. Allison Marie offered up a celebratory prayer
for us. Later, with our small family including John seated at the
dining table, Dylan delivered his own spontaneous prayer of hope
and thanks that he was actually moving through what he called
"recovery." As a mother, my heart rejoiced to see him responding so
positively. Two years of Drug Court didn't seem so long now, and
the past three and a half months had been preparation for the long
haul ahead. Dylan was signed up for classes in the new semester
starting in January. In no time, he'd be a student again. There had
been setbacks, but now it felt like we were finally coming out of the
woods into more familiar territory. And when Dylan blew out the
twenty-four candles on his chocolate birthday cake in December,
I felt a wave of gratitude that we had all somehow made it through
such a tumultuous year.

After dinner, we pulled on our coats and went outside into the
bracing night air. "It feels good," Dylan said. John liked it, too; the
cold reminded him of winters in Canada where he grew up. Before
he set off, though, John wanted us to see the constellation Orion,
now right above us. Amazingly, that night the sky seemed so clear
that even though the stars were far away, they seemed closer and
brighter than usual.

"Do you see those three, perfectly aligned stars up there? That's
Orion's belt," John pointed out. All three of our heads tilted back
to take in a huge swath of the sky overhead. The bright star belt
shone like diamonds. "Orion's the Hunter. Look down now from
the belt and you'll see two other bright stars; those are his knees,
so you can imagine him standing there, strong, solid." We admired
the bold pattern, which John had shown me many times before. It
was one of his favorites. I knew he wanted to share this ancient star
knowledge with my son.

"And, if you look above the belt, you can see another bright
star, there, on the right, that's his left shoulder. Then, look across on

his right side at those two stars above the shoulder level. See that one way up above where his head might be? They say he's holding up a spear in his right hand—as if he's poised to throw it across the sky with all his might." We were all scanning the inky darkness far over our heads, trying to trace a man's body in this far-flung array of stars. I glanced over at Dylan, calmly taking it all in. Did he see himself as the hunter, too?

Well, probably not tonight. I was just happy that he seemed relaxed, like things were going right for once.

John and I hugged him before he set off down the street. He turned and waved to us, and we waved back.

I've looked for reassurance many times in many places. Sometimes, looking for Orion's belt on a cold winter night, knowing that it will be there, right overhead—that's as close to certainty as a person can come by in this world. Sometimes, that's reassurance enough.

CHAPTER 11: FORGIVE US OUR DEBTS

Shortly after all this positive change, one day in mid-January—not long before classes were to begin for spring semester, with Dylan aboard this time as a student—I received a phone call from my son. He told me casually that he wanted to discuss a time to meet with me to talk about how he was going to pay off his court fees. Aha— the topic of finances again! It was like Billy the Kid ambushing my stagecoach on the road. My blood pressure shot up: *What now!? Was there no plan? Why am I involved in this?* Nonetheless, with great difficulty, I managed to keep my cool and agreed to meet with him at my house.

The gist of the situation: Dylan was ready to move up to Stage Two of Drug Court, but he had to have a plan for how to pay off his court fees by February. He showed me the Court payment sheet: he owed $700 of an original $800 fee. (Later, I found out he was $200 behind in his payments, which were $100 a month.) I was not liking this. He began talking about a plan whereby, as with the moped repair, he would have me deduct a certain amount from his weekly allowance, and that would go toward his court fees. John and I were seated at the table across from him, since I'd taken the precaution of having reinforcements. I asked Dylan if he'd looked into getting a job at the car wash or at a local restaurant. All of those jobs were close by. Even if his moped conked out, he could get there; he could work on the weekends. Dylan told me he had looked but didn't see any jobs available. I explained about the neon sign at the car wash flashing "now hiring" in bold letters. Resistance. I heard the usual statements: "I've looked for jobs, I have felonies on my record, and I don't have reliable transportation. People think I'm too aggressive, not docile enough; they don't want to hire me. I don't like to walk; I don't like to sweat, etc., etc. " John chimed in: "You can get a job; you CAN earn the money."

Despite January chill, the temperature in the room rose. Dylan was cornered and he knew it. Or maybe he felt outnumbered. He walked out of the house but came back after a few minutes to launch a new diatribe.

"John doesn't have any right to say anything to me; I'm not his son. I'm nothing like his sons; I'm not smart; I'm a screw-up. Things are hard for me. I have anxiety problems, and I don't get along with people."

He cried out from frustration one second, then gathered up his anger and poked his horns into an imagined enemy the next.

"And then John was looking at me with a little smile on his face all during our talk." Dylan grimaced for theatrical effect. "That's being disrespectful."

The smile. This reminded me of the scene with the moped in the abandoned scooter lot when I smiled at the wrong time, too.

"It's not disrespect," I countered. "I know John, and he does that sometimes when he feels uncomfortable." The scene went on, but not for long. Dylan left again, threatening to blow it all up—quit Drug Court, quit college. I was upset, but by then I'd seen lots of these dramatic scenes come and go. Best to lie low and wait for it to pass. Even the imperturbable John said he should have put on his bulletproof vest that morning. He wasn't used to household explosions—or at least he wasn't until he met me and my son.

A bit later, my phone rang again. Dylan was now defiant. "I'm not going to jail because of you two. I'm going to figure out a plan. If I had come to you calm and with a good plan, you would have gone along with it."

I talked to him and steered clear of showing anger myself. I stayed calm no matter what, using my mantra, "Be The Rock." I remember saying, "You're not a screw-up, Dylan; you're very competent. You're a smart person who's made some bad decisions, and you're not good at managing money." Before we hung up, I added one more thing: "I don't feel sorry for you."

Not long afterward, he called again matter-of-factly—as if nothing unusual had happened—to request assistance with taking two giant tubs of possessions over to his new apartment to help finish off the move. If this were anyone other than the child I gave birth to twenty-four years ago, I would not have given him the time of day. However, John and I decided to comply. Dylan was calm now, looked shaken, but was doing what he needed to be able to take up residence in the new apartment over several days. There was a limit to how much he could transport on a moped, especially in the rainy season. When we arrived at the new apartment, John got out to open the hatchback and then to help take out a tub chock-full of household possessions, following Dylan upstairs. Dylan thanked him politely. We took him back to his former residence and then left without further discussion.

A day later, Dylan called with another financial proposal: he mentioned a lump sum that he would forfeit from his weekly allowance money. I said he should draw up a plan. I also asked him the burning question that came to me in the middle of the previous night.

"Where is the $380 you got from selling the Kona bike a while back?"

"I bought a TV set."

I fume. "Why didn't you spend that on the court fees?"

"I forgot about them."

"That was really dumb. You can't forget court fees. You have to have a plan for paying them."

He agreed calmly enough that he should have had one before, but he was making one now. He was only $200 behind in his payments. The day before, Thursday, he had met with Darlene Winchester at Drug Court, so he undoubtedly unloaded his frustration to her about his encounters with me. He'd already alluded more than once to his "mom issues." According to him, Darlene said we should all three meet to talk and work out something. "Fine, sign me up," I said. Overall, I noticed he sounded more together, more upbeat. As if to counter the pessimism of what he'd said before, Dylan told me he wanted to finish college. He believed he could get a job afterward, maybe at a restaurant, and work his way up. I detected that behind all his bluster and blowouts was a lot of fear. He was afraid of failure.

I left a message for Ms. Winchester at Drug Court. If she wanted to talk to me, I would like to talk to her, as Dylan proposed. When she called back, what she said reassured me somewhat.

"Dylan is making moves toward taking more responsibility," she told me. "Things aren't as bleak as you might think at the moment. He knows change is in the wind."

It was if she could read my mind.

"Yes, I do think we need some help in establishing a healthier pattern of working out disagreements."

Ms. Winchester went on to say that she couldn't legally reveal anything to me until he signed a release form, which she would request. Then we could set up an appointment.

While out on another errand, I found out Dylan was having second thoughts about the threesome meeting. He wanted to take another try at just the two of us working this out and mentioned another plan.

"OK, I'll look at it, but I still want to have that meeting. I've already called Darlene's office."

He jumped in. "Yes, she told me you had called and for me to sign some release papers. Why didn't you call me to ask if you could call her?"

"Because you already said that the three of us were going to be involved in discussions, so I wanted to know what was going on."

Later, after a five-minute trip to Auto Zone for a new moped part, Dylan requested to pass by Drug Court to sign the release papers, hesitating—probably to put it off until Monday—but then quickly deciding to go ahead. Soon, Darlene would contact me to set up a time for all of us. The important thing, I realized as the day wore on, was not to agree to anything until we all three met together. I began to see that having Darlene as arbitrator could be a real benefit. It would enable us to get beyond a confrontation and help keep me from being railroaded into something.

"I don't feel sorry for you." Now, there's a statement for you. The way I saw it, ever since his teen years, Dylan had been telling a hard-luck story to, and about, himself. Strangely, he seemed to take a familiar comfort from it. In the narrative, he got a bad deal from life. First, he inherited a few scrambler genes that gave him mental health issues. Next, he got stuck being raised by incompetent parents. Nature and nurture both set against him from the get-go. After that, bad friends, bad breaks, bad luck. Because of this, his parents—and the world— owed him big time. Even God owed him (if Dylan believed in God). It was as if there was a huge chip on his shoulder that he was always carrying around, as if he'd cribbed his lines from Tupac Shakur, "Me against the world." He saw himself as a marked man. Because of all this unfairness, there was a grudge debt out there, always accruing interest. But what he didn't realize is how this accounting system, where it's the other person who pays, kept him from taking charge of his own life.

The worst of it was that, as his mom, I bought into that grudge debt for a time myself. I admit to feeling guilt that I didn't spend more time with my son when he was very young, that I wasn't more patient, more understanding of this little kid who was so different from me. I'm sure I've got more than a couple of black marks on my slate to account for. Why was I trying to write articles in the summer instead of being caretaker of my four-year-old son? Would things have been different on an emotional level, at least? Then there was the guilt I felt about not doing enough to make the marriage to Mike work out. Had I been immature and selfish? Probably. But I remember the choice I made back then: to do what I could be good at, where I could be rewarded for my efforts. I put a lot into my career, where at least I had some control over outcomes. There wasn't much of that in my home life.

After the divorce, I wasn't too pleased with the way Mike used his time with Dylan to explain why he left, probably detailing all my emotional high crimes and misdemeanors. Years later there was the undergrad psychology course Dylan took at the University of Cincinnati, the one on the importance of childhood bonding and what happens to kids who don't have a good bond with their parents—especially, crucially, all-significantly, with their mother. That clinched it: I fell from trusty mom who stood by him to doghouse mom who abandoned him. The scales fell from Dylan's eyes, and he saw the real me, a fallen creature. Now I owed him, big time.

My temperature rose as I thought of this. I saw now it wasn't just about the endless streams of financial support for Dylan; it was about emotional debt—barge loads of it. Regarding his childhood and early teen years, it seemed to me he had a selective memory for the "bad parent" stuff. After all, if as a parent I'm held guilty of cherry-picking only the most mutant, ancestral genes to pass on to him, then he can be held guilty of picking out only the worst of times to remember and hold on to. That's more of a real choice, isn't it?

It all made me want showdown time with Dylan—the kind you can have in a therapist's office. There's a technique in which two chairs are set up opposite each other with a five-foot space between. The client sits in one chair, and the other one remains empty. You can imagine anyone you want in the other chair. The idea is to tell that person everything you want to say, all the resentments you've been harboring up inside for years. You can wave your arms, yell, punch, whatever . . . but mostly, you talk. Of all the people on the planet they could possibly choose, most individuals will put one of their parents in the hot seat before blasting away for half an hour. There's seemingly no end to that person's crimes and shortcomings, no end to the repressed venom that has to come out. This power wash is not needed by everyone, of course—just people with emotional residue to clean out of their drainpipes.

In my twenties, I myself would have hauled my own dad into that chair for sure. As for emotional grudge debt, I've kept my share, even over small stuff. When Dad was a poor grad student with bills to pay, he wasn't always the most even-tempered person; I remember plenty of irritation spilling over, mostly onto me when I was recruited as the hapless assistant on household repair projects. Then much later, as a college student, I remember being bummed that while all my peers had driver's licenses, I didn't. This was because my dad took us all out to the West Coast for a semester during the time I would have taken Driver's Ed at my home high school. Of course, the whole family experience was way more educational than a mere driving course, but later I added that example to my growing list of "Dad aggrandizing his career at the expense of his family" wrongs. I held on to that grudge for a few years, too—still not driving—until one day a friend said, "Well, you could always sign up for a Driver's Ed class at the university. I know someone else who did that just last semester and now she's getting her license." Even after this blazing lightning bolt of revealed wisdom struck me, it barely put a crack in the hard, little shell of my grudge. It took a while for the juice to run out. But by the time I started my first driving lesson in a snowy football stadium that next January, my resentment had mysteriously disappeared. I was free to take action for myself.

Now, for me as a parent, the shoe was definitely on the other foot. I knew what it felt like to be in that hot seat across from Dylan as a Bad Mom, and I'd felt the burn. But that day I wanted a role reversal. I was putting my son in that chair and doing a riposte. I'd look right at him and say this: "Look, you may think you had it rough and were miserable one hundred percent of the time, but your picture of things is NOT accurate! What about all the memories (not to mention, documented photos) I have of you—yes, you— smiling, running, climbing, and laughing your head off? Do you remember any of *that*?

"You had great visits with grandparents and friends, went to wonderful schools with attentive teachers. We parents may not have been ideal, OK, but at least we showed up. We did as well as we could at the time. What about all the fun trips we took to places where your dad worked on gardens? How about the time you and I went across the sagebrush desert outside of that town in Colorado on our mountain bikes? After pursuing the trail, we bravely went along a precipitous roadway edge all the way down to Woody Creek Tavern where you had a grilled cheese sandwich in the shape of a teddy-bear face and some root beer. Hey, now that's living! You were only about seven years old, doing ten miles or so on a bike. Talk about adventure! We made it there and all the way back, too, which wasn't so easy in the heat, but we took sips of water from our bottles and found a tiny bit of shade under one of those scrub bushes—just enough—until you could go on. And later, we were proud of our accomplishment. You did an amazing thing for a young kid. With me. Did you forget all that?

"And what about all the trips you took later, after the divorce, with your dad to Arizona or Arkansas, when you got to operate a little Bobcat to help move rocks and soil around, just like the garden work crew? Or the time you went with your dad to Maine and got to float out on a boat with his friend Lennie to haul up fresh lobster from a wooden trap? No, let's face it, kid. Your young years were pretty good—privileged, even. So, while it's true that Mother Nature might have dealt you a wild card, you've still got plenty of good cards left to play. What you choose to remember, Dylan, is your own affair. I don't feel sorry for you! Make your own life out of what you have."

And for once, Dylan would be speechless—without reply. And then he would think about it all, maybe for a long time.

Well, there was no such showdown at the therapist's office, but the two of us did have an appointment with Ms. Winchester coming up. By then, John had to leave for Blue Valley again, so I was on my own for the January 12 meeting in Darlene's office at Drug Court. I felt a certain amount of apprehension as I made copies of Dylan's proposal and my counter-proposal and stuffed them into a brown envelope to bring with me to the meeting. I felt like an attorney for an environmental group headed toward a confrontational meeting with a corporate officer and her agent. I wanted to be ready with documents to distribute all around. I picked Dylan up and we arrived, probably both equally nervous, at Drug Court headquarters. Darlene greeted us, offered us coffee, and took us into her office in a back part of the establishment. The office was paneled in dark wood and lined with bookshelves and stacks of papers everywhere. It could have been any professor's office on campus. A vintage lamp shed a soft glow as we pulled up our chairs to Darlene's desk, side by side.

Things didn't go as expected. Instead of refereeing a battle, Darlene instructed Dylan and me to each write down our goals and expectations for him over the next few months. Then we discussed in more general terms how Dylan was progressing, what was holding him back, how he could move forward, how we were all working together as a team. It really was more like being at the therapist's office. Not that it was exactly a piece of cake! The whole meeting took two hours and moved through some difficult landscapes. We talked about emotions: Darlene asked each of us what we thought love was, what did love look like? I said it was about taking care of each other; for Dylan, it was a feeling. As we responded, I could sense him pulling away from me; he had to assert his difference. The old hurts came out as Dylan remembered his childhood. I grew impatient as all these tightly held emotions surfaced, saying in exasperation, "I'm sorry your childhood wasn't perfect, and I wasn't always there for you, but can't we move on? What about all I'm doing for you now? Haven't I shown you that I care about you? If I didn't care, I wouldn't be doing this. I wouldn't be here."

Through this confrontation, I could see Darlene's social-worker skills coming to the fore. She listened calmly and with empathy to both of us, but intervened at one point, saying, "That's all in the rear-view mirror, Dylan. We're in a car and we're going forward; we can't just continue to gaze in the rear-view mirror—yes, a glance now and then, but overall, we've got to look ahead to be able to steer this vehicle forward." She talked about new choices, new possibilities—not in a grandiose way, but very practically. Small steps, day by day—as in, "How do you eat an elephant? One bite at a time." This was a message my son needed to hear, and from somebody else besides me. Darlene reminded Dylan about a story one of the other Drug Court members told in group the other day, about how he was driving intoxicated and had an accident that injured his best friend. She talked about how others share about their painful experiences; we can feel empathy and compassion for them and so start to feel the same for ourselves when we need to. She talked about how we have to forgive.

I started to relax and step aside emotionally. Maybe I didn't have to fight this out after all. It started to dawn on me that maybe I couldn't save Dylan. Not alone, anyway. I couldn't, but it was OK. He had probably already learned all he could from me. Now he needed to learn from others. And I knew they were out there, lots of good people: Darlene, for example, and Arlo, his sponsor in AA. Who knows how many others were in the different group meetings every week? Dylan would get to see he wasn't alone. Others had their struggles, too, and they were all in there together, wrestling with them.

When it was time for us to adjourn, Darlene moved toward a conclusion. "So, do you feel comfortable working out your financial discussions on your own now?" Darlene asked. "Or do you need me to be present on another occasion?"

Dylan and I glanced at each other. I let it be his call, and we agreed to hash out payment proposals on our own. In any event, Ms. Winchester asked Dylan if it would be helpful to have a three-way discussion again periodically, just to clear the air from time to time. He thought it might, maybe spaced out every two or three months. We agreed to that.

As we left Darlene's dark office and entered the cloudy light of day outside, a group was gathering in the courtyard, mostly consisting of burly guys. The whole Drug Court crew was assembling for a general meeting. Among them was a familiar face I nodded to. I couldn't place him at first but I soon remembered this was Fred, the small-engine, moped guy who had the shop south of town. Even Fred was in Drug Court? Yes, yes, it was the men's group, and they were of all ages, and Connor was there, too. Walking along through the gathering, it felt like the Red Sea parting, probably because I was with Dylan, and he was one of them. I even felt a rush of greeting and welcome from these assembled faces—one or two, anyway. What a tribe! They were greeting each other, standing in small clusters near a huge, gnarled tree in the front yard, hands in pockets or out to slap someone on the shoulder, ruffs of collars turned up against the cold. I noticed it was starting to snow, with thick flakes swirling around us, contributing to a feeling of celebration. Now, this will sound strange, but coming out of Darlene's dimly lit office into this scene, it almost felt like those accounts of people who report near-death experiences and later say they went through a dark tunnel with a light at the end of it. People report feeling a mysterious, welcoming warmth coming from special beings who appear in order to escort them through a portal into a better existence beyond. Though I admit it seems doubtful that any of us in the courtyard were near death at that moment—or that the special beings referred to in these accounts were former members of Drug Court—still, you just never know how mysteries may be revealed in this world.

Right before I reached my car, Connor approached and said that he had a rent payment for me. He held out his hand and put several bills all neatly wrapped in half into mine, quite a wad. It was Thursday, payday at the engine factory where he worked. He was usually late in his payments, and I frankly wasn't expecting this last one at all. As always, he looked me right in the eye with a steady gaze as he handed me the money. I took it and thanked him. I asked if he had found a new place to live, and he said yes. Dylan came up and was standing there, too, as if in solidarity. Snowflakes fell on their hair and jacket shoulders. By the time I finally drove away, I felt a completely unexpected sense of wellbeing. It wasn't simply that I thought maybe things could work out after all. It was more in the nature of a revelation, an awareness that Dylan had sources of support in the world beyond himself—and way beyond me.

The following weekend, Dylan and I met again and ironed out a payment plan. With classes starting, we agreed he would forfeit a portion of his allowance "income" in order to pay, over time, the remaining court fee. He'd have to give up a chunk each week for a good while in order to make up the amount of the payment. We agreed he would bring it in person to the court. Fine, I thought to myself, and if you feel the pinch in your pocketbook, then maybe you'll cast aside your fear and get a side job.

Then, a month later, in the middle of February, right before the next payment was due, a miracle happened. After my 11:30 Wednesday class, I read a text message from Dylan saying he'd received a restitution payment of $1,100. Amazed, I called him, but he wasn't available until later. Eventually, I learned that this amazing windfall was related to the robbery in Fairfield, just north of Cincinnati, three years ago. My mind flashed back to that occasion: Dylan was visiting a friend in a suburb; as he was leaving the apartment building, a thug and his accomplice who knew he had money on him held him up at gunpoint. Against the odds, Dylan fought to keep his money, but during the wild scuffle, which ended on the floor, the thug's accomplice managed to grab the cash. (Don't ask what Dylan was doing with $1,100 in cash on him; I've tried and haven't gotten a straight answer. He agrees it was one of the stupidest things he's ever done.) When they fled, Dylan was left alone on the floor, with a shoulder out of socket and a scalp wound. A friend drove him to the local hospital where he checked himself in. He survived the ordeal—another miracle—and Mom got to hear about it later. What a nightmare!

Now, though, I had to shake myself back into the present. "So, how in the world did it come about that you received a restitution check for that amount?" Dylan told me he had been working on it for weeks. Right after the incident, he'd reported the crime to the police, and a detective had come to speak to him. After that, he hadn't heard anything and assumed the thieves hadn't been caught. But recently, he'd looked up his name once again on Google, and he found among the listings of past traffic fines that an Ohio court listed him as having received a restitution payment for a theft. Dylan called the court in Fairfield County and told the clerk that his address had changed. He hadn't lived in Cincinnati for over two years, and so hadn't received any restitution payment that had apparently been sent there. The clerk said she would investigate the matter. Next thing he knew, a check from Fairfield County arrived in his mailbox here in town, right after he had taken the precaution of getting a mailbox key for the new apartment.

"I can't believe it," I told Dylan, dazed. For sure, I rejoiced with him at the good news. But in the very next moment, I also realized the danger of Dylan having a huge check in his hands. I asked him what he planned to do with it. Maybe I didn't even have to: he volunteered that he at first wanted to keep it—what a prize! But then he remembered the large court payment hanging over his head ($734), $500 of which (or some of it, at least) had to be paid that very Friday. He said he'd pay off the whole fee, then wanted to put the rest into the bank. He even decided to put it in a savings account that would be harder to get to and would charge fees for withdrawing. I heaved a huge sigh of relief. As if to prove his good fortune, Dylan even sent me a scanned copy of the check via e-mail, and later showed me the receipt for paying off the court fee in Doran County. Even staring at the receipt, I could still barely believe all this had actually happened.

Later, I was of two minds on the whole restitution affair. On the one hand, I wasn't so sure this *deus ex machina* resolution of the court fees was altogether for the good. What if it taught Dylan the lesson that he could avoid having to manage money wisely because some miracle would crop up at the last minute to save his ass? How would he learn to sacrifice what he wants now for what he may need later? Despite two parents giving numerous lessons on budgeting and looking ahead, these lessons hadn't taken hold yet. On the other hand, I empathized with Dylan's point of view that he had suffered an injustice earlier and, by reporting the crime and meeting with the detective, he contributed to the crime being prosecuted. Dylan had shown persistence and ingenuity in getting the money back.

For now, I could only be thankful, even with reservations.

Overall, I hoped this new adventure would give him a bit more confidence in the workings of the world—namely, that not ALL the cards in the deck were stacked against him. This unexpected restitution of lost money from the past, one enabling him to pay off his own debt now, might even start something. It might start to knock off some of that chip he carried around on his shoulder, the one as big as the state of Massachusetts.

CHAPTER 12: ATTILA THE HUN

For a long time, while my son was very young, I thought he was a smaller version of Attila the Hun. I thought he had only three settings on his dial: brash, bold, and barbarian. Every day there would be a whole list of transgressions: "Don't eat all the chips on the table; don't pull the dog's tail; don't yell so loudly!" Only gradually did I discover how sensitive he was. And despite his often unruly behavior and high-energy antics, I found out that this little kid had a core of common sense, even of justice. On occasion, he was capable of delivering some keen perceptions. At times, he stopped me in my tracks.

For example, there was the incident of the fish bowl. One day I was cleaning something downstairs, and when I turned around, I saw that Dylan was not just watching the fish in the goldfish bowl but starting to grab the bowl to give it a shake. I could tell he knew he wasn't supposed to be doing that, but the temptation to riffle the waters proved too irresistible. In no time, the fish was subjected to earthquake tremors of alarming intensity. Not being the calmest person myself, I immediately reacted in alarm: "Don't do that! That's being mean to the goldfish; he doesn't like it." Of course, I zoomed right up to my son in a moment. When he just laughed and continued his earthquakes, I got very angry at him. I removed his hands roughly and shook his arms to show how it felt to the fish. "That's what it feels like," I said loudly. My son was surprised, especially when he realized how mad I was. My technique was working, but not quite in the way I imagined. It was more that my impromptu lesson in teaching Dylan empathy toward other creatures was starting to backfire. I realized that I had used way too much noise and force to make my point about being gentle. Even I was startled by my own anger. Dylan was scared and started to cry. "Mom, what you're doing to me now is worse than what I was doing to the fish."

At first, I was frozen in place by the truth of what he'd just said; in the next instant, I melted. I bent down and just hugged him while we both cried. He was so right.

There weren't any more fishbowl quakes, but I found out it takes more than one rough lesson to learn empathy in life. And as often happens with a young parent, it's not just the adult who's giving lessons to be learned. So who was the barbarian that time?

CHAPTER 13: DEEPAK AND TUPAC

When Dylan reached school age, things seemed to be calmer, but there would still be episodes of extreme stress due to the pressures of two careers, childrearing, householding, and matching up all our schedules. In an attempt to solve some of the complexity, we decided to build a new house and move into town. When Mike first suggested this, I had been opposed. How could we give up our little house in the country? For me, it fulfilled a dream. But even I had to admit eventually that the dream was hard to maintain amid the pressures of real life for the three of us. Most of what we needed was in town. If we all lived there, I could walk to work; Dylan could soon walk to school. This would free up Mike's schedule, allow him to do more projects and sometimes travel during the year. And soon, instead of Dylan needing one of his parents to take him everywhere, he could ride his bike. There would be other young kids in the neighborhood for him to play with, instead of just one little boy his own age nearby. We were all for independence, but living in the country often meant being isolated.

For a while, the design plans and the move kept us creatively occupied. The new house was an enormous work project. Then suddenly our lives were in place, but only on the surface. It would be easy to say that the difficulties of balancing two careers while parenting a child who could, at times, be difficult were the forces that did in the marriage. But even though these were both factors, I doubt they were the deciding ones. You can never know everything you need to know before you face challenges; the knowledge and skills need to be developed in the throes of the situation. At that point, I wasn't learning very fast. My husband and I didn't always agree about our ways of parenting when we faced difficulties. Sometimes it felt like we were pulling in different directions. In general, Mike was in favor of strict rules for Dylan, while I was often more lenient, more ad hoc in my judgments. Naturally, this led to arguments. More importantly, Mike felt I wasn't putting as much effort into my family as I was into my career. I felt maxed out in both categories. We sought counseling, which worked for a while, but that didn't address the fundamental issues between us. Instead of trying to be mutually supportive or flexible, we became stubborn. Mike would insist that he was the reasonable one, he was right, while I was the emotional, wayward one. My anger and frustration went underground. I tried so hard to keep the lid on my true feelings that half the time I didn't even know how volatile they were.

Things escalated. Instead of our differences complementing each other, they started to build up a residue of grievances and resentments. On occasion, there would be angry standoffs; each time, we would be set in our roles. First, he would goad and then, in a fit of self-righteous anger, I would explode. It was the opposite of taking conscious action—more like being swept into some diabolical mechanism beyond my control. Predictably, the delicate Jenga tower of our marriage fell apart. The uneasy truce was over. Coming back from a work-related trip, Mike quietly announced that he wanted us to separate. Things had changed; he was giving up on us.

Then came the terrible evening when, together, we told our son. I will never forget this; it was one of the worst days of my life. I remember Dylan hearing the news, then bursting out in tears, then coming up to each of us, his dad and me, to hug us—still crying. We were all crying. It was excruciating, and so touching that my son would try to comfort both himself and us. At that moment, I would have given anything to be able to go back in time to change this outcome. I would have vowed to do the impossible: change us, do whatever was necessary to build a better family, either with his dad or by myself, to make everything work for all of us. But I didn't have that power. Besides, it was too late.

Initially, after the break-up, we worried about how our son would take this. Would he be OK? When Mike moved hundreds of miles away to Cleveland, I scheduled appointments with a therapist for myself and for Dylan. The therapist met with me for a good six months or so, with Dylan maybe three or four times. After that, Mr. Baldwin determined that the boy was resilient and didn't seem unduly upset by this turn of events. He would weather the storm and adapt. I remember the therapist was impressed by ten-year-old Dylan's vocabulary and his ability to discuss his life and emotions. Baldwin said he didn't often encounter that in a rural area. But truly, at that age, Dylan was probably the calmest and best-adjusted he had ever been. He was articulate and rational. He knew how to do a lot of practical things, like simple repairs. He loved tools and was always taking gadgets apart and putting them back together. I learned to save whatever strange, small metallic objects I would find around the house, remembering they would probably be needed to fix a toy car or be useful for some project or other. Dylan was talkative, too; we had many long, lively conversations, and he was a great companion. It seemed like we were bonded beyond all adversity.

During the first couple of years following the separation, my son and I were very close. We had to stick together; we were shipwrecked on the same island. At least we had each other. I helped him keep up with his homework; we did things together on the weekends; we sat close together at church. When he developed a passion for BMX racing, we deliberated on all kinds of bike parts and enhancements. I drove him to the closest BMX bike track, thirty or forty miles away, so that he could try out his skills. He loved the rolling bumps, the zigzags, the jumps—everything that took physical effort and brought strong sensations. Sometimes, he would persuade a friend to go with us. BMX was still a little new in our region at the time. I was worried at first about the dangers, but then I figured he had to express his daredevil nature somehow, so this was as good as anything. At least I knew what he was doing. Most kids were on sports teams, so they had strict schedules of weekend participation in games. He had been that way, too, for a number of years. But gradually, from maybe eleven on, he started moving away from soccer and wanted to do an individual sport. I think he wanted to test himself, do something that not everyone around was into yet. He had to find an area where he could excel in the way he wanted to. He won trophies, and I cheered him on.

It must have been right around this time—or maybe right before it—that I wanted to take the photos, the ones before the major transformation that I knew was coming. In trying to catch my son in an image that I could look back at for years, Dylan would say I was trying to hold on to him and to the past, hold on in a way that wasn't possible or wanted by him. At age eleven or twelve, he was all for growing up, coming of age and into his full powers. It's probably true I was holding on, trying to capture some quality of youth and innocence that was going to be lost. Maybe I remained haunted by the last sentence of Marjorie Kinnan Rawlings's novel, *The Yearling*, a book I read when I was the same age he was back then: "A boy and a yearling were gone forever," she wrote. And part of me didn't want that to happen.

I spent the first year or so after the break-up doing inner reconnaissance—to understand better what went wrong in my marriage and to restore some sense of balance. The therapist, Mr. Baldwin, assigned M. Scott Peck's book *The Road Less Traveled*, which I read and discussed with him. He suspected out loud what I only dimly sensed: a lot of my emotional life had gotten buried, and I would have to search my way through the ruins before rebuilding. I wanted to transform myself from the inside out. Withdrawing as much as possible from excessive career responsibilities while still working, I took up Tai Chi and yoga; read Rumi, the Sufi mystic poet; poured cascades of confused feelings onto the pages of several journals. I also listened to the neo-Vedic advice of Dr. Deepak Chopra. A Massachusetts internist who had grown up in India, he felt it was time to bring the ancient wisdom of Ayurveda to the attention of ambitious, stressed-out Americans. Alarmed by how narrowly focused—and intrusive—standard medical practices were becoming, Chopra talked about health in a different way. Health meant finding ways to balance the natural rhythms of what he called the "quantum mechanical human body." Rather than being mere machines of flesh and bone, in his view our bodies contain "rivers of intelligence and consciousness" that are always flowing, always influenced by thoughts as well as events.

Whatever else of use I may have learned from Chopra, at least the three Ayurvedic *doshas* offered me a conceptual shorthand to explain why my marriage failed. Health in relationships, too, was a question of finding balance and counter-balance. *Doshas* are basic human types, based on body build, temperament, energy patterns. Like many readers of his early book, *Perfect Health*, I took a quick questionnaire to find out which *dosha* best described my own characteristics. Checking my assessment, I found out I was mainly a Vata type, meaning dry, nervous, alert but easily agitated. According to Ayurveda, warm, buttery, or oily dishes could help to balance such qualities, which meant completely revamping my cuisine. Meanwhile, I couldn't help but notice that my ex-husband would fit that category too. That didn't bode well for us from the get-go. Two brittle, anxious Vatas co-habiting? It didn't seem like it would be too comfortable over the long term. Then I discovered my son was a Pitta type: being hot and temperamental, he would do best seeking out cool, refreshing foods and avoiding spices, especially during the summer, when a tendency to overheat could send Pittas over the edge. Aha! I marveled at the accuracy of these descriptions. No wonder our household had been so incendiary, with two dry, airy Vatas around a fiery, hot Pitta. That was practically the formula for explosions. Call it Vedic voodoo, but all this made perfect sense to me. It explained the family dynamic as well as anything else. For counterbalance, what each of us needed was a calm, earthy Kapha type—someone of the third *dosha*. Unfortunately, cool-headed, steady Kaphas were in short supply within our immediate vicinity.

While at first I was content to pursue the road less traveled, I eventually found myself facing quite a few diverging paths in the yellow wood. For one thing, I had to look around to rebuild my social life. Old friends from my married past had drifted away during my seclusion, and besides, I needed to seek out new people. In that regard, Dylan and I were in the same boat. And so, for one memorable period, we both ended up spending quite a bit of social time with members of the Hassan family.

The Hassans were new in town, and their international background made them unusual for a rural area in west Kentucky. I first meet Lena in my department, where she had applied as a full-time lecturer. She was an American who had grown up in a military family stationed in Europe and who spoke Spanish and French fluently. She also knew Arabic because she had recently lived in Saudi Arabia for several years, and her husband was Sudanese. It soon got out that if you ever met one of the Hassans, you were bound to meet the whole clan sooner or later. True enough, I found out that her older son had been that sole native-speaker student in two of my advanced classes, and her second eldest son had just enrolled at the college, too. It was because their sons were students here that the parents decided it was a propitious time to relocate and begin a new life in the U.S. Not long after that, I learned that one of Lena's younger sons happened to be the same age as my own. In fact, Dylan had just told me a story about a new boy from Saudi Arabia, named Ramul, who was in his class at school.

Through these interconnections, Dylan and I ended up spending many a late afternoon or early evening with the Hassans. We were all in transition, and both sides were eager to make friends. Lena was the welcoming matriarch, holding court at the center while her husband phoned his business contacts or moved about the house with various hobbies. She didn't pretend that her household was anything other than improvisational. For me, her home felt like an open tent of hospitality in a social desert, and I took refuge there. While our sons rode together on bikes outside or dealt cards indoors, the two of us would sip mint tea and talk. We could discuss anything at all openly, whether we agreed with each other or not. Of course, there were endless interruptions: cooking, kids, the salty commentaries of the family's talking parrot. For me, Lena's opinions were endlessly fascinating and contradictory. For example, she had become a devout Muslim who practiced Ramadan even with a busy teaching schedule, but she was also a staunch feminist, especially when it came to workplace rights and salaries. She told me many stories about the family's recent years in Saudi Arabia, where she had taught English to Saudi women, dressed like them in a black robe and *hijab*. I could barely picture such a robust, outspoken woman wearing these clothes, let alone working in them. Having grown up as an American in France, she valued independent thinking, but at the same time, she'd grown fond of Arabian-style community and hospitality. I found her critical of our stateside brand of individualism; she preferred her own particular blend of both worlds.

Before Lena, I had never met a fellow American citizen who had not, until coming to our town in 2000, actually lived in the U.S. It seemed to me that during her first year here, she was in many ways a foreigner, someone who looked at our culture from an outsider's challenging perspective. Then, too, so many basic elements of small-town America were new to her: Fourth of July parades, fireworks, school sports, picnics—even rain. With great delight, she would tell me how her desert husband loved to sit with her on the porch watching the fascinating phenomenon of a steady spring rainfall.

Given my newly divorced status, it wasn't long before Lena took it upon herself to become my romantic advisor. However hardworking and dedicated to family she might be, it wasn't beyond her to issue statements that sounded like something from a fortune teller in *One Thousand and One Nights*. "Love lite, that's what you should look for," she told me. "You have an interesting career; you have a child. You don't need interference or distractions from those. Believe me, love lite is the way to go." And then she concocted a rare, exotic perfume I could use in my conquests. I took a whiff of the musky potion and laughed. This was something for Scheherazade, not me, but in any case, it couldn't hurt. My prior, intermittent romances hadn't exactly flourished; I concluded it was going to take a while before the right person came along.

This friendship helped me regain confidence; it offered support to branch out in new directions, try new ways of doing things. There were new opportunities on the professional level, too. When she successfully applied for a grant to develop her language teaching skills in France, she encouraged me to do the same. I applied and spent four weeks with teachers from many different countries taking classes in Grenoble the next summer. I was able to find ways to balance my parenting responsibilities at home, while relying on

Mike's summer trips with Dylan and two or three weeks of summer camp to cover times when I traveled. Shortly after this, the chair of our department announced a magnificent windfall. The dean had secured a generous grant from a major health corporation to support international travel for faculty and students in our department. This was a special gift that many of us could use. Over three or four years, after attending a summer conference in Martinique, I was able to return on the grant to interview two authors from this unique island culture about their novels. Each project taught me something valuable and led to other opportunities. It was a time of expansion.

And Dylan, what did he perceive back then? In those years between ten and thirteen, did he feel insecure, lonely? He didn't seem that way to me. He hung out with different friends, mostly guys his age who lived nearby. A couple of those I worried about sometimes, but I liked Paul, the boy who lived in the house directly behind ours. I found out his mom was the Methodist campus minister. I enjoyed her sense of humor and could identify with her being a single mother, raising a son and a daughter by herself. We all hit it off, and I wanted to get to know her better. She told me she felt a little isolated, though, being away from family and living in such a rural community. Not long after, Beverly accepted the call to a metropolitan church in Denver. I knew this would be a better fit for her, but both Dylan and I were sad to see them leave.

Now that I think about it, quite a few of the boys he spent time with back then were also sons of single moms: Cory, Logan, and then later on, Ryan and Lonnie. Not all the boys, but most. It's as if when his dad and I separated, our son somehow decided that he was going to have to shift social identities. He was going to have to move from the success track, where all the cool kids had intact, professional families, to the outlier track, the one where kids were mostly from single-parent households, meaning that Dad wasn't around. Was this a decision he made, or did it just happen that way? He always had friends, but they weren't the long-term, solid kind you would expect to have in a small town. Some of that was due to a friend moving away with his family, like Paul. But other times, the choice to "move on" to another friend was Dylan's choice. That's what happened with Ramul. After a while, Dylan felt this new friend wasn't proficient enough in biking. In fact, he was a "disaster on wheels" who could actually cause accidents to happen for anyone in his way, Dylan claimed. After a while, it became clear to both of them that Ramul was more introspective, more of a person who liked reading and quieter pursuits indoors. I regretted Dylan's attitude, because I found the younger Hassan to have a calm temperament and an understanding that far surpassed his years. If only some of that would have rubbed off on Dylan! Maybe Lena's family members were the much-needed Kapha types that were in such short supply nearby. It didn't surprise me to hear a few years later from Lena that Ramul was thinking of becoming a doctor.

It seemed Dylan had contradictory impulses when it came to friends: on the one hand, he wanted to be with the "cool" group, but on the other, he seemed drawn to kids who were somehow on the fringes, maybe new kids or someone not as integrated into any group. As I look back, I wonder if that ambivalence was due to the way he began perceiving himself.

The inner shift to seeing himself as an outlier was something I didn't notice back then—not sufficiently. It was only years later that he spoke about that. And this ambivalence about where he fit in socially showed up, I think, right around the time he began realizing that things were going on for him internally that other kids didn't have to deal with: racing thoughts, fluctuating energy levels, mood changes, temper flare-ups that went out of bounds. I knew about the red-hot temper, but I didn't know much about the other internal events. He didn't talk about them much, only a few times. I should have paid more attention to those, should have sought help, but I didn't. Everyone knows preteens go through mood changes. Even the hot flare-ups seemed like "normal" anomalies.

Meanwhile, I was taking on more career responsibilities. I took my son's adjustment for granted. He was so smart, so articulate, so resilient. He was getting good grades. I was proud of all those things. Mr. Baldwin, the therapist, saw that too, didn't he? To me, it seemed completely inevitable that Dylan was going to grow up to go to college and become a professional person like his parents. It was his birthright.

Our tight dyad lasted a while, but shortly after Dylan turned twelve, I think we both sensed that the sands were shifting under us. My son was growing up fast, moving from a more or less secure childhood toward a more uncertain adolescence. He, too, had to test his powers in a widening world. He also had many more choices to make, and it wasn't clear whose influence he would be under in making them. Looking back, I can see the two of us were living under the same roof, but our worlds were diverging in ways I couldn't predict. While I was practicing yoga and tuning in to sitar music for meditation, my son was turning on to a whole other type of influence from the external world. It was Deepak versus Tupac.

Dylan had two powerful tools for expanding his possibilities: his bike, which could even take him into distant neighborhoods, and the internet, a gift from Grandpa. My dad was convinced that this was the wave of the future, and Dylan had to be aboard. Mike and I had been skeptical—we'd put it off as long as possible. Computer, yes, but the internet? Ready or not, when Dylan turned thirteen, the bulging computer arrived in a gigantic black-and-white box, soon to be ensconced in part of our wide living room. From there, I felt I could keep up with what he was doing. Dylan's main interest was in finding music and later, films. There began his huge interest in hip-hop, R&B, and rap. Within a short time, he was an expert in this domain and started taking in cash by burning his own CD collections for friends and acquaintances. Occasionally, though, I got hints through the grapevine that some of the parents on the receiving end were not so appreciative of the productions.

There were many rappers he listened to over the next few years, but one rap artist he especially admired was Tupac Shakur. Most likely Dylan listened to him more often a few years later, but his interest started early. I try to speculate on what, exactly, it was about this music—and rap in particular—that would so attract a young teenager like my son at that time. First and foremost, it had to be the sheer intensity of it. Dylan loved beats. He liked his music loud and vibrating, wanted to feel the impact of it in his body. He received music from the same place a Digital Underground musician said that Tupac rapped from: the solar plexus. I remember once he wanted to me to listen to some music, and he positioned me right where he himself liked to be, body right in front of the speakers so that each of the beats and rhythms would hit me full in the chest and abdomen. I remember the visceral impact of it almost knocking me out of my chair. The beats struck like a boxer's hits, only they were strangely coming from the inside, as if reverberating off my own heartbeat. "Yeah, that's it, Mom," he told me.

But sound was only part of it; the rest was the legend, the questioning, feeling persona of the rebel, Tupac. The rapper had already been dead for four years, but his musical legend—along with his tragic rise and fall—was very much alive. Maybe Shakur's world, so different on the surface from Dylan's own, held more of the sharp contrasts, the highs and the lows, he was feeling in himself and didn't see reflected around him anywhere else. At the time, I couldn't see why my son would identify with a rapper who talked about tough times on city streets, but elements of the attraction became clear as time went on. I remember Dylan said he didn't like the "sugar coating" of reality. For him, the real was rough and ragged. I believe he sensed that intuitively because that's how he was starting to experience it in his preteen years. In fact, Dylan was drawn to bold stories of meteoric rises and spectacular falls wherever they occurred. He was particularly struck by the film *Blow,* the story of a Los Angeles cocaine mogul who built an empire, then took too many risks and lost it all. Alarmed by some of Dylan's "tunings-in" via internet, I set the parental controls and tried to steer him toward what I considered more edifying cultural events, like plays or musicals at the university theatre. But he would only get restless in the middle of them, and we would have to leave. He couldn't sit still long enough, or maybe they just weren't gripping enough to hold his attention. Things had to pack a punch, or he wasn't feeling it at all. At the same time, he loved hilarious comedies, the kind that would set him off laughing until he was doubled up in spasms on the couch. Clearly, I needed to redesign the house complete with gym equipment, punching bags, pool table, and giant trampoline outside for teen energy release. But even that would only have worked for a while.

As for any parent of a rebellious teen, there were plenty of comic moments amid the fray. Among the myriad phone calls from girls asking for Dylan, I picked up the phone early one Saturday evening to hear a concerned male voice: someone's dad. "Did you know that your son crawled through a window of my house into my daughter's bedroom?" the father asked calmly. "Please come by and pick him up." That was a new one. I found out that Dylan had been invited by the girl to do so, but that certainly didn't make it OK—especially not for her dad. Apparently, she was grounded at the time and decided it would make the time pass faster if she had a young male visitor. Her father handled it masterfully: he remained calm, all the while looking my son in the eye and telling him he would be welcome to knock at the front door like any other visitor but not to sneak through any windows. It made him look like a cat burglar. He also explained that this was his house and he needed to know who was there. Toward the end of our visit, the dad invited his daughter out to say hello. Then it was time for Dylan and me to take our leave. The dad shook our hands and made sure we crossed back over the threshold. To my knowledge, there were no further illicit visitations by my son—not to that house, anyway.

I remember back in my own teen days a parental male voice would come on the TV: "It's 10 p.m.; do you know where your child is?" Yes, a good question, and how about we add 2 a.m. or 4 p.m. or 8 p.m. as well? I have to admit that, as my son grew older, I couldn't always answer that question with complete accuracy. It's not that I was oblivious. But my philosophy of parenting was that young people didn't have to be locked into a strict after-school schedule, with parents chauffeuring them about from special lessons to sports games to friends' houses. I believed they needed more creative freedom than that. Nonetheless, I made sure Dylan would call me to check in, as I knew other parents did. I knew who his friends were and kept in touch with their parents, too. Dylan was home before dark on school days and went out with a friend—and a curfew—on weekends. Yes, my son was growing up fast, but even though we were moving into a new era for both of us, I was pretty sure we could work things out.

CHAPTER 14: OFF TRACK

In the years after Mike left, I found out that it was one thing to be a single parent when the going was smooth; it was another when we hit the rough spots. One day, Dylan was racing on a brand-new BMX track in our town. He loved being able to practice on it so close to home. But on this day, there were way too many racers lined up on the hill for the start. Even from the stands, you could see that the track downhill and over the first rollers was barely wide enough to accommodate the field of contestants that came charging down, each one trying to get ahead as they gained full momentum for the course ahead. Sure enough, an accident occurred on the first set of rollers. Two or three bikes were down, one of them Dylan's. My heart sank for him. Among the spectators on the far side of the track, I watched to see how quickly the riders would get up, if anyone was hurt. Usually, they were only shaken and bruised, but real injury in this sport was always a possibility. I held my breath. This time, it was clear that Dylan was in pain. His knee. He was helped from the course so he could sit on the sidelines, feeling not only the pain of the injury but also angry and defeated.

My first impulse was to go down immediately to talk to him and see how he was doing. I could commiserate with him, check out the knee, tell him things would be OK. But at the same time, something else was stopping me. I couldn't be sure of Dylan's reaction. Would he accept my attempts to talk to him quietly? Or would his anger and frustration erupt and make a scene? Probably some angry explosion at home or in the car with him earlier that week made me fear the same thing could happen right here, now, in front of all these people. I flashed back to scenes throughout his childhood, going all the way back to his earliest years, how it could happen that my attempts to help him when he was upset could backfire. Not always, but often enough. From what I knew of my son, I could just as well become a lightning rod for all his pain in that moment. What good would that do? My courage left me. I wanted his dad to be there; he would know how to handle this situation. Reluctantly, I waited. My fear of an emotional blow-up was equal to my own self-disgust at staying riveted to my seat, as if I were a mere bystander, not a mom. From what I could tell, though, my son didn't seem seriously injured, thank goodness. He didn't need to go to the hospital. The announcer stopped the race for a restart, and the downed racers gradually dispersed.

I looked around. There weren't too many single moms out there, mostly dads. This was a rough sport, after all. I wondered about myself. A concerned parent should be down there in the trenches with their boy. Why was I so worried about my son's reaction and what other people thought about it? You're supposed to do the right thing, regardless of how the world sees it or what the reaction is. Why did I think I could do this single parenting job, anyway? Wasn't I just a lightweight, fair-weather mom? Somebody who could handle parenting only when everything was going fine? Yep, that was me, all right. The old feeling moved in as it so often did when the chips were down on the home front: incapable, ineffective, not up to the job. I was a person who could do just fine back at the office, in my department, where things tended to be neat and tidy.

But real life out here on the crash track wasn't like that. Out here, people broke bones, took a punch, cracked their teeth, got flattened.

Eventually—I don't remember how he made it—Dylan somehow limped around the track to the spectator side, which was also near the final straightaway. He sat on a mound near the track and watched the proceedings. I was scouting a path to climb down from the stands when I noticed a man down below approaching my son. I could see the stranger was talking to him, probably to ask him how he was, to tell him he was glad it wasn't any worse, and not to worry—it was just one race. Dylan said something, nodded his head. I was thankful. From Dylan's reaction, I judged he was staying calm. By then, I was on my way to talk to Dylan myself. We sat together for a while, then I asked if he wanted to watch the rest of the races or go home. He wanted to watch for a while. By the time I helped him up, he could walk, slowly, favoring his left knee. When we got home, we knew it was important to get ice, prop his leg up, get movies to watch. Back then, my thirteen-year-old son seemed so indestructible, had come through so many scrapes and falls, I thought he'd heal up and be back at it in a few days. It would be a week later before Dylan would tell me, "Mom, I have to go to the doctor. My knee feels strange; this is different." He was right. The doctor said he had a torn ACL; the ligament would eventually require surgery to fully stabilize the knee again. It would be advisable to wait until the bones finished growing, however. He'd have to wait a few years. For now, he should keep icing it for the swelling. After that, he could continue biking for casual transportation and fun. But as for BMX racing, no. Too hard on an injured knee.

Other things were changing, too. Gradually, from twelve to thirteen to fourteen years old, Dylan's behavior became more unpredictable. I couldn't count on him to follow through with rules or agreements we'd made. In eighth grade, he insisted that he wanted to switch from fall soccer to football. I wasn't keen on the idea, but we discussed it, and I agreed to let him try it. Things went well for a while, but then one day he didn't show up for practice. The coach didn't know where he was, so I went looking for him in the neighborhood. I finally found him nonchalantly visiting with a friend. "Hey, Mom, what's up?" he said, as if nothing was wrong. I explained that skipping football practice wasn't an option. I found myself having to mete out "groundings" and punishments—that or taking away privileges, things he would look forward to. It was like trying to train an unruly horse. Hadn't we been through all this before when he was younger?

For his part, Dylan felt I wasn't holding up my end of the deal. Why had I been among the last parents to pick up their kid at soccer practices? I told him it wasn't easy to work full-time and be a parent-chauffeur, but these rationalizations fell on deaf ears. Everyone else's parent was doing it, so why couldn't I? My assignment: try harder, Mom. I made it a point not to be late.

Problems cropped up at school. He didn't always do his homework. Sometimes he was tardy; on occasion, he didn't show up for school at all. This shocked me. He knew how important getting an education was. Why was he doing this? When I quizzed him on where he went and why, his answers were sketchy; they didn't make sense to me. None of these behaviors seemed to fit who he'd been. Whereas before we'd always been able to talk and work things out, now we had loud disagreements. I talked with him and tried to understand, but I was losing a clear sense of who my son was. Our relationship became less trusting, and I felt more like an inquisitor—or even, at times, a jailer. "No, you can't go out tonight. Not after what happened today. You have to stay home," I'd tell him. Little did he know that this was as bad a punishment for me as for him. Once, after a particularly frustrating episode with my rebel son, I asked Rev. Patrick to intervene, and he came to our house to speak with him, too. They had had a good connection since he'd been Dylan's soccer coach when he was younger. It helped to have the outside support, but we needed more.

I began to sense I really couldn't do this all alone. Dylan's dad lived far away in northern Ohio, and though Dylan visited him every school holiday and during the summer, I didn't feel this new stranger was getting enough guidance. In retrospect, all these incidents (the tardiness, the truancy) should have been waving red flags for me—and for the school counselor. It should have been standard practice for the counselor to intervene, to suggest Dylan have a mental health screening to investigate possible causes for the changed behaviors. We both could have been interviewed. At that stage, with the school's help, we could have found out about medical treatment, appropriate counseling, and maybe even alternative options for doing classwork. This we can see clearly in hindsight. But in those years, a "zero tolerance" attitude toward behavior problems was still widely in place. I can only hope a more comprehensive approach, along with early intervention, will be more common for kids and families in this situation today.

Toward the end of turbulent eighth grade, incidents were coming fast and furious. By this time, given the prevailing wisdom of the era, I should have had him on a strict schedule, under lock and key if need be, with me as warden. Would that have helped? One day, he'd climbed with a friend up to a high floor of the college's Fine Arts building. According to witnesses at an outdoor café across the street, a folding chair came careening off a balcony to crash on the sidewalk below. Fortunately, no one was injured, but someone certainly could have been. The campus police took the call and found two kids, one of them my son—he'd been the one to throw the chair. When I later asked him why he did it, he said he didn't know; the idea just came to him. He thought it would be exciting to watch it fall. An impulse. I couldn't believe he didn't think about the consequences.

Because of this event, Dylan was assigned a juvenile court representative. He had to attend after-school and Saturday meetings and do community service; together, we met with his counselor several times. One would think such a regimen would cause a kid to change his behaviors, realize that every action has a consequence, but that wasn't happening. Dylan would say he was going to do better in the future, and say so sincerely. But then . . . a new incident. I began to feel that my bright, curious son wasn't learning anymore. Or that he wasn't learning one of the most important lessons you have to know in life: self-management. Why couldn't he? What was wrong?

Dylan had always been prone to tantrums and inexplicable fits of irritability. These weren't going away, either. In the past, Mike and I had learned to remain calm, impose a time-out, keep him in his room until he calmed down. When he was in a rage, you couldn't talk to him. No communication was possible—this had been true since he was a little child. I maintained the same policies as before during these troubled years, only now my son was older, bigger, stronger. It wasn't so easy to persuade a kid rapidly growing past my height and weight that he needed to keep himself under control. My tools for maintaining discipline often seemed too small for the job. Once, in an angry outburst, Dylan struck the inside arm rest of the car on his side, shattering the plastic. I noticed that behind posters, there were holes punched in his bedroom door. He had already patched up a hole in the wall by himself, where he had kicked in the drywall. That happened earlier, when Mike was still there. We learned to be calm and matter-of-fact; if you ruin it, you fix it. I used the same methods, but I was getting more and more worried about these explosions. Even his hard-won BMX trophies weren't safe. They could be smashed in a rage, along with other easy targets. What Dylan really needed was help in anger management, but that would not come until later, after things spiraled out of control. Back then, none of us understood why.

The worst thing was that I no longer felt I could trust him. He had always been a volatile kid, but now he seemed like molten mercury. He seemed to be at least two different persons, depending on which moment I intercepted him. As for myself, I wasn't a dictator-type; I wanted Dylan's involvement in thinking through what could work better. And he would come up with good ideas that I could agree with. There were actually days when we were on the same page. So it was that we could have a perfectly rational conversation about something on Tuesday, make an agreement about what to do, and then by Friday all bets would be off, as if the discussion had never occurred. I began doubting my methods, my whole approach. Were all my cherished ideas about parenting wrong? Was I supposed to become a dictator? The rules that worked well enough at age nine or ten were now being unilaterally overthrown. I'd tried to be a creative person, think outside the box. Now the box I really cared about had grown powerful legs and was running away from me. When the phone rang, sometimes in the middle of the night, it could be the police. "We picked up your son with a friend of his. They were caught driving on Highway 141, and the officer pulled them over." Dylan had snuck out at 2 a.m. for an adventure in the car his friend Doug had "borrowed" from his mom. I called Mike in exasperation. He knew things weren't going well.

I thought maybe Dylan needed a stronger father presence in his life. True, Mike would call Dylan every week to talk to him; Dylan could call him anytime. And true, the boy always visited his father during his school breaks and vacations, maybe three of those, plus maybe three weeks during the summer. But Mike lived twelve hours away—too far away to be involved daily. As the difficult school year wound to a close, we began to talk about Dylan spending more time with his dad. In fact, would Mike be able to take over the major parenting role? What if Dylan moved up there to live with him and his partner, Linda? I admit I latched on to this option with fervor, which wasn't good for my pride, but it did calm my anxieties. I could no longer defend any of my parenting ideas; they were failing miserably. Besides, trading with Mike seemed fair to me. I had done my share of solo parenting. Now it was right for Mike to do his.

And what about Dylan? Would he go along with this? I talked to him about it. I brought up everything that had been happening and presented the case to him. Maybe he would like to be in a larger place, make a fresh start? If things weren't going so well with Mom, maybe it would be better with Dad? He wasn't enthusiastic about it. He didn't think his dad would understand him as well. I was dubious about this. Wasn't his objection just a ploy to be with the less strict parent? Maybe he was better able to manipulate me because I was easier to deal with. When it came right down to it, over the weeks of deliberation with Mike and Dylan, I decided not to let my son's preference hold sway. The way I saw it, Dylan had already exerted too much of his own out-of-control authority, and it was time to try something different. Even if—maybe even especially if—Dylan didn't like it.

The upshot was that Mike worked out with his partner that he would live separately with Dylan during his high school years. The two of them would relocate to a suburb of Cleveland with a good school system; they would rent a house. It would be a fresh start in a new community for both of them. They would be a team. It was a tremendously generous and bold move on Mike's part. One day in July, he pulled up in his blue van, and we all loaded it up with Dylan's things. By now, he was used to the idea. He had visited his dad, seen the new school, realized that this would be his (and his dad's) next challenge. He wasn't overly emotional at leaving. He seemed in a good mood, ready for adventure. They both did.

By the time the van slowly pulled away, loaded to the brim, and I waved goodbye to both of them, I felt my brave front start to slip away. As I sat in my newly empty house, I was barely able to take stock of what had just happened, the implications of it all. An overwhelming sadness and defeat threatened. Two important people in my life had said goodbye to me in this very place. But behind this, there was also the hope that things would somehow get better. Deeper, yet sheer relief! I was truly on my own now. It was scary but exhilarating. I was free!

I didn't sit there for long. I'd made a plan in advance for how I was going to spend the weekend so that I wouldn't feel completely devastated. I packed up my own bags in twenty minutes and drove two and a half hours to the big city, got the hell out of Dodge. I had signed up for ballroom dance lessons. As frivolous as it may sound, dance was a lifesaver for me at that point. It was expressive, fun, and challenging to learn. Of course, this could have been sheer escapism. Or maybe it was my chance to capture lost Cinderella-at-the-ball moments from years earlier.

I knew I had to do something to fill the void in my life. At least it wasn't drugs or alcohol. The only contact I had with police now was for my own occasional speeding tickets, miles out of Croftburg.

CHAPTER 15: ROAD WARRIOR

However impressed I might have been by the vision of bonding and solidarity I witnessed at the Drug Court gathering on the snowy lawn, I began to sense that for Dylan, the whole experience of recovery felt like an ongoing battle. There were daily skirmishes with such topics as surrender and resistance, ones that challenged his concept of who he had been, who he was, and who he could become. A sign of Dylan's internal struggle were the comments he made to me that winter about the AA classes he had to attend as part of Drug Court. Dylan was ambivalent about these. "So many personal stories you hear," he said. The confessional aspect of the meetings was riveting for him. So many falls, then so many rescues and turnarounds at the brink of disaster! He could relate to that. Each one was a testimony of having surmounted long odds, of surviving.

On the other hand, he was militantly against what he saw as a defeatist attitude at those same meetings. A lot of what folks called "recovery" sounded to him like surrender. "I hate how you have to wallow in this philosophy of 'I am nothing' or 'I'm a weak, stupid nobody who needs help,'" Dylan said. "People at these meetings are always saying stuff like 'I have to rely on God or a Higher Power to get me through life's tribulations,'" he complained. "Why does a state-run program push this kind of fundamentalism? I really don't believe in God, and I don't believe all this stuff that people say. I've tried to go along for a while, and when I start to believe like they do, it messes me up. I don't think I got into the trouble I did because I'm stupid. I think it's because I couldn't handle my emotions. I just let myself make some bad decisions. Or maybe I made those decisions for the wrong reasons. But I don't accept that I'm a poor, dumb person."

I took this in, later realizing that his struggle wasn't just with some type of local fundamentalism; it was about spiritual surrender itself. I could understand why this would be so difficult for him. He had always, always sought to control his external world, and that's probably because he felt he had so little control over his own internal world. I didn't know exactly how that worked, but I sensed it was true.

And then I puzzled over the irony of his attitude. "I'm not a poor, dumb person," he'd said, when not more than a few weeks ago he had so fitfully proclaimed to John and me: "I'm not like John's sons; I'm a screw-up. I can't take the stress, I can't do everything perfectly, I have anxiety—it's hard for me to do what is easy for them." I wanted to ask him, "OK, Dylan, do you not see there is a contradiction here in how you see yourself?"

In early February Dylan began to get seriously interested in body-building. This became clear the time he and I went out to dinner at a sports bar to celebrate the restitution money paying off his court fees and his re-entry into college life. Dylan was talkative; he'd earlier told me that he was hoping to approach the trainer of the body-sculpting class at the gym about getting a construction job during the summer. The trainer happened to be a contractor as well. Dylan had always been an active, physical person. Over the previous fall, I waved at him when I occasionally saw him whisking by on his Kona bike to the fitness center in early evening. But now, he was avid about getting himself in super-shape, not only through exercise but through protein supplements. As he talked, I must have expressed some misgivings about his "bulking up"—not getting fit, but turning into a Mr. Johnny Atlas mountain muscle man. My son never did anything by halves: it was all or nothing.

Well, this set him off; I could see it wouldn't take too long for the fuse to detonate. Right on cue, the blast occurred. "What's wrong with bulking up and getting muscles?" Dylan asked with raised voice. "I'm not like you and Dad. I have a muscular build, I'm athletic, and this is something I can do that's good for me. Other guys at the gym are impressed when they see me work out. They say, 'you could really get strong' and I know that's true." His main critique of my remark: "You and Dad are always trying to get me to be like you; well, it's not going to happen. I'm completely different. Let me be who I am."

I felt wronged by this statement but decided to back off. Might as well try to cut off a Mack truck doing 80 mph. So I kept quiet, my eyes leaving his to scan the six or seven TV sports channel screens around the room while Dylan, in turn, checked his smart phone. What I saw were torpedo-like hockey players slashing across the ice, all trying to slam a small, round puck into a net, when they weren't smashing into each other. On other screens, impossibly tall, limber athletes were bobbing, dribbling, ducking, and shooting a basketball through a hoop. The sheer fluidity of the moves was dazzling. Didn't all these sports screens prove how important it was for men to focus on improving their strength, speed, and performance? The whole world was watching them. *Sure, sure, it's all true. But, what about the inner life? What makes a person strong on the inside?*

Since then, I've reflected on something Oliver Sacks, the beloved British neurologist, said about his own Muscle Beach phase of young manhood in his book, *On the Move*. Writing about his training days in California, he says, "I sometimes wonder why I pushed myself so relentlessly in weight lifting . . . I became strong— very strong—with all my weight lifting but found that this did nothing for my character, which remained exactly the same."

So, what does it take to build your inner strength and flexibility? That sounds at least as useful over the long haul. Many would say it takes cultivating a spiritual life, and there are many shapes that can take. According to Brené Brown, a professor of social work who has studied the problem, what it takes to weather the storms of life is paradoxical: it's the courage to be open and vulnerable. The author of *Rising Strong* tells us that, according to her research, the most resilient life practitioners were those who were courageous in making themselves open to change and learning. That's how they found creative solutions. To describe how this courage works, she uses the word "rumble"—as in, you get down and rumble emotionally with the dilemma you're facing. This word feels more active than the older word "surrender": for many, that sounds too much like giving up. When you rumble, it involves rolling around, tussling—getting pushed and pushing back. It's more along the lines of wrestling with some kind of force, and the opposing forces are usually within yourself.

Ah, rumbling with vulnerability. Just try to sell *that* to any young person, especially a young man! But at the same time, I knew my son was intent on building physical strength precisely *because* he felt so vulnerable—and he wanted to flee as far as possible from that. My thoughts turned to a story Dylan had told me just recently. When flying along on his scooter, he frequently felt so exposed, whereas everyone else was enclosed in their comfortable metal capsules, behind dark glass. "There's no margin for error on a scooter," he told me. "One moment of inattention, and you've had it." An incident had occurred where he'd had to stop suddenly, and he'd been concerned the car behind him wasn't going to stop soon enough. He'd had to shoot ahead on the soft, roadside shoulder and, as a result, got thrown unceremoniously to the ground. It was either that or risk taking a serious hit. Not a great experience for his shoulder, or his pride.

So yes, I could see why muscle building was important to him. He loved the exertion of it, the way it relieved stress. But more important, it was a way to put on armor. Dylan actually used the term once. "I feel like I need armor out there." Vulnerability? No way! Not persuasive when he was at risk of getting run over because he didn't have enough metal around him.

And internal issues? Look what happened to Fred, the moped salesman. About a month or so after I'd seen him in the yard before the Drug Court meeting, Dylan told me that Fred was getting expelled from DC. And that was after he'd been in the group for three years; in fact, he was in what they call "After Care." Who knows why it happened? Maybe Fred had come under some kind of stress, then started drinking again and tried to cover it up. Addiction sneaks up on people in different ways. And while you could have a relapse in DC, you couldn't lie about it. Dylan shook his head as he told me. "It was horrible," he said. "Fred broke down; he cried; and then he told us all he loved us, and he was so sorry. We couldn't believe it; it was like he was just standing there, naked."

I was sad, too. What would Fred do now? Would he have to serve time? I imagined that being dismissed from Drug Court was like falling off the planet into outer darkness. My son must have been shaken, too, for a man who had helped him, someone who had come so far down the road with the group but now had to leave on his own. It was a hard lesson in what could happen. Small wonder Dylan felt he needed internal armor, too.

By the time our food arrived, we both abandoned our screen thoughts and resumed our conversation. The steamy cloud of conflict had dissipated. I decided to take a strategic detour and ask more about the gym, ask Dylan's advice on what clothing would be good for somebody like me to work out in. Other topics might get us out of bounds, but we were usually game, both of us, for a conversation about clothing styles. My thirty-six feet of over-stuffed closets more than qualified me as an expert in that category.

"We all go to Fitness Forever gym club. Even Darlene trains there. You need spandex capris and then two or three layers of tops you can take off when you overheat," Dylan advised me.

I smiled at that one. Even though I was quick enough to overheat, somehow I didn't see myself becoming the Queen of Spandex anytime soon.

All this talk about armor and bodybuilding wasn't going to slow down, as I soon found out. Dylan was pulling out all the stops when it came to vitamins and supplements. He said he couldn't afford to buy what he needed, so would I help him out? Guess he knew how, as his mom, I would be supportive of whatever came under the rubric "Health and Human Happiness." So, on occasion, I'd spring for large bottles of fish oil capsules, de-mercurized and loaded with omega-3s, reputed to help with brain health and any metabolic problems. Of course, vitamins were necessary—even if he was eating right, there would always be something lacking that could use a boost. Then, before long, came the biggest booster of all. Dylan showed me the much-needed item as he led me one day into the supplements aisle at Walgreens: two humongous canisters of protein powder.

From the size of the packaging, it looked like something you'd pour into a diesel engine with a funnel.

"What?! You expect me to pay for THAT? How do you even know what all is in that stuff? There could be whole dissolved cow bones in there with some concrete dust."

"No, it's not calcium. It's Isotone Zero Carb. No bones, Mom, but it *is* made from cow's milk," he said. "Look at the ingredients: it's protein derived from whey."

He started reading off the list of ingredients, then gave a mini-lecture right then and there on protein supplements and why they were necessary, how no one looking to build muscle could hope to do it on regular food alone. Instead of building up, you'd be tearing down.

"But I've seen plenty of people out there who are strong and who don't use any powders. My dad and your own dad were very strong in their younger years, and they never took supplements. You get strong by doing exercise."

Dylan waved my comment aside as completely antiquated and inconsequential.

"I've done lots of exercise in my life. But you'll remember when I did a workout routine to get strong last year, I was always tired out afterward. I couldn't keep up. But just recently, someone loaned me some of this. It did wonders! Everyone serious about working out and getting strong takes a good product," he said.

It was Fate. Despite my best intentions, I was witnessing a live commercial by an ace salesman. Of course, I had to be bowled over by the sheer velocity of it. All common sense had to be scattered like ten pins. Besides, this was for my only son's health and wellbeing. How could I go against that?

The results didn't go unnoticed by John. He probably got a glimpse of the dollars flying out of my bank account, even as I was complaining about Mountain Man going overboard.

"Look, you can buy him all the supplements you want," he said. "And he can lift all the weights in the gym trying to turn himself into Spider Man, the strongest guy on the block. But how will that help him deal with his Peter Parker frailties?"

I wasn't too sure about that.

Later, I was reminded of Darlene's assessment during one of our meetings together. Joking with Dylan, she'd said, "You know what I've told you before. You have the demeanor of a sophisticated thirty-year-old, but inside on the emotional level, you're about ten years old still. All those teen years of escaping into marijuana clouds, that was a way for you to deal with the confusion of your feelings. But now, as an adult, you get to start figuring them out and finding other ways—more productive ways—of dealing with them."

The director of Drug Court knew how to say these things to him.

"Darlene's tough," Dylan remarked to me sometimes, shaking his head. But I could tell by the way he said it that he admired her for it. As if he knew that's exactly what he needed to hear, even if he didn't always like it.

CHAPTER 16: A NEW START WITH DAD

When Mike and fourteen-year-old Dylan started living together in Berea, Ohio, an older suburb of Cleveland, Dylan had to adjust to going to a new school. The phone calls and reports I received from that time indicated that Dylan was busy, involved in a number of activities, many of them with his dad. His physical skills were in demand for odd jobs, and his computer skills, too. He helped an older couple living downstairs set up their e-mail accounts and sort through technical glitches. He accompanied his dad on tree and bush pruning jobs. Growing tall and capable during these years, he helped his dad with major garden-design jobs in other states during the summer. Parts of that were fun for him, like getting to drive a small front-end loader around to deliver rocks and soil. But other parts required careful planning and skillful negotiating with clients, qualities Dylan didn't exactly have in spades—not yet, anyway. I always hoped that he would one day use his strength and artistic skills to make gardens himself, but—like most other things I suggested to him—he pushed that one away.

I later found out that other things were happening behind the scenes. For one, Dylan had thoroughly researched marijuana on the internet and had decided this was just the right calming drug for him. In fact, it wasn't really a drug, he told himself. No, cannabis was a plant, a very special plant that had been bred by people all over the planet for years, so that it would contain the right combination of cannabinoids to smooth out unsettled minds. Smoking it could help keep anxiety at bay, and Dylan felt he had plenty of that to deal with. Of course, he tried regular smokes as well, but cigarettes didn't have nearly the same therapeutic effect. As if he said to himself, "Can't trust anyone else to help me deal with my problems, so I'll find my own way."

Then, too, he was living in a postindustrial metropolis near the great, northern expanse of Lake Erie. I tended to play down the fact that this would be such an enormous change for him. After all, we'd spent plenty of time there visiting Grandma Louise and the rest of Mike's family, especially in the summer. But to actually live there, go to school there, that was like being relocated to a whole different universe. For sure, it was one that had a much wider variety of citizens in it. The old social rules and divides of a small town gave way to a much larger playing field. But you had to figure out where you fit in.

I later found out that here, too, Dylan had made his own arrangements. For guy friends, he was interested in types who'd had a rougher kind of life, who were street-smart. He described one friend to me years later who, apart from being a high school student, worked at the zoo, smoked pot, knew guys who had been in jail. No doubt, they discussed rap music. Dylan probably burned CDs for his friends there like he did here. The urban scene only reinforced his attraction to street rap: a huge poster of Tupac went up on his bedroom wall. The rapper's lyrics, the titles, became his mantras to live by: "Only God Can Judge Me," "All Eyez on Me," "Keep Ya' Head Up." Neither Mike nor I saw this clearly at the time, but Dylan was taking up his stand. Deciding he could never be one of the mainstream guys, he chose to identify with the rebels.

Part of this was regular teen angst, but there was another angle to it, a class identity angle. Instead of seeing his move to the city as one expanding his worldview—and his options—Dylan saw this move to a rental house in Berea a lot like the divorce, as a further sign of his life being disrupted, of him falling into a déclassé zone. Our house in Kentucky had been far from fancy, but it was new and special in a way the rental house in Berea wasn't. To him, living in the older suburb seemed like a big step down. He hadn't had the chance yet to see how the northern lake city of Cleveland would reinvent itself, how the derelict downtown would be transformed into interesting new museums, markets, nightspots, parks, refurbished neighborhoods. All that was still to come. At age fifteen, Dylan could only adapt to his changed circumstances as he saw them, but he was resisting, too. Inside, he maintained a solid nostalgia for Croftburg.

During that year in Berea, moments of open conflict erupted between Dylan and his dad, the same as I'd experienced. Mike caught Dylan smoking weed and came down on him about it. Dylan exploded; for him, marijuana was the way he was keeping himself under control. Who was his dad—or anyone else—to tell him otherwise? Sure, it was illegal, but he knew there were plenty of people working their way around that one. Then came one nasty incident when Mike "got in his way." Mike told me about it. He'd had to confront Dylan about smoking a joint or some other infraction. Dylan lost it. He picked up his dad's CD player and crashed it on the floor, then he crossed over to where his dad was standing and pushed him roughly backward, where he hit his head against a wall. When, not surprisingly, Mike received a cut on his head, Dylan immediately apologized and helped him with the wound. After the dust settled, Mike had to work out a plan for Dylan to contribute toward replacing the broken CD player—more computer tutorials downstairs to earn the money. It wasn't unusual for the teen to take his anger out on objects: over the years, he'd graduated from busting up pencils to more significant objects like trophies, answering machines, phones, lamps, car door handles, chairs. This latest incident, though, was a frightening example of how Dylan's explosions could physically harm one of us. It could have been me; it could have been a teacher or any authority figure telling him he couldn't do what he wanted to.

Mike now knew what I'd discovered. This was a fractious kid who was getting seriously out of control. Somehow, he'd have to be reined in or he'd be in jail. Mike took Dylan to counselors; Dylan agreed to attend anger-management classes. They discussed thoroughly his need to manage his white-hot temper. What amazes me now is that no one suggested that he get a mental health review. In 2002, such reviews for teens were not common. Who suspected that this oppositional behavior might be caused by an insidious illness called bipolar disorder? Instead, people talked about "bad" kids and "good" kids. Behavior problems were cases of "flawed" character, bad parenting, or both. As a parent, if your kid "acted up," you applied "tough love"—that and maybe a strong dose of Ritalin— then popped some tranquilizers for yourself.

Toward spring, Mike and I both wondered if Dylan's underlying anger was due, at least in part, to the Big Move to Cleveland. His dad took him to counseling sessions, tried to work with him, asked him about the next school year. How did he want things to go? It came out that Dylan wanted more than anything to return to his hometown. Mike thought hard; it was not an easy proposition. Dylan had three more years of high school left. Yet if Dylan felt more positive, things would go more smoothly. Perhaps he could consider moving back to Croftburg, renting a house there. Dylan would be back with his old friends, back on familiar turf. His mom was there and could help out. Would it be worth the sacrifice for him? Mike didn't know but was willing to try. He asked me to help him locate a suitable house. Late that summer, they moved in, just in time for another school year at the local high school.

At first, the move back appeared to be a wise decision. Once again, Dylan had his regular pal, Lonnie—the nice one—to do things with, girls once again calling at all hours. He was doing his schoolwork, maintaining his curfew, doing chores. Things seemed in balance, more or less, as far as we could expect with a moody, difficult teen. Both of us parents attended regular counseling sessions with Dylan. In the counselor's office, everything seemed so manageable. Mr. Evans had a good rapport with Dylan, could take things in stride, break down a contentious area, and suggest ways for us to reach a compromise. I remember thinking, "I bet this will work out." But not for long. During that first fall of tenth grade, several incidents occurred, ones that were far more serious than anything else that had yet happened.

One evening, Mike called me over to their place because Dylan was late for curfew (again), and he wanted us to have a three-way talk. Not long after I arrived, Dylan came in, feeling fine—too fine, in fact. He was stoned out of his mind—eyes glazed over, words slurring in the simplest of sentences. We grounded him, talked to him, but I'm not sure anything got through that night. On other occasions, though, he could still be perfectly calm and reasonable. Between scenes like this, we could still go out and have dinner together with good communication. At times, Dylan could be perfectly self-reflective. What he said, though, was disturbing.

He talked about feeling anxious, feeling sometimes depressed, like he couldn't do what he needed to at school because he couldn't focus. He talked, too, about having racing thoughts—sometimes he couldn't slow down what was going on in his head. In late October, Mike took him to see a doctor who prescribed the antidepressant Lexapro, which Dylan started taking every day. In return, Dylan agreed to give up marijuana. In general, though, he made light of any problems. Mike and I were worried but remained optimistic. Truth is, we were confused; we had no explanations. We didn't know what it was, exactly, that we were up against. There were still good days, too, and it always seemed that there was one more option we could try to stabilize the situation.

During the fateful months of November and December, within only a few short weeks, Dylan managed to accumulate several charges. First came the fourth-degree assault charge brought by another boy's parents after a school fight. According to Dylan, it all started when a kid misinterpreted something he'd said in the lunchroom and punched him. We told him we were glad he'd restrained himself and hadn't punched back. The situation seemed to calm down over the weekend, but the following Monday morning, as soon as Dylan saw the boy again, his rage flared and he retaliated. Another fight ensued, along with an assault charge. A week later, Dylan shoplifted a pair of shoes by walking out in them after trying them on (which he agreed was a completely stupid thing to do). Not long after, he was charged with possession of marijuana and a glass pipe when an officer stopped a vehicle in which he was a passenger. In yet another incident, he got into an altercation with some other boys at Lonnie's house when he was taking down a tent they'd been camping in, which resulted in the police being called. Riled up, Dylan was in no shape to talk calmly to the officer and answer questions. Instead, he became confrontational and did the unthinkable. He actually fought with the first officer, and it took two other officers arriving on the scene to subdue him. Of course, he was charged with resisting arrest. When his pockets were searched, the police found a pocketknife and some pills. By now, Dylan was getting a reputation with the city police. They learned never to approach him alone.

In the last, decisive incident, Mike, Dylan, and I were having an evening together in December. I was visiting because Dylan had just turned sixteen. He and I were sitting at the computer together, discussing which songs to burn onto a gift CD for Christmas. The next thing I knew, Mike and Dylan were in the kitchen, and an argument was flaring. Mike asked me to come, and I could see that Dylan was in a rage. I found out later that it all had to do with Dylan horsing around, but it was too forceful for his dad. The efforts Mike made to ward him off made Dylan see red. Coming into the kitchen, I tried talking to him to get to calm down, but it soon became clear that wasn't going to happen. Instead, his rage escalated. I was genuinely scared of impending violence and called 911. I didn't even speak, just held the phone. The dispatcher could hear the shouting, the threats pouring out. Dylan was using his imposing physical strength to push his dad into a corner.

Before long, three or four policemen were knocking on the door. They knew all too well who they were dealing with by now. His dad and I watched in stunned horror as the officers loomed over him. We were afraid that, though vastly outnumbered, he would fight them—but thank God, even in his anger he must have had some shred of rationality telling him it was impossible to resist this time. I still remember that as they handcuffed him and led him away, he suddenly looked so alone and fearful of what would happen. He actually called out for his dad, as if he were a little kid again. Things had turned radically wrong—and it happened in just a few seconds. Such confusion and anguish for all of us! We didn't know what to do; it was devastating. Dylan was on his way to jail and then to the juvenile detention center in a neighboring city. This was the last straw.

In Juvenile Court, the judge in our county ordered a psychological screening for mental health issues. "It's unusual for a young person to have this many charges in one month," she said. No kidding! I was given a list of psychologists to consult. Since it was very near Christmas by now, Mike had returned to Cleveland to be with Linda and the rest of his family up there. Now the ball was back in my court. We had until January 5 to get some results to show the judge. I spoke on the phone with my dad in North Carolina, who encouraged me to seek the best specialist I could find. He would pay. I made an appointment with Dr. Barnard, juvenile and forensic psychologist at Vanderbilt Medical Center. Then I made special arrangements with the court to pick up my son from the detention center at 5:00 a.m. before driving two and a half hours to Nashville. We had just one day to have the screening, then I'd drive him back. Dylan was quiet for most of the trip, probably still half asleep. I remember his face when we were both having breakfast before our appointment at Vanderbilt. "I think I'll always be in jail," he said despondently. "I'll always be locked up." I told him no, it wasn't always going to be that way. The information the doctor would give us was going to help. Meanwhile, I didn't feel even half as confident as I tried to sound. Would this screening help or wouldn't it?

Later that same day, after a round of independent interviews and separate in-depth questionnaires, we received the first hint of a diagnosis. Dr. Barnard spoke to both of us individually, then together, and said that he was fairly sure that Dylan had all the signs of a disorder that he called *cyclothymia*. It's an old word for a mood disorder; it could be something like pre-bipolar, specifically for an adolescent.It didn't matter what you called it, he said; the term referred to a cluster of psychic phenomena that affect behavior. It was characterized by racing thoughts, quick changes of mood and energy level—the feeling that you were invincible and on top of the world for a while and then, a few days or maybe hours later, a sense that you were doomed and would always be depressed. Those patterns, which sounded so familiar, were part of the exaggerated mood shifting so characteristic of this psychic condition. There were also times when the person experienced fuzzy cognition, could barely think his way out of a cardboard box. Other times, thinking would be extraordinarily quick and focused. It was an intense, chaotic situation for a person to deal with.

There would be biorhythmic disturbances, too—sleep was affected, for example. At times, a person with a mood disorder would need to sleep hours longer than usual; at other times, they could barely sleep at all. This also sounded familiar. In hearing this, I recalled how years ago, Dylan would have such trouble falling asleep sometimes, and then on those occasions when he woke up at night, he seemed so distressed and had great difficulty falling back to sleep afterward. Another symptom could be panic attacks, anxiety out of control—these could frequently occur along with this disorder, too. I could never understand where they came from. But Dr. Barnard pointed out that a person experiencing *some* psychic anxiety could, on occasion, *feel* like he was experiencing something much more physical, more intense, almost life-threatening, affecting breathing and heart rate. At times, the person could fear he was going to have a heart attack. I thought of the times Dylan had told me or his dad that he needed to go to the emergency room. We'd taken him there, too, because it was the only way to calm his distress. The doctors never found anything wrong, but just going through the check-up was a way of coping with the situation.

The combination of all these symptoms could certainly make a person highly reactive, afraid first and foremost of losing control. Dr. Barnard quoted Hagop Akiskal's article on pre-bipolar indicators in children and adolescents for us, stating that "intermittent intense emotionality" was one of the hallmarks, and under that rubric, "irritability that could degenerate into explosive anger" stood out for Dylan. This last part correlated with his recent episodes edging into violent behavior.

Alone later that evening, I looked up more information on the internet. "Cyclothymia" didn't sound too bad, but from what I could find online in late December 2003, "mood disorder" and "bipolar" did. Especially when I read about outcomes for people who had these disorders. Bipolar was designated as one of the most debilitating mental illnesses anyone could have because it affects emotions,

energy levels, reasoning, impulses, and decisions. What part of your
life would NOT be affected by those? Not to mention it was a life-
long condition. This illness impacted a person's ability to hold a steady
job, to have long-term meaningful relationships, and to keep personal
finances in order. Reading more, I then came across the psychiatric
term "co-morbidity." The technical meaning is having two or more
co-existing illnesses, a primary one and then another linked to it. For
example, a mood disorder and anxiety, augmenting distress. Another
typical combination would be a mood disorder and substance abuse
leading to addiction. Today, the preferred term is "dual diagnosis,"
but back then, the earlier word etched its skull and crossbones on me
as I finally closed the internet pages for the night. *Co-morbidity*: how
could anyone recover from *that*? Yet, Dr. Barnard had been calm; he
was knowledgeable. He said there was no cure, but treatment was
available. His counsel for us would come in a follow-up report.

After putting together the results of the separate interviews
(including a phone interview with Dylan's dad) and the psychological
survey questions all three of us answered, Dr. Barnard and his accom-
panying psychologist sent a full report to Mike and me several days
later. We studied it with interest, and since Dr. Barnard invited our
comments or corrections, we each sent those, too. I felt reassured by
their professionalism. I spoke to Mike and my dad about what we'd
learned. The written diagnosis didn't sound nearly as frightening as
what I'd read online. At least there was a name for this strange phenomenon we had been dealing with all along, not knowing what it
was. A mood disorder. I believed that Dylan had always lived with
this, but that in his teens, the condition had become much worse,
much more pronounced. The diagnosis was scary but it was also, at
the same time, a relief.

I remember when Dr. Barnard spoke to Dylan and me after the
consultation, he said not to put too much stock in a specific term.
In an e-mail to us, he wrote that "psychiatric diagnoses are not cut

in stone." Nonetheless, data from the screening provided a better understanding of the cause for the behaviors—and a treatment. He expressed a hope that Dylan would get the help he needed to deal with his behaviors and his moods. Dr. Barnard's final comment in his e-mail comforted all of us: "The main purpose of this report is to convey to the judge that Dylan has some significant (and treatable) mental health issues. Your main goal is for the judge to allow treatment to occur (whether it's outpatient or residential) rather than place Dylan in a juvenile detention facility." Amen!

When I told my dad about Dr. Barnard's report, he remained thoughtful. He hoped, too, that now that we had some kind of professional diagnosis, Dylan could receive the treatment he needed to regain his health and get his life back in order. As we were talking, he made a comment: "All this makes me wonder how many other people who are locked up now in the prison system have some similar kind of mental illness."

Probably quite a few. During the time my son was detained in a juvenile detention center in Kentucky, an important study was being carried out by the national Office of Justice to find an answer to the very same question. Researchers visited a series of representative state and local jails as well as federal prisons from 2002 through 2004 to interview inmates about their mental health. The data was compiled in a written report, "Mental Health Problems of Prison and Jail Inmates," from the Bureau of Justice Statistics, published in 2006. In it, more than half of all state, federal, and local jail inmates reported experiences within the twelve months prior to their arrest of what clinicians would consider mania, severe depression, anxiety, or a psychotic disorder. These self-reported symptoms aligned with criteria described in the then-current *Diagnostic and Statistical Manual of Mental Disorders* (DSM-IV). The study also reported high levels of prior substance abuse within this same population of inmates with mental health problems—nearly 75%.

Similar studies of youth in contact with the juvenile justice system during this period yielded comparable information. In 2007, the National Center for Mental Health and Juvenile Justice published a report stating that close to 70% of such adolescents had a diagnosable mental health disorder that hadn't been found or treated yet. Of those, 20% had a disorder severe enough to impair their daily ability to function in social settings such as school. The underlying problem could be a psychiatric illness, or it could be a reaction to trauma or abuse that the child had suffered and needed help to surmount emotionally. Following the pattern of jailed adults, 60% of this population also had a co-occurring substance use disorder—their attempt to cope. Studies like these launched efforts to provide communities with a blueprint for policy changes. The goal was for youth with antisocial behaviors to be directed to mental health assessment and ongoing care *before* they got locked up for serious incidents. Needless to say, the challenge continues.

As a parent with a teenage son in a detention facility back in 2003, I could only wonder: who will be the catcher in the rye to keep young persons with mental health issues today from eventually falling into the coils of the criminal justice system tomorrow? Who, if not our physicians, our therapists, our healthcare delivery? Surely, these services must become widely available to the many persons who so desperately need them. It couldn't happen soon enough.

During the weeks of Dylan's incarceration, Mike and I researched possibilities for a residential school that he could attend and found a program that we thought could work. It would be hugely expensive, but my parents agreed to help out. We discussed it and agreed that each of us would pay a third of the total expenses. It was a tough decision, but at the time, Mike and I were too exhausted and frightened to consider any other possibility. We hoped that when

Dr. Barnard's report was given to Judge Cassidy in January, along with our proposal to enroll our son in a residential program, she would agree to release him to do this.

Dr. Barnard had made it clear that Dylan needed to have some kind of medication to modulate his symptoms. He wrote about that in the report, too, mentioning lithium, but there were others as well, such as Depakote or Lamictal, for example. He said it might take some experimentation with a trained psychiatrist to find the right medication or combination of meds that would work for him. We made sure the school had a psychiatrist who could prescribe these. When I told Dr. Barnard that we were thinking of sending our son to a residential school, he remained pensive for a moment. He said that generally, it was better to keep the child in his familiar home environment and work with him or her through counseling. "But," he added diplomatically, "an appropriate residential program could be a good solution, too." After all, considering Dylan's emotional conflicts within the family, he had suggested that alternate sources of emotional support from adults (foster parent, teacher, other relative, friend's parent) might be explored.

When presented with the report and our plan, the juvenile court judge agreed to permit Dylan to be released. It was January 5, a new year, and hopefully a new chapter opening in all our lives. Sending our son away from home to a residential school may not have been the wisest thing to do, but it felt like the only viable option at the time. Initially, Dylan experienced more stress, I know. It was yet another huge change for him to adapt to.

Back in that cold January when Dylan was sixteen, we parents had a diagnosis and a plan, but we had no idea how much more there was to learn about our son's mood disorder. We were only at the edge of that mysterious territory we would all have to cross.

CHAPTER 17: JAMAICA

When we saw our son again for the first time after his January juvenile court hearing and release, it was at a small facility in Jamaica. How did he get there? Well, the in-between steps had been rockier than we anticipated. Actually, Dylan had first gone to a different residential school in another state, but after he punched one of the staff in an angry outburst, his choice was either to leave altogether or agree to go to another, stronger version of the program in Jamaica. That's where the toughest cases got sent. Dylan agreed to the transfer, largely because the alternative would be more jail time in Juvenile Detention. Though drastic, the event seemed to convince him he needed to take his next opportunity seriously.

In fact, his new destination was a former resort hotel on the Jamaican seacoast that had been converted into a residential school for troubled teens—the most troubled. Almost all of the personnel who worked with these American adolescents were Jamaicans: they served as counselors, teachers, librarians, cooks, supervisors, monitors, and cleanup crew, although the teen residents (who saw themselves as "inmates") did a lot of their own cleaning and laundry. Despite the laid-back island ambiance, this was a highly disciplined place with strict guidelines for behavior. Girls were housed on one side, boys on the other; the two seldom interacted. Everyone had a daily schedule of classes and activities. Teens could move up and gain privileges in the program according to how well they worked and followed the rules. It was old school, like something out of another century. Yet we parents knew that no young person was sent to that school lightly. You had to be desperate. We all feared for our teens' lives back home. "This isn't exactly a resort," Dylan had reported in his first letter to me. True, if it was any kind of resort, it was a last resort.

From the beginning, parents and their son or daughter could communicate by letter as often as they wished. Kids were, in fact, required to write their parents at least one letter per week. Counselors who worked with the teens reported also at weekly intervals via phone conversations with parents. Despite the distance, we didn't feel cut off; there were progress reports, and kids were relatively free to express what they were feeling. If they cooperated and moved to a higher level, the teens could eventually earn the privilege of phone conversations with parents once a week. Most Jamaicans—contrary to what employees at big resort spas in Negril, for example, might convey—believe in rules and strict discipline for kids in their family lives. Adults and seniors are respected. Each person works and fills a role in supporting the household.

In my interactions with the Jamaican teachers and counselors at the school, I found them to be refreshingly direct and down-to-earth. Still, it could be a very tough job. The two therapists who worked at the school were American women, and they each held a deep respect for their Jamaican colleagues as well as for the culture of the area. The school also had a psychiatrist—very important to us—also a Jamaican, trained in the UK, who came in every week from Kingston to consult with teens. I had to be assertive to make sure he met with Dylan, though, as he was in high demand. It took a few weeks before Dylan was on a lithium regime and meeting with

Dr. Bishop regularly to monitor his symptoms. I remember feeling relieved that my son was finally getting the medication that the psychiatrist in Nashville said would help him.

We parents had our own program meetings, too. In fact, we worked through a curriculum and performed many of the same transformative group activities with our peers as our sons and daughters did with theirs at the school. While I went to these on my own, Mike attended with Linda. Over the months, many letters were exchanged along with weekly progress reports by phone with Dylan's counselor, Ms. Taylor. It felt like a big step up when we could finally have our own calls with Dylan, hear his voice. Then, after several more months, the counselors told us it was time for the first round of parent-teen visits that would take place at the school. Everyone was very expectant; we parents hadn't seen our kids for a long time. What would they be like? We had letters from them to read, phone calls, but what would our interaction with them be after this transition? Occasionally, we parents would get to see a photo of our son or daughter. *Is that my son actually smiling?* To us, this seemingly everyday occurrence was a miracle, coming from a rebellious, exiled teenager. And most of us had never been to Jamaica before. We needed advice as to how to get to the location, where to stay. By the time our group arrived at the school and toured the grounds and classrooms, we were all slightly dazed and charged with emotions. The long-awaited meeting time was at hand.

The event was choreographed in a structured way. First, groups of parents stood in circles within a large room. We were told to close our eyes and to face inside the circle. Next, counselors ushered in a group of teens who each scanned the room to find their parents. When each teen was standing behind his or her parents, we were told to turn around and to touch the shoulders of the person in front of us, still with our eyes closed. Finally, we could open them. Amid hugs, and cries, and tears, a great sense of relief and jubilation burst out into the room. Dylan's face looked surprisingly radiant; he was relaxed and beaming. I hadn't seen him this way for a long time. When Ms. Taylor, his Jamaican counselor, came up to us, she hugged Dylan, too, and I knew they had the kind of close relationship where they could joke around with each other. Sunlight streamed through slits in the window blinds, and for those first few moments, I'm pretty sure we all felt we'd died and gone to heaven.

The students could take their parents on a longer tour of the premises, and Dylan showed his father and me the room he shared with five other guys. He showed me the neat shelves where they kept their belongings, and I noticed an ordered assembly of shoes on the floor nearby. He showed me the beds, how they folded out at night and folded back up into the wall with a clip during the day to free up the space. Dylan pointed to a little cut on his forehead: "That's where I hit it on a bed corner the other day when I was putting it up." It was just a small mark in his smooth skin. I was happy that he looked healthy. The numerous windows of the room were wide open with sunlight pouring in. It seemed that the building was completely permeable to the outdoors—just like the resort hotel it had once been. "Well, you wouldn't think it was so nice if you lived here like we do, Mom," Dylan remarked. True enough. For him and his fellows, it seemed like international boot camp.

"You should have been here when Hurricane Charley blew through here, Mom," Dylan said. "It happened during the night. We didn't get much sleep. Remember how I told you how the rain was blowing though the slats in the shutters? It was right here."

He showed me the large window facing the sea that was outfitted with pull-down blinds inside and, on the outside, shutters. I recalled the night he'd described; it sounded frightening. They'd stayed at the school for Charley, but when powerful Hurricane Ivan approached a short while later, they all evacuated to take shelter further inland, away from the coast. I recalled all too clearly how worried we parents were that Saturday; a number of us communicated by e-mail, straining for news. Then, finally, we heard about our kids by satellite phone from the school director. "Everyone's OK," he said. "The school will need some repairs, but thank God, everyone's safe." A collective sigh of relief filled the airwaves.

Later on the grounds during our visit, Dylan pointed out the trees and shrubbery we passed. "You wouldn't believe it, Mom," he said, "but the hurricane blew most all the leaves off these plants. By now, though, they've grown back and you can barely tell it happened."

I found out the Jamaicans in the surrounding countryside were just as resilient. When hurricanes blew the metal roofs off their houses, neighbors got together to help locate and reattach them. Afterward everyone swept up the debris, rounded up their chickens and goats, tended their gardens, planted new rows of callaloo. Hurricanes were just part of the usual drama of living on the island. That was another reason Americans on the staff admired their Jamaican coworkers.

After casual tour time, we parents had scheduled meetings with our teens and the counselors, to talk about their progress in schoolwork and in the program. We could visit their teachers, too, but mostly Mike and I spent time separately and together with Dylan, talking. He was seventeen now and I couldn't believe how much more relaxed he was. The rebellious wild tension that used to course through him was gone. He was expressive, as he always had been, but under control. I knew from Ms. Taylor's reports that he still had outbursts, but they were minor in comparison to those before. They had discussed anger management, and Dylan said he'd seen enough of peers being out of control to know that he didn't want to be in that situation. He was working on it.

What he wanted more than anything was to come back home, return to high school, have a normal life. But Mike and I had talked about it from our respective places; we also heeded advice from the program directors. We felt that Dylan was doing well there, and we thought he would do better if he graduated from the program, which would mean slightly over another year. In retrospect, I'm not sure at all we made the right decision. Were we shaking the fragile bond of trust we had just built up with our son? I do know Dylan was upset when we gave him the news. It was a terrible letdown for him, the likes of which I can only imagine. A year is a long time to a teenager. At least the three of us were all together at the time we told him; we could share the tears. We could be there to reach out and touch his arm, look into his eyes, tell him it would be hard, but consider how far he had come already. We wanted Dylan to be ready to start a new life, not go back to the old one. The old one scared us too much.

All the times when Dylan was playing football in middle school at Croftburg, and I was sitting in the stands with other parents under the glow of floodlights on autumn evenings, I took for granted that I would be doing that for years. That he would be playing sports or playing in the band, he would be going out with girlfriends, attending the prom in a tuxedo—all those teen stops on the road to adulthood, all those cozy, hometown bonding experiences. Instead, I'm sure he felt exiled in this Jamaican school so far away. We felt exiled too. That whole nostalgic chapter of teen and parent life together had been ripped out of our book forever. It was a different kind of hurricane.

On our second day at the school, Mike and I had the chance to visit one of the program classes my son was attending, presided over by Ms. Taylor. I thought I would be sitting on the sidelines listening, but after a while, Ms. Taylor introduced us as Dylan's parents, and we were both given the opportunity to address the assembly. There were probably about fifteen young men there, sitting in their khaki shorts and shirts before us, cross-legged on the floor. Because of the tan uniforms, they looked like a troop of budding French Foreign Legionnaires. As I later found out, some of them probably were destined for the American armed forces. That was a popular career choice for guys in the school, and their families thought military discipline would be a good fit for their wayward sons. When I stood up to speak, I remember their faces—so young, so vulnerable, so open and attentive too. It was hard to believe that these teens had been stoned out of their minds with street drugs, had probably stolen money from their parents, had maybe been violent or at least disrespectful, had destroyed property, broken laws, been out of control. They must have been, or they wouldn't be there at that school.

Maybe I thought of the French Foreign Legion because I had once visited a Legion base in Nîmes, France. I knew that the recruits came from everywhere, and some young men had even gotten into trouble with the law, but the Legion would take them in anyway. Each recruit was assigned a new name and a buddy who spoke French and taught them the ropes. Once you got into the Legion, you took on the identity of a Legionnaire. It was the army of second chances. Even when you were off-duty and went into town, you wore your uniform because your new identity was not something you put on and took off again. Your first loyalty was to the Legion. It was a lifetime pact. Even the commandant spent holidays like Christmas first with his men, then later with his family. That summer, I remembered seeing Legionnaires walking, either alone or with a buddy, on the streets. How disciplined and self-contained they looked!

Well, I didn't talk to those young men in front of me about the Legion, but I did talk about how the program at the school offered them a chance to become a new person. I knew I was addressing them mainly as a mom—that was the most important thing. Not all of the teens there had their parents visiting; that was clear. For some of them, being reunited with their families, even for a few days, was still a distant hope. So out of all the things I may have said on that particular day, the one thing that would resonate for them was telling them I knew their parents cared about them. "How do you know that?" they asked me. I told them it was because I had been talking to other parents for a while now. Mostly moms. That I was in touch with a whole network of moms who had sons or daughters—mostly sons—in this school, and we wrote messages to each other for encouragement. I had even met a number of them. That what I knew was this: these parents wanted their sons to do well. They wanted them to be able to come back home and live good lives. When I told them this, looking into their eyes, I could only hope that somehow my words (and Mike's too) lifted their spirits a little. Some of them would have a hard road ahead.

I've often wondered what happened to those young men in the room that day. Where are they now? I only found out about a scattered few: one went back home and did well, went to college, had a girlfriend, stayed clean. Another seemed to be doing well, but then he had a fatal car crash—probably drug or alcohol-related. Yet another had gotten out of the program and, fearful of resuming his old ways, signed up for the military—against his parents' wishes. I wonder how many of them had—like my son—mental health issues to deal with. Probably more than a few. My impression is that families were each struggling to find their way. There weren't clear maps for how to deal with these complexities, but we offered each other support, shared whatever we knew.

From a parent's point of view, was this program worth all the time, all the money, the emotional risk of sending our kids away? In extremis, given the circumstances, yes. Sometimes there has to be a major intervention, a new perspective. But had I understood more about my son's particular mood disorder—how his particular brain chemistry affected his behavior—and *if* he had been diagnosed and treated sooner, before things spiraled out of control, then such a drastic intervention might not have been needed. Was there a better way? Yes, a closer program, an alternative school with informed counselors so that we parents could have received more training and support in how to deal with this earlier. Maybe group therapy for teens with similar issues so that they could face problems together, with guidance, and not feel isolated. There needed to be interventions that all parents whose kids needed it could afford.

Still, both Mike and I felt we learned a lot from our experience. The directors never promised us a rainbow. They never said the program would "fix" our kids. Instead, the counselors always told us this: "When your son or daughter comes back home, that's when the real work begins. Get ready."

CHAPTER 18: WHITE RABBIT

Imagine it's August 17, 1969 in Woodstock, New York. Jefferson Airplane is on stage. The musicians look out and see 500,000 young fans blanketing the fields around them. Soon, the electric guitars begin their hypnotic, Bolero-like rhythms, as Grace Slick steps up to take the mic. A cloud of long, curly hair surrounds her face; she's dressed all in white with a long, fringed tunic and fluttery bell-bottom pants. Her unmistakable voice floats out over the crowd. They already know the words.

> *One pill makes you larger*
> *And one pill makes you small*
> *And the ones that mother gives you*
> *Don't do anything at all*
> *Go ask Alice*
> *When she's ten feet tall*

Grace Slick's lyrics from "White Rabbit" refer to her generation's experimentation with psychedelic drugs to "expand consciousness." According to legend, she was apparently tripping on LSD and listening obsessively to Miles Davis's *Sketches of Spain*

at the time she wrote it. Maybe more than a few in the crowd at
Woodstock were sharing the same acid-induced trip that morning
in 1969. By the time Grace built up to the song's pulsing refrain,
"Feed your head! Feed your head!" everyone in the crowd could
chant it together and knew exactly what it meant. But today, these
words could take on a whole different meaning.

Of course, "Go ask Alice" in the song is a reference to the
young heroine of *Alice in Wonderland*. I remember my dad reading
this story to me when I was about six or seven years old, and I was
way too young to understand all of Lewis Carroll's puns and innu-
endos. I certainly didn't make any connections to altered mental
states. The problems Alice encountered once she chased the White
Rabbit down the rabbit hole seemed related to the strange fact that
she would change sizes, sometimes very dramatically, and not always
when she wanted to. For example, early on, she finds a key on a glass
table and is delighted to think that it must fit one of the closed doors
she sees down a long hall. But by the time she finds the little door
the key fits, she realizes that she is not the right size to go through
it and into the lovely garden she glimpses beyond. Dismayed, she
goes back to the glass table and finds, mysteriously, a small bottle
on it that says "drink me." After reassuring herself that the bottle
doesn't have any poison warnings marked on it, she decides to drink
and soon finds herself shrinking down to just the right size to go
through the little door.

But then, she finds that she's left the key on the table high
above her, and she can't reach it. Not to worry; she eventually finds
a small cake nearby with the words "eat me" on it, which makes her
grow taller, but—so true to human experience—this sudden change
causes more disorientation, so by the time she finds a way to shrink
enough to get through the little door, she finds she has once again
left the key on the glass table. Many of her adventures subsequently
have to do with her being an unusual size (either too big or too

small), leading her to many strange sensations and a dream-like flow of encounters with various creatures.

Though it may seem far-fetched to some, Alice's adventures now seem like a close metaphor to describe untreated bipolar disorder. Because an unregulated brain chemistry puts the person experiencing this on a wild ride—"curiouser and curiouser," as Alice says—it does ring true that she would always be trying to get herself to the "right size" in order to be able to do what she wants or needs to in that moment. And because of this, the person would—like Alice—be having some unusual perspectives on her surroundings, as well as some surprise encounters. She would also want a way to control all this crazy stuff.

The rest of Alice's adventures occur after she meets an imperious, if somewhat spaced-out caterpillar smoking a hookah atop a mushroom. By the time he crawls away, he gives her some advice to address her inappropriate sizing issues. He tells her to eat pieces of the mushroom: "One side will make you grow taller, and the other side will make you grow shorter." Now, armed with a piece of the mushroom from opposite sides in each hand, Alice has the tools she needs for administering her own adjustment. She can self-medicate.

With all the changes going on inside and all around them, it isn't surprising that young persons with bipolar often become amateur pharmacologists. When your own mental thermostat isn't working right, you rapidly start looking for compounds that can help adjust it—not to mention that you also have to be able to manage your social persona in various situations, ones that become increasingly demanding as you move beyond your family circle. You certainly don't want to show to the rest of the world all the internal management problems you're having! Cigarettes, alcohol, marijuana—at least, you'll try those. After that, you can consider other possibilities. Yes, in no time, a person could become like Alice in Wonderland, looking around for that piece of mushroom, that little bottle that says "drink me" so she can get herself to the right size. After all, who knows when you might have to attend a Mad Hatter's tea party, run on top of a chessboard, or play croquet with a deck of cards and a hedgehog? Life makes a lot of demands.

These reflections relate to conversations I had with Dylan during his first winter in Drug Court. From time to time, Dylan commented on incidents that happened when he was a student at the University of Cincinnati, and I realized that I knew only a small part of what had actually occurred there. During my frequent "Mom Missions" after the robbery, for example, I didn't realize that he was smoking pot regularly (still!) and that he was drinking. His doctors had always told him it wasn't a good idea for someone in his medical situation to drink, but that apparently didn't faze him. So when I once saw a whiskey bottle on his kitchen shelf, he assured me that was for his friend Neal who liked the stuff when he came over to socialize. He himself didn't drink it, didn't even like it.

Now in Drug Court, though, Dylan was quite open about his past drinking and pot use. He matter-of-factly recounted how, for example, I would comment back during one of my weekend visits to Cincinnati how he seemed to be doing better and in good spirits. "You didn't know, Mom, but I'd just been smoking a joint to mellow myself out right before you got there," he told me. And probably the night before, he'd been with friends in a favorite neighborhood bar drinking the night away—all this when he knew he was supposed to be taking only his meds, nothing else. According to him, it was his right as a young adult to go out and socialize in bars. Danger? No, he didn't see any danger in doing that. He felt he could handle his liquor better than most.

After the robbery in 2008, I knew he was shaken; I didn't even know if he could stay in school that semester. We talked about

whether he should continue to live there. He wanted to, so I ended
up going to Cincinnati almost every weekend. Mike was out of the
country that fall teaching, so he wasn't able to share the load of visits.
It was seven hours on the road from Croftburg, one way. When I
got there, Dylan and I had long conversations during those early
weeks about how to deal with his moods, his anxiety, his lifestyle.
Once, when he was feeling highly anxious, I insisted that he go to a
clinician at the local primary care center for help. By this time, he'd
managed to convince himself that he had ADHD, not bipolar. He
was no longer taking a mood stabilizer. The clinician asked Dylan
questions, and when he received the answers, was kind but direct
with him.

"You have a complex mental health situation," he said. "And
you need to have continuous care from a psychiatrist who can monitor how things are going."

"But my psychiatrist closed down his office," Dylan protested.
"He left town and since then, I've had trouble finding another one
to give me an appointment."

"No matter," the young doctor said. "You have to be patient.
This is a major city. There are psychiatrists out there; you just have
to be persistent and find one and keep your appointments."

The doctor's voice was calm, but the common-sense clarity of
his words struck me like a thunderbolt. Of course! How in all this
crazy tumult could we have lost track of the obvious? Well, unfortunately, it happens. To a person with a mood disorder—especially
one in his early twenties, eager to try to fit in with his peers—there
can be a long list of distractors. And we parents were often so busy
just putting out brush fires in Dylan's life that we could easily miss
addressing the root cause: a complex brain disorder that needed
steady, ongoing treatment. At that moment in the doctor's office,
I felt guilty that I hadn't done enough to help my son find a psychiatrist to replace the one who had left his practice. I'd let Dylan

take the lead. The path hadn't been easy; he'd tried, but there had been obstacles. So instead, he took charge by self-medicating. Who knows? In his situation, I may well have done the same thing.

Dylan's White Rabbit Diary as a second-year college student in Cincinnati, 2008:

> *8:30 am, Monday: Feeling anxious this morning. Again, no reason—just the way it is. Drink a shot of whiskey from the bottle Neal left behind on Saturday night. That will smooth me out enough to get dressed and ready for class.*

> *2:30 pm: Have to get to work on my assignments for tomorrow and my night class later this week. Feeling a little tuned out; it'll be hard to concentrate. I'll make some strong coffee and drink a few cups to sharpen up.*

> *5:00 pm: Too wired. Got my work done for tomorrow, but feeling anxious again. Time to come down. I'll go out for a walk to the corner store and pick up some cigarettes—maybe find a guy there to sell me a joint. That'll help even me out. No way I could eat anything in this state.*

> *8:00 pm: Time to work out at the gym. I need three protein bars and two cans of Red Bull to rev up.*

> *10:00 pm: Feeling mellow now after the workout. Time for dinner. This is great, but I won't be able to do much on my assignment for Wednesday. Just hope I'll be able to get some sleep tonight. Yeah, I think there's a good chance of that. I'll get up early tomorrow and finish my work then.*

But if by chance I have a rough night, it's going to take a bomb-sized alarm clock to wake me up.

9:00 am, Wednesday: Got a presentation coming up in my speech class. That professor can really be a hard-ass, too. She can really get in your face. To tell the truth, I think she's entertaining in the way she does the class. But man, she can really put people on the spot: she can GRILL you! And today . . . well, gotta take a Klonopin or I'll never make it through my speech. When I get uptight in front of the class, it's all over. Ideas go straight out of my head; I start to sweat; I'm sure everyone can see I'm on pins and needles. I'll need a Klonopin to keep myself calm.

3:00 pm, same day: Well, I haven't taken a mood stabilizer for a while now. No lithium, no Lamictal. I'm not so convinced I have a mood disorder—think it's more like ADHD. I have trouble focusing and being able to concentrate. That's why I can't get my work done on time. Sometimes, I'm still half asleep and can't get my mind awake. Other times, I get all these racing thoughts, sometimes going around in circles, too. If only Dr. Adivan hadn't closed his practice and taken off for another state where he could make more money! Now, I can only go to the clinic and get the type of drugs any GP can prescribe, like Lexapro or Wellbutrin. Those help some, but maybe what I really need to focus my mind is Adderall.

9:30 am, Thursday: When I look around at all these other students going to class, I wonder how they do it. They look so calm, so together. And then in class, they always have their assignments done. To me sometimes, it just seems they're friggin' robots! It's like they're pre-programmed to do every-thing just on time, just on cue, just the right way. Not me! No way I've ever been like that. Never will.

9:30 am, Saturday: Mom's coming for a visit. Better call Neal and have him stop by with a joint before she gets here. She means well and all that, but she can be really irritating, too. She just doesn't get it, what all I have to deal with. No one else can really know what it's like unless they have the same thing going on. Not to mention, now instead of having my own car, I have to rely on her driving me around. It's crazy; I have to cue her on every turn, every move. She's such a small-town driver! She doesn't have a clue how to drive in a big city. All the more reason I'm going to need that joint—yeah, maybe two.

The only problem with all these little hits and fixes is that the person starts to rely on them. Self-medication becomes the main way of trying to take control in a chaotic state. Often, what the person doesn't see is that these are just yo-yo adjustments delivered by ingested chemicals, not a way of stabilizing the situation or learning to ride the waves. Instead, if the pattern continues, these "fixes" can start to alter an already off-kilter brain chemistry. If we go back to Alice, it's as if she changed sizes so often for so long that she entirely lost any sense of her normal-sized self. So, instead of being able to modulate the highs and lows, the person with a mood disorder experiences peaks and valleys getting steeper and deeper. Far from gaining control, she drifts further out—often without realizing, or even caring. Addiction can set in. Soon, the person may have two monsters to deal with: bipolar *and* addiction. Today the usual term for this is "dual diagnosis." I've learned, however, that not everyone living with bipolar veers toward drug addiction. Apparently, that tendency requires a special set of pre-disposition genes—yet another throw of the hereditary dice.

Over the years, there had been several "off" periods before Dylan stayed on board with his diagnosis and his meds. Thank God, at present he seemed to be keeping his appointments with Dr. Peltay. When it came to meds, I couldn't see why Dylan didn't just stay on lithium, but he always wanted to try some new combination to see if it would work better. Usually, this meant taking a mood stabilizer and another pharmaceutical to calm his anxiety. Sooner or later, though, he wouldn't like one of the side effects, like weight gain or interference with sleep. Other times, he said he didn't like how a certain medication dulled his emotions, made him feel like a zombie. He said once it was as if before, he'd been watching the world through a high-definition, wide-screen color TV and then, after taking the medication, he'd have to get used to a standard 1950s-style TV model in black and white. It all seemed so fuzzy, so drab by comparison! Carrie Fisher, the late actress of Princess Leia fame, would confirm: "Being high on bipolar is way better than any drug—believe me," she's said in interviews. "And I've tried quite a few."

Dylan's history of self-medication vs. medical treatment made me wonder about how my son viewed his mood disorder during his time in Drug Court, how he was either moving toward reconciliation with it or staying in resistance. Most people think of an illness as something to fight, something to vanquish. This is a fine strategy for hostile microbes, a virus, or cancer. But what if you have a disorder that affects your consciousness, your decision making? What if it is something so embedded in your concept of yourself—your personality and identity—that you can barely distinguish what part, exactly, is the disorder and what part is your essential self? As for mood swings, shifts from euphoric highs to listless lows, with bouts of extreme irritation and anxiety thrown in, racing thoughts, restless emotions (spaced out by periods of relative normalcy) —a person in Dylan's situation often cannot remember a time when he didn't have them. So then, when you try to even out, go on meds, try to have a "normal" life, impose limits on yourself, check out your own thinking—how do you get used to all that? Does "normal" feel like a strange glove you're putting on, a buffer that separates you from the skin you've come to rely on as your sentient contact with the world?

After I read Kay Redfield Jamison's book *An Unquiet Mind*, the dilemma became clearer to me. Dr. Jamison is a professor of psychiatry and a clinician who not only studies mood disorders but also has bipolar herself (she calls it by its earlier term, manic-depressive disorder). Jamison courageously "came out" in the 1990s, writing an astonishing memoir about how she struggled against—and eventually learned to live with—this serious illness. Frequently describing her personality as "mercurial," she tells the harrowing story of how her passionate curiosity, hard work, and boundless energy degenerated into full-blown psychotic madness in her twenties, almost before she knew what was happening. After that, predictably, she fell into a deep depression. Even with expert medical care, this condition lasted a year and a half. When she finally recovered, she was glad to find her mind working again, but then began what she called an ongoing battle with lithium, the medication she needed to keep her moods under some semblance of control.

The paradox is this: she didn't like the control, and that's what always surprises people. In her chapter "Missing Saturn," she tells us what she missed the most: riding high on the wonderful waves of "white mania"—those sudden whirlwind enthusiasms, the transformational gusts of energy and inspiration that allowed her to sweep through the world without touching the ground. She calls this euphoric mood state "flying through the rings of Saturn." For Jamison, a California girl with a test-pilot dad who flew fighter planes, Saturn was the wild blue yonder of your dreams and daring.

Of course, she believed you could get there if you were special and flew high enough.

Only gradually did she learn that these euphoric states were not infinitely repeatable. Her illness was progressing; the white manias were morphing into manic states of psychosis—often mingling with severe anxiety or irritation. Her illness, Bipolar I, was not going to stay within the bounds of a livable life without two things: medication and effort. She had to learn, however reluctantly, to accept softer waves, a new self. "In my case I had a horrible sense of loss for who I had been and where I had been. It was difficult to give up the high flights of mind and mood, even though the depressions that inevitably followed nearly cost me my life." The way she tells it, she had to give up high flights through the rings of Saturn for a more practical life here on Earth.

So now in Drug Court, was Dylan was ready to give up his own version of "high flights?" He didn't have a test-pilot dad, but from stories he told me about his life and loves in the Cincinnati days, I was pretty sure he spent a fair share of time flying through the rings of Saturn, too. No wonder he still held out hope he would return there someday! I knew he'd had his first intense romantic involvement in that place, with a girl he'd met on day one of his freshman year. With her or with friends, he'd driven his car everywhere and discovered a whole, huge hilltop metropolis. He'd learned how to find scores of businesses, repair shops, workplaces, clinics, restaurants, concert halls, cafés, gyms, hangouts. He had met and gotten to know all kinds of people from all walks of life—not just students. After what he called his two "exile" years at the special school, he wanted to know and be friends with everyone.

The second year, he withdrew from classes to support himself by working at odd jobs provided by a temp agency. For him, college courses at the University of Cincinnati were too slow; he was looking for a lucky break. We didn't like it, but for him, this was a learning experience. He'd met an even wider variety of city residents—guys who'd worked in car factories for years, worked graveyard shifts, weekend shifts, any and all shifts, just to put some cash in their wallets. And while in the metropolis, he'd also met a few of those special breeds of slick, cool guys, the kind who went to clubs, dressed in the most amazing clothes and dropped the best lines. They were *never* short on cash, or so it seemed. The stories some of those guys could tell!

To Dylan, it was all intoxicating—worlds within worlds to discover. And all this was something we presumably dull family members plodding away in our conforming lives wouldn't have a clue about. No, we didn't. I'd only read or seen this stuff in movies. I didn't know anyone who actually *lived* like that. But Dylan did. I remembered Saturday visits when we'd be down on the Ohio River waterfront, strolling in a park, and he would tell me about some of his adventures—only the milder ones he thought I could handle, of course. Even then, I was aware of trying to steer him back to some kind of a regular life.

"Look, all that is amazing," I would say, "but you need to think about earning a living, having a real life, not about becoming a millionaire or some kind of blackjack champion in Vegas. Be realistic. You need to go back to college."

Back then, he would nod his head, but that was probably only to comfort me a bit. Trouble was, he wasn't convinced of the necessity to have a regular life at all. It took things like living on his own terms, doing well for a while, making big bucks, then being totally down on his luck because it had all somehow disappeared. When he finally called us months later, he was facing disaster. It's strange to say, but right before this, he was convinced that his life was turning around, that after a whole series of temp jobs he was "on the way up" in a new one with promise—if only he could get the car fixed and pay off his fines so he could get his license back. When the family went to the city to meet him, we saw the state of the car. When I drove it out of the city lot to a repair shop, it sounded like a B52 bomber that had flown too many missions and spent the last twenty years of its life rusting in a field. How could he not realize that his car—along with his life back then—had fallen into shambles? We told him we would help, but only on the condition that he return to his studies and sell the car. He took our offer.

Now, three years later, he was in Drug Court and living in a small college town in what has to be one of the most conservative areas of the country. This was where he was born and grew up; in fact, he's a native son. Yet in a lot of ways, he was also a wild seed from planet Saturn who had to find a way to grow here—at least for the duration. It wouldn't be easy for him to adjust to a toned-down, "simple" life. It wasn't just about adjusting to the rules of DC, not just about adapting to life in a small town after being in a big city. No, as Jamison tells it, the hardest part of all is the internal resistance: giving up a version of yourself that you secretly really like and admire. That adventurous, charismatic self doesn't want rules, doesn't want blandness, doesn't want routine. *But Dylan, you have to adjust; you have to learn to be responsible, even if means working with less. Focus on what you need.*

Somehow Kay Jamison learned how to declare a truce with normal, civilian life. She learned how to accept the person she was when ill and the person she could become when well. She says this didn't happen easily. She credits her psychiatrist's patience in her long battle with lithium; she acknowledges the healing art of psychotherapy to deal with the deceptive thought traps she fell into. But she also makes it clear that another powerful source of her healing was the network of loving relationships that sustained her. "This medicine, love," she calls it. The love came from family, yes, but also from persons who surprisingly, when they got close enough, did not turn away when she told them about her illness. Instead, they made the courageous decision—even while knowing what they were up against—to accompany her on the uncharted trail of a difficult life.

From Dr. Jamison I found out that accepting your truth, knowing you need help, then learning where to find it and from whom—that's already a miracle.

I could only hope Dylan would find the same in his own life someday. At least he was still alive. He'd made it past twenty-four years. My brother didn't.

CHAPTER 19
YOUNG MEN ON THE ROADSIDE

When it happened that I had a twenty-four-year-old son in Drug Court, I found myself increasingly aware of other young men out and about. In our small college town, there were many young people on the streets from all walks of life. So if I happened to see someone roughly the age of my son, I would notice his demeanor, his attitude. Near the campus, young folks would be out for fitness jogs on the sidewalks. Other times, though, I'd spot someone walking in a perilous place alongside a major road. Then I'd find myself speculating: did he lose his license? Did he have substance abuse issues? If the guy looked slightly scruffy, I'd wonder if he just got out of jail or was headed that way. Did he have any kids already? Was he looking for a job or just his next meal at a fast-food place? Heading for his next class or his next fix?

A glance would make me wonder: Was this just another day for him? Or did he sense that he'd somehow arrived at a turning point in his life? What lay ahead on his road?

No doubt, these existential speculations are due to the impact of my son's experiences. But on another level, they're due as much to those of my brother, Mark, born eight years after me. I remember one summer day a few years ago, I was driving in Tennessee, approaching Nashville. Suddenly, I saw a hitchhiker on the right side of the road. This wasn't too rare near Music City; it looked like he had a guitar case with him. What captured my attention, though, was his amazing resemblance to my brother, Mark—same body type, same longish, curly hair, same glasses. It was uncanny. I almost turned the car around, wanted to go back and look into his face to see if it was really him or not. But of course, I didn't stop. For one thing, my brother had been dead for twenty years. He had died suddenly in an alcohol-related incident, had been found dead in his apartment. At the time, he was twenty-three years old, still in college and working a summer job. Long after I passed the hitchhiker, I couldn't shake the memory of Mark. What if he had somehow managed to come back to the world in the form of this other young man out there? An irrational thought, but very real to me, as if I had somehow driven right through a space/time portal into another dimension of remembered reality.

It was my mother who first told me about my brother's drinking problem, how it had started when he was a teenager out with buddies on Saturday nights. I had missed all that while away at college. My dad found the beer cans in the trunk, but he thought that was just normal teen guy stuff—nothing to worry about. For some it isn't, but you never know what kind of genetic predispositions you've inherited. By the time Mark was in college, his roommates decided one day they needed to take him to detox. Things were getting out of control. He eventually had to take a medical withdrawal from school, but not before his grades had taken a nosedive, probably for missed classes.

When Mark came back home to continue recovery and attend AA, for a while it was touch and go. Visiting one summer, I felt that an invisible circle of shame had been drawn around my brother.

He didn't talk about what had happened, not to me. My dad only alluded to events in one blunt sentence to explain why my brother was home again. Only Mom would talk about matters, but always privately, in hushed tones, as if no one was really supposed to hear about it. Dad had trouble accepting the situation. He couldn't see why his son couldn't handle alcohol, why he had "flunked out" of school like that. If Dad had only thought about his own father's weekend binge drinking, it wouldn't have seemed so strange. But I believe our dad's refusal to look at family history had to do with protecting himself. Like many men of his era, he didn't find it manly to show any vulnerability. Back then, he felt it was threatening, even dangerous, to probe painful feelings from the past. He didn't realize how dangerous it would be *not* to. He didn't cry.

Meanwhile, my mother had been crying all along. When I visited home from grad school, she told me stories of my brother's secret illness that shocked me: how Mark had snitched scotch whiskey from the cabinet, how sometimes he had fallen into *delirium tremens* on withdrawal, how he pleaded with her to give him wine or whiskey. She would not. Instead, she brought cold, wet cloths for his forehead, stayed with him, spoke to him, prayed by his bedside. I couldn't believe how much she had been through. And I couldn't imagine my sweet, shy brother being so sick, so unlike himself. How could this be? And my dad barely spoke about it, closing his heart.

When Mark joined AA and made a recovery, it took him at least a year at the local community college to work his way back up to being eligible to enroll at NC State in Raleigh. By then, he was a student in their landscape design program and doing well. Then another year later, in the spring of 1984, came a relapse. It apparently started on a group field trip to the Biltmore Estate in Asheville. One night, the class was enjoying their camp setting outdoors, sitting on a mountaintop under the stars, drinking beer. Mark wasn't far enough along in his recovery to say "No thanks, I don't drink." Not easy for a young man to say to his peers on such a tempting occasion. That night must have triggered the addiction. Three months later, he was found dead in the apartment he shared with a roommate. My father received a phone call from the Raleigh police one July morning. After the shock, all he and my mother could do was cry. Later that same morning, I picked up the phone: I remember my father's usual bright, confident voice sounding strange and flat on the other end—the space, the silence, the effort to talk, to breathe. He told me simply that Mark was dead and asked me to come home. Hardly anything more. Dazed, Mike and I made reservations for Greenville, packed our bags. How could this be happening? A strong young man, my brother . . . dead at twenty-three.

My parents were comforted to have us there. Along with funeral plans, there were other difficult ordeals to go through. The hardest was entering Mark's apartment to retrieve his possessions. My mother and I were there, but we didn't go in. A police detective stood by with keys. Though it was a hot day, he was dressed in a dark suit and as he opened the door, held a neatly folded white handkerchief to his nose. The apartment was now a crime scene since someone—my brother—had been found dead there. "The apartment will have to be professionally treated by a forensics unit," he told us, "but please feel free to remove whatever you want that belongs to your son." Then my father and Mike began the process of gathering Mark's belongings and bringing them outside in armfuls while my mom and I loaded them into the car. The work was grim; our clothes were soon soaked with sweat. Mike later told me that he couldn't believe how many empty bottles of cheap wine he saw. The floor was lined with them. And hovering over it all was the hot, sticky smell of death.

The next day at the funeral, the dark casket at the front of the church was closed and covered completely with an immense bouquet of white flowers, my brother's favorites. Amid the pale green of spring woodlands, he loved the brightness of white dogwood blossoms. I knew Mom chose them to honor her son's spirit. Their whiteness, their purity, somehow cleansed the ghastly experience of the previous day.

My mother told me afterward that her prayers for Mark had been answered—but not in the way she had hoped. She said what she wanted for him was to heal, to be free, to be at peace. And now, though he had lost his life, he was. When she told me this, the tears were flowing. I tried to comfort her but felt so awkward at it. As if my arms couldn't encircle so much grief.

For several years after Mark's funeral, whenever I went back to North Carolina to visit my parents, I noticed my mom still kept some of his clothes in what had been his bedroom. A portrait photo of him held its place on top of the chest of drawers. The same curly hair, the same features, the light brown eyes, the unguarded gaze looking out, as if he'd just asked us an open question and was waiting for us to answer.

Mark was the gentlest person I ever knew, and believe me, being eight years his senior, I was not the nicest sister you could imagine. I still feel guilty for all the times I was less than kind to him. For me, growing up, he was often just a pesky boy I could tease and lord it over, someone who wasn't nearly as accomplished or sophisticated as I was. Later, when we were both older, I tried to make it up to him, and I think he forgave me. But I realize that I didn't understand at all what was going on for him during the years he was becoming an adult. How could I know, how could any of us know that Mark would die so young with his whole life in front of him? Most painful of all was my awareness of the intense loneliness he must have felt that last weekend. Questions haunted me, haunted all of us: Why did he not reach out for help? Was he too ashamed? Did he secretly want to die or was it an accident? We didn't have answers.

A family tragedy reverberates far out in time. More than a decade later, when our own son became a teenager, Mike and I couldn't believe how closely he resembled my brother in the photo. We told our son about Mark's fate; we wanted to ward off disaster. Dylan's personality was completely different, but the physical resemblance! It scared us. We learned from Mark that sturdy young men could disappear overnight for reasons that were hard to understand.

It was after my son's arrest that I would think back to stories my mother had told me about Mark: her anguish, her prayers, her feelings of helplessness at watching her son struggle with addiction. At the time, how could I have guessed that I, who had spent so much energy trying to be different from my mother, cultivating a completely separate life, would walk down a similar path? That my heart would crack open, much like hers did? Later, I wanted to go back in time and talk to her again. "Mom, now I understand more of what you went through. How in the world did you and Dad survive it all? How did you both heal?" I wanted to look into her eyes and hear her voice. I wanted us to cry together, to comfort each other. But by then, she was already gone. My dad, too.

No, I didn't know yet what would happen to my own son, but I always held a silent fear in my heart—a fear that history could repeat itself.

CHAPTER 20: NAMI II

Laura's Story, Part I

Our February meeting started with news of our group becoming an official NAMI affiliate within our state. Next, our leader Sandra reminded us about plans for our upcoming advocacy trip to Frankfort, the state capitol, while the legislature was in session. We wanted to support the passage of Tim's Law, which would mandate court-ordered outpatient treatment for the severely mentally ill, helping people like Rita's son, Brett. Then we discussed when to schedule a group trip to Louisville to visit a place called Bridgehaven, a special center offering counseling, activities, and fellowship for persons with severe mental illness. A date was set for the summer. By the time we went around the table to give our self-introductions and updates, I noticed there was a new person there, sitting next to Joan. It was her daughter, Laura. Sandra greeted our visitor warmly.

Joan attended regularly, but a visit from her daughter was a rare and special event. At this period, a visit from anyone actually living with a mental illness was exceptional. We were a small contingent, a new frontier outpost in the mental health network. So at first, even for us, it was still unusual for someone to show up at a meeting to say, "Yes, I have a mental illness and here's how it is for me. I want to tell you about it." Though I hadn't met Laura before, I knew from Joan that she'd been living at a special treatment facility in nearby Chesterfield after life-changing events. Joan had told us several times that her daughter was getting along well at the residential center with the support of medication and counseling. But as it turned out, there was much more to know.

It soon became clear that Laura was going through a tough time. She was forty-nine years old, had gone to college, lived in Texas, and now was back in the area, trying to get her life back in order. She had Bipolar I with a severe anxiety disorder that upped the voltage of her illness considerably. There had been no diagnosis until she had her first psychotic episode, and that was over twenty years ago, before she knew she needed to stay on certain medications to control the illness. The other parents, who had known her longer, felt a genuine affection for her. They also felt respect, because she could articulate for us what she had gone through, what she was still experiencing. It helped us understand.

"Yes, lately I've been getting into a crisis situation again," she told us. "I've found a new boyfriend, and for a while, it was great, but now—I'm finding out he just doesn't understand what I need to take care of myself." One of her most immediate problems was getting enough sleep. She was a morning person who'd agreed to start living with a night owl who thought nothing of turning on the TV in the bedroom when she was already asleep, waking her up. He didn't see why she couldn't adapt to his schedule and sleep when he did. He also didn't understand her illness or what she needed to do to stay well. Without reading about the illness or listening to her, he wouldn't know that for a person with bipolar, being sleep-deprived is NOT a situation you want to get into. It's one of the triggers that can bring on a manic episode.

"Zach doesn't think I have any illness. He says I'm fine," she went on. "But that's because I've been taking my medicine and trying to keep a healthy lifestyle. But now I feel if he's not going to accept this about me, if he's not going to allow me to take care of myself, then I need to break up with him."

From what Joan had told us in the past, I knew she'd had more than one partner similar in attitude to Zach. It was a pattern. Once she started feeling better, she would get involved in a new relationship and, for one reason or another, leave behind the regimen that would keep her well. Since Laura was one of those who, with self-care, could "pass" for neurotypical most of the time, even people close to her didn't realize that she had to manage a serious illness every day. Her previous Texas boyfriend certainly didn't. He'd told her she wasn't sick at all, didn't need those fancy medications. She should just eat right, exercise. Besides that, she needed protection, which he was happy to provide. After she stopped taking her meds and became more anxious and unpredictable, he advanced to thinking it was a good idea to lock the doors of their house, so she couldn't get out and "get into trouble" while he was gone. Joan tried to warn Laura that her boyfriend had some control issues, but from there, the situation rapidly went downhill. "I kept getting more anxious, and my boyfriend was getting more controlling. It felt like I was starting to live in some kind of horror movie," Laura said. That's when she knew she had to get away from him, permanently. At least the new predicament with Zach, though similar, wasn't nearly as bad as that. Not yet.

"So now," she said, looking anxiously at Joan, "I've temporarily moved back in with Mom, and I'm trying to be strong to deal with all this . . . but, you know, it's pushing me over the edge. So if I act a little strange, a little over-dramatic, it's because I'm way over my stress threshold right now."

I was sitting close by, and as Laura spoke, her hands spoke, too. Her fingernails tapped on the table in front of her. Her hands curved arcs in the air to convey frustration. In a way, the long, tapered fingers with the red nails didn't seem to go with the rest of her, dressed as she was in jeans and western boots, her hair cropped like a boy's. But when her fingers exploded outward with barely contained anxiety and emotion, we all felt the tension. Probably Joan brought her here tonight so she could release some of her distress, get some comfort. Just when it seemed Laura might be able to find a little happiness and security in another relationship, things were going off the rails again.

"I do NOT want to have a meltdown," Laura said. "I know how horrible that is. And I can feel one building up inside. It's like a pot that's about to boil over." Those red-tipped fingers flared out again before tapping on the table in front of her. "But I'm just not going there." She repeated like a mantra, to calm herself: "I have to take care of myself now. I have to do what's right for me." What that meant in this situation was that she needed to get a separate residence away from Zach and resume her therapy sessions. The relationship could wait. Maybe Zach would understand, maybe not.

We all felt drawn to her, but what Laura was saying was scary for me. Like her, Dylan also had a stop-and-go pattern in his wellness regimen. Like most, he had a love/hate relationship with his meds, so there was always a reason for why he'd stop taking them at some point. Then, too, the physical expression of Laura's anxiety reminded me of times I'd witnessed in Dylan the same about-to-boil-over behaviors, only he was a lot louder and bigger. With other people, he would try to keep himself under control, even under duress. But with someone he was close to, he'd be more likely to bluster and fume his way through, letting out the tension. Sometimes I wondered if he even noticed he was going overboard. Probably not. Not when he was talking ninety miles an hour; not when he couldn't stop to listen for five seconds.

But from what Laura said, I gathered there were often two struggles going on simultaneously for people like her. First was trying to deal with a tricky, debilitating psychic state. Second was trying to deal with the person right in front of you, who didn't necessarily understand what was going on for you internally. It took skill to ride the bull, and usually someone got left in the dust. But the main thing it took was self-awareness—and that was even harder to hang on to than the bull.

I knew parts of Laura's story because Joan had told us, but now she told the whole story herself—what she had been seeing and feeling during the psychotic episodes that began when she was in her late twenties and a young mother. Laura hadn't even been diagnosed yet with a type of bipolar when she experienced her first psychotic break. It happened after an argument with her husband in a restaurant. When she ran to the restroom to try to cool down the blaze in her head, she suddenly saw red blood instead of water running from the faucet. Terrified, she screamed repeatedly and had to be taken to a local hospital. In the late 1980s, there was no psychiatric care at all in rural areas like ours, so she had to go to Nashville and eventually to Memphis for long-term treatment. Her children were taken in by her husband's relatives because he felt he couldn't work full-time and take care of them alone.

Months later, she eventually recovered some stability, but by then her marriage had broken up, and her kids were estranged from her—the "crazy woman." She had to start over. At least by then, she had a diagnosis and a treatment plan. There was an explanation for what had happened, even if it wasn't exactly comforting. When she felt strong enough, she decided to move to Texas and look for a job, make a fresh start. That's where she met the man she fell in love with, the one who didn't understand that she had a chronic illness, that she needed to keep herself well by, among other things, taking her meds.

I already knew the part about Joan agreeing to take Laura in— with rules— when she called from the Texas lock-in disaster. Her mom had seen it coming. "Geez, if your boyfriend locks you in to keep you *safe*, doesn't that tell you there's a big problem coming on?" Joan asked, shaking her head. Now, both of them were in complete agreement about that one. When the distress call came through, Joan had told her daughter she would welcome her back home, but one of the rules was this: "If you try to commit suicide again, you're not doing it in my house. I can't stop you, but you're not doing it in my house. Do you understand?" We already knew that Joan's own mother had taken her life at home when her daughters were still living there. She'd swallowed a whole bottle full of sleeping pills. So now, Joan's attitude toward her daughter's illness was strict: *I'll help you as much as I can, but you have to want to help yourself—and look for what you need.* At least now there was some small assistance for mental health in our area, unlike twenty years ago. Laura and Joan searched together for a place that could provide the services Laura needed: Medicaid, a psychiatrist, meds, counseling. That's what she found at Chesterfield.

As Laura gave her own version of these events, Joan sometimes touched her arm lightly, as if to steady her. I could picture them together years earlier, imagine Laura as Joan's expressive little girl, a five-year-old with blond curls and a vivid imagination. No one would suspect what destiny awaited her. Decades later, her blue eyes were still bright, now surrounded by the inevitable crinkles brought by years of an unpredictable life and turbulent emotions. She talked about being an educated person, having ten years of college and about "what I had once been," as if so much of her had been lost somewhere. We were all reminded of that terrible sadness, the awareness of what such an illness can take from you, and the courage needed to combat that. Laura had to hold on to that courage now. We were there to listen and to encourage her; it was a rare privilege. For all of us, she was a heroine.

"This illness, it's not a death sentence," she said. "But it *is* a life sentence. And you have to deal with it every day, no matter what comes."

Joan chimed in. "Listening to Laura and helping her makes me realize what my own mother must have gone through." Joan was always the strong mom among us, and we admired her for it. She was the widow of a navy husband who served long tours of duty across the seas all during their marriage. Where she got her strength, Lord knows, but she'd come through fire herself growing up. Her own mother had been battling a mental illness with no name while raising three kids— that must have been a big part of it. And now Joan was witnessing her own daughter going through some of the same episodes. The struggle was cycling through the generations, and Joan was standing at the center of it all, holding on. Better than most, she knew how to strike that balance between giving support to a loved one and keeping your own boundaries, your own sense of what's right and what not right. She told us she'd had to learn that as a child, to survive.

"And this group is so important to me," Joan said, looking around at us. "To both of us." She glanced at her daughter next to her and smiled. After all the tough things she'd told us in the past, I was moved to see how much emotional support she was giving to her daughter now.

Sandra was in tears.

"We're glad you came," she said. The rest of us nodded, listening in silent solidarity.

"Well, I do know this," Joan said with a steady voice. "With you all here, I feel I'm not alone. And maybe what I've learned can help someone else."

When the meeting was adjourned, some of us stayed to talk longer. Laura even smiled some; I could tell she was feeling a little better. Everyone thanked her for coming; she'd been heard. After our farewells, I went out into the cool night air, taking in some deep breaths to decompress. This evening had been intense. Out of the stories related in the group, Laura's roller coaster ride with her bipolar seemed to me to be the closest to Dylan's, although her case was more severe as she had slipped at least a few times into psychosis. Like her, he could be intelligent and rational, and could do well until he stopped taking his meds or got derailed by deciding he didn't have to follow a rule that got in his way. Was he learning fast enough how to deal with his situation?

Human stories like Laura's shook me to the core, because my son could just as well have to face such crises someday: have a rough life, like hers, have to come back from a crash and burn, just like she did. I marveled at how brave both Joan and Laura were, and how honest and open their relationship had become, even through the troubles. I knew it was important for me to hear it all, to see what had to be seen and not get caught up in wishful thinking or denial. I needed to hear and remember everything these people were saying, so I could be prepared for whatever lay ahead.

Driving down dark streets, I wanted so badly to get back to the light and comfort of my own house, my own life. I felt as if I'd just witnessed the opening of Pandora's box under a full moon. Many demons had come flying out, ones I'd prefer to leave in there or not even know about. But wait a minute—didn't they say that, way at the bottom of the box, hope was somewhere in there, too?

CHAPTER 21: TWO STEPS FORWARD

The arrival of summer brought with it a time of transitions for both Dylan and me, though we were in very different times of our lives. For my part, the end of the spring semester marked the conclusion of my eight-year stint as Chair of the department. I would serve until June 30, then change roles. Though a colleague had made this same move before me, it hadn't been easy to make the decision to step down; it felt like letting go of something important. I'd be giving up a respected, sanctioned form of responsibility, of guidance. People defer to you as the Chair, ask for your advice, your assistance, your signature on documents. Your office is frequently visited by faculty and students alike. It's as if you're wearing an invisible robe, so deciding to remove it feels like a divestiture, a letting go of professional credits you've built up over time. Nonetheless, my plan was to return to being a full-time college teacher for two more years, then retire from the profession. I wanted to be open to other possibilities.

Amid the flurry of activities closing spring term 2012, Dylan called to invite me out to dinner for my birthday. He wanted to do it with just the two of us, so we waited until the second weekend in May. It was nice: we were both celebrating the successful end of an important semester. For him, too, it was a major step. He had managed to continue with Drug Court obligations as well as getting reintegrated into college courses. It hadn't been a smooth road, but he'd stayed on it. In fact, the semester had taken fewer hairpin turns than most of his previous college terms; sobriety agreed with him. Especially in his business and communication classes, which he enjoyed and which included interactive projects, he had done very well, earning A's and B's. This was definitely something for us to cheer about. Yes, the long winter was finally turning into summer. But how would it go? During the next few weeks, Dylan would be facing a transition, too, one he hadn't always handled well in the past. I recalled the fateful May and June of a year ago.

According to Drug Court mandates, since Dylan wouldn't be taking a full load of classes this summer, he would need to have a job lined up. Arlo, his AA sponsor, provided odd jobs for him occasionally at his family's farm and on apartments they owned, but that wouldn't be enough to keep him busy or bring in money. So Dylan was looking around for something else, something more steady.

"Well, why don't you try applying at a restaurant or maybe at a store? There's lots of jobs like that for young people in town," I suggested.

"No, that doesn't pay enough, just minimum wage. Not only that, but I don't look the type to do those jobs. I'm a big guy; I look too physical," he replied.

"Yes, but you like talking to different people, and you're persuasive. I can see you working in a store, explaining the merchandise," I countered.

"Yeah, but I want to make a better wage," he said. "I have plans."

"Oh?"

"I want to make some money, enough to save, then get a vehicle," Dylan said. "A friend in Drug Court says he's been doing some masonry for $15 an hour, and the foreman is looking for more laborers this summer. So I'm putting my name in for that. Hope it works out."

"Enough for a vehicle?" I asked, trying not to sound incredulous. "Sure you're ready for that? That's a big step, and it's going to be expensive."

"Yeah, I know. But if I have a job that pays, I can handle that, as soon as I can get my license back."

He explained to me that Drug Court wasn't just about staying on the straight and narrow to avoid getting negative sanctions. The point was if you did well, you could move to a higher level. You could get a reward. Instead of being monitored all the time, you'd start charting your own course, taking on more responsibilities.

"That's how it works," he informed me. I got it: the carrot and the stick. It takes both to motivate most people. All the same, a vehicle seemed to me a pretty big carrot. How would this happen? And how soon would he be able to get his license back to drive a vehicle? It seemed to me this would all take a while. My head reeled, thinking of all the hoops to jump through, but Dylan was all for charging full speed ahead.

Later, I couldn't help but think back a year last June when my son had been cultivating cannabis in his closet to make big bucks. Then, due to an alcohol incident involving a firearm, all hell had broken loose and he'd been arrested. Just remembering it all made me want to reach for a nitroglycerin capsule to stave off an impending heart attack. "Hey, that was last year," I reminded myself firmly. "Last year, Dylan probably thought he didn't have much to lose. This year is different. Now, he has a lot to lose. He has to stay on his path or get locked up."

Clearly, we were both reviewing our options, setting a course forward. So how was it all going to play out?

As June rolled in, I became excited about a trip John and I were planning for the last two weeks of the month. It would be part of our own celebration of my sixtieth birthday. We were going somewhere in Europe I had never yet been. At first, I was reluctant to be away at this time. "Nonsense," said John. "You can go away for a while; you aren't on 24/7 guard duty. You have to live your life!" Besides, John had already made the reservations; we were going. To assuage my misgivings, I called Mike to see if he and Linda could come down and stay in town for the time I'd be away. That wasn't too difficult to arrange, because Mike had plans to do some more work on the memorial garden at St. Alban's that summer. In fact, if he came at that time, Dylan could help out while he'd be there. Linda would come, too, and do photography in the area. I felt reassured.

Before preparing for the trip, though, I had to apply myself rigorously to doing another type of packing. I had to begin the long process of leaving one office to take up residence in another, one floor down. The physical labor was only part of it: along with endless steps up and down stairs with armloads of boxes came interminable debates with myself about the contents. I wasn't just moving stuff, I was paging through years and years of my professional life. Every day brought new decisions: Will I ever need this document, this book again? If I keep it, where will it go? It felt that just as I was dismantling my former office organization and rebuilding another, I was also peeling away layers of the past, lightening up for the next part of the journey.

During the last part of June, John and I travelled to a completely different world: strolls on a medieval stone bridge, long hikes up rocky hillsides, wonderful roast duck dinners at an ancient inn by a river, busy market days full of local products, friendly chats with the innkeeper every morning at breakfast over the best bread, coffee, and fruit. By the time we left, we were already dreaming of our next visit and where else we would explore in the area: caves, vineyards, Romanesque churches, perched villages. Not to mention thinking about our future lives. We eventually wanted to live in the same town together, after six years of a long-distance relationship across the state. In two more years, this could actually happen. It didn't seem so far off now, and that, too, would be part of the changes to come. When it was time to go home, John accompanied me to the airport, then we said our ritual goodbyes. He'd be staying for another month to teach study-abroad courses, which he loved to do. I wouldn't see him again until August.

Driving back home from the Nashville airport, I felt refreshed from our trip together. I took stock of the fact that very soon, on July 1, I would be officially released from my Chair's duties. As for my other life as a parent, my secret identity as a Mission Impossible Drug Court mom—well, that alternate career would continue for a while. But I was anticipating it too would phase out gradually. Yet even while dreaming of freedom, with every passing mile over rolling hills toward Croftburg, I felt the grip of that invisible mesh of home-front responsibilities closing in on me once again.

Sure enough, in my first talk with Dylan a day or two later, he started complaining about Mike. The communal work at St. Alban's had gone well enough; Dylan had brought a friend to assist a crew placing stones for a walkway his dad had designed. But then, as so often happened, the two had a disagreement. Dylan's main gripe was that his dad wouldn't let him do things his way, didn't have confidence that he could do things another way and they would work out fine. Dylan had gotten so frustrated that he'd had to call and make appointments with Darlene Winchester at Drug Court just to let out his frustrations.

"She probably thinks I'm an idiot, but it doesn't matter. I just needed to vent," he told me, already working up some steam as he spoke.

I was beginning to be very glad I hadn't been around during this episode. I was only half-listening to all this, anyway. I remembered what Darlene had said earlier, when we three were together at our meeting: that Dylan, emotionally, was still like a teenager, still battling against his parents. I wondered: would his emotional age ever catch up to his actual one? How long would it take for us to get past all this conflict?

My ears perked up, though, when the topic of work and money came up. Apparently, Dylan had done quite a few odd jobs here and there, but his main job—the one he was counting on to fill his bank account—was the bricklaying job, and though he'd started it a couple weeks earlier, it had been on hold for a while. Just last Friday, though—finally—the crew was back in business. That meant the pay would once again start rolling in.

"Too bad this masonry job isn't steady. I made allowances for irregular work, but even my lowest estimate was way off," he told me. He'd been thinking that the first wad of cash he'd earned would multiply every week, only it hadn't turned out that way.

"At this rate, it'll take forever to make any dough."

And to get a vehicle, I thought.

A few days later, Dylan came over to mow. But after two weeks of 105-degree weather, only brown, crispy stubble lay underfoot where the green lawn should be. The whole country was in the grips of a dry, red-hot July heat wave.

"Looks like we'll have to wait on the grass," I told him. We were both brushing away beads of sweat from our foreheads as we surveyed the scene.

"Yeah, a friend asked me to go to the lake later today. That sounds like a better idea." He was munching on a sandwich, waving his arm for emphasis, as he often did. After another bite, he told me that he had a girlfriend now, and her name was Amanda. He met her at AA, and they "really hit it off," even though she was a little younger, twenty years old.

"That's good," I said.

"Yeah, that *is* good." I figured he'd had his own dry spell when it came to girlfriends.

"Did you guys know each other for a while and then you decided to spend time together?" I asked.

"Sort of," he replied, wolfing down the last two bites of his sandwich. He indicated he had to get going, so I knew no more information would be forthcoming.

"Oh, and by the way, my AA group just celebrated my first twelve months of sobriety." He dropped it casually, just like that.

"Wow, that's great!" Of course, I cheered this milestone for him and for the support others were giving him to stay on his path. Did Dylan realize how fortunate he was to have that? And here he had me thinking all his plans and projects were going awry just a few days ago! Unwinding the hose to water a parched flowerbed, I fell to wondering how this new girlfriend situation would unfold. If they met at AA, that could be either good or else really bad.

A few days later, during one of my office-dismantling episodes, I fielded a call from Dylan. Again, he was frustrated about how things were going. A whole litany of woes spilled out: he didn't have steady work, hadn't been able to save much money for a car yet—and, to top it off, the promising relationship he'd started with Amanda in AA just ended. She said he "didn't have his act together quite yet," and she needed to be with someone who did. I listened to the avalanche, trying hard not to get swept away by it myself. Instead, I uttered what I hoped would be consoling words. "Don't worry. Things will get better; you just have to have patience." But how consoling would they be? Not to mention, I felt an edge to some of what he said, an edge directed to me as his parent, something along the lines of "Hey, don't you see how hard I'm struggling here? Why aren't you helping me more?" Was I imagining this?

Things got worse the next day when I stopped by Dylan's apartment in the late afternoon to pick up the utility bills. Come to think of it, I was already helping quite a bit. I'd agreed to pay his rent and utilities for the summer. That way, any earnings he could keep for a future vehicle. He came outside, his spiked hair still wet from the after-workday shower. His construction site work buddy with the maroon truck was somewhere inside. Despite the shower, Dylan didn't seem very chill. He noticed that one of the bills he handed off was already past due.

"Well, I can only pay them when I get them," I said. Next, he launched into a jeremiad.

"It's not fair; Fate is against me, I do everything right and then I'm punished! Every guy I know has a car, a girlfriend, and then look at me. Look, I've got a job, I'm working, look at my hands all torn apart laying bricks. Do you see that?" He held his hands with broken skin near the open window of my car to make sure I got the point.

"And then, you expect me to save money. Don't you get it? I don't make enough money to save anything!! How is that supposed to happen? All I'm asking is to have a normal life for a guy in the U.S.A.: a car, a girlfriend, and money for a change of clothes or some shoes every now and then!"

Before I could respond, he stepped back into the apartment and then, with the flourish of a trial lawyer, produced Exhibit A, a torn pair of tan chino shorts. According to him, this was the second or third instance of very nice $65 shorts getting split open by his doing a heavy moving job recently. Clearly, his clothes weren't holding up any better than his morale. In different circumstances, I might have laughed at the distressed-beyond-all-functionality shorts, but as I sat in my car, surveying the scene, I happened to notice that Dylan was swinging his laniered key chain around like a high-speed propeller, his jaw set in barely contained anger. I decided this was not the moment to laugh—or even smile. One wrong word, one misplaced inflection or gesture from me, and he would launch the nukes.

It was clearly my turn to speak in court, and I had to some-how deflect the whole weight of the world's injustice in the next two minutes. Directing my attention to the sorry-looking chinos, I gamely launched the idea that for the rough work he was doing, he should get some cheap but sturdy clothes from either Goodwill or a local consignment shop. That way, he could save his regular clothes for other occasions. Given his agitation, it took several moments to bring him around. Finally, he acknowledged that maybe this would be a good idea. But it was clear that a few sand bags of common sense were no match for a tidal wave of financial angst—and I was right in the path of the deluge.

Dylan went on to inform me that he was getting tired of depending on other people for transportation. I wasn't surprised. As one of the transportation providers, I was getting tired of it, too. I had grown suspicious that Dylan was asking for rides because he wanted to convince me how hard it was for him to get around without a vehicle. By summer, he'd decided to sell his moped because it was becoming a liability; he didn't want to be tempted to drive it without a legal license. In order to get his license reinstated, he needed to finish his alcohol-counseling classes. He'd been attending those at $25/week, and Dr. Beaumont, the instructor, told him the license he could probably get would be a hardship license, which he could do by August . . . maybe. The special license would allow him to drive only to work, to classes, to his Drug Court and AA meetings, and to buy groceries—only necessary trips. But from Dylan's standpoint, that would be a big improvement. He could be independent.

Dylan made it volubly clear that he wanted to be able to save money this summer so that he could purchase a vehicle "sometime before doomsday." He intimated it was time to "get another plan in place." Remaining as steady but flexible as I could manage, I suggested that we should get together when we were *both* calm with some ideas to see what was reasonable.

"Well, it better happen *soon*," he said. Then he took a new turn. "How about we meet with Darlene Winchester and have a three-way talk? She keeps telling me I should be able to work this out."

"OK, see if you can arrange it," I said, brightening my tone. The idea of having a third person arbitrate seemed like a useful idea. From what he just said, it seemed Dylan had been over some of this ground with the Drug Court director already, and I just hadn't heard about it. It sounded to me like I was out of the loop, but very much caught in the net—at least from Dylan's perspective.

I complained to my friend Sandra later about this exchange. We often observed that somehow our kids thought they deserved to have everything they wanted. Provided for them, by us. Entitlement. Sandra commiserated; she'd heard many such irritated demands from her own son, Brad. Despite his irrational tendencies due to schizophrenia, Brad remained an unerring accountant when it came to comparing parental favors for his sister or for him. Disregarding the difference between their situations, he judged simply that if his sister had a car or a vacation, he should get one, too. Whenever a confrontation happened with his mom, which it did fairly often, Robert (Brad's stepdad since he was five years old) would step in to declare the discussion over.

"So if you have the chance to have a third party there to arbitrate, that will be a very good thing for you," she told me. "It will keep things on track with his expectations."

"I hope so," I told her. At least I'd gotten the chance to vent. And I really *did* want to know what Ms. Winchester thought about all this. Time for another visit.

Just when it seemed our conversation was about to wind up, suddenly Sandra brought up a new topic, one that made my blood freeze.

"Did you hear about that violent crime that just happened here in town? A murder; it was just around the corner from Walgreens in a building on that little street near Dairy Queen," she said.

"No, what murder?"

She told me a fifty-five-year-old woman had been stabbed to death in her apartment at about 7 p.m. the previous evening—by her son, who later told police he'd heard voices telling him to kill her. He was obviously not in his right mind, and it sounded like schizophrenia.

"Rita called to tell me about it right after she heard it on the Channel 12 news last night," Sandra said. Rita's son had schizophrenia, too; the two women had bonded like sisters. Very scary stuff for us NAMI moms, especially those whose sons had that particular illness. Who could imagine such a ghastly crime right there in the middle of town, so close to a place hundreds of folks went on a summer's evening?

"Well, maybe we'll find out more, and we'll talk about it at our next meeting. Remember, this Thursday," Sandra added.

"Sure," I said, still feeling the tremor. "Take care."

I checked the online newspaper, read that the neighbors were shocked. According to them, the mother and her son, who visited every week for dinner, had a completely normal relationship. No particular warnings, nothing suspicious. That evening, they heard cries, then shouts. A man came out of the apartment with a knife, then someone called the police. The man cooperated with officers and was taken into custody. A detective had been assigned to make an investigation.

"I wonder if the public will hear much about the mental illness behind this story," I thought. About how the illness wasn't being treated.

At our next NAMI meeting that same week, parents were eager to talk about the incident.

"That's one more reason we have to lobby our legislators in Frankfort," Sandra said. "Nobody else is going to connect the dots, explain how it is that if someone like Burke doesn't get the right psychiatric care when they need it—before they have violent, psychotic episodes—there can be big trouble ahead."

"Someone at work knew this man was a war veteran, too," Nancy chimed in. "You'd think at least a veteran would get good medical care, some psychological support. Look at what all they go through in combat. And then they come home and can't get the care they need." I wondered if and when his mental illness had even been acknowledged. Schizophrenia isn't usually diagnosed until a person hears voices or experiences an hallucination. How old had he been when that first occurred? Had he ever received a treatment plan? Had he gone off it because no one was checking up on him?

It wasn't lost on any of us that it had been a mom who was on the front lines of this particular battle. That's who the terrible voices in Burke's head told him to destroy, and he didn't know how to quiet those voices, how to get away. So many times it was either the mom, or the wife, or the girlfriend facing this terror.

"Burke wasn't the one who killed his mom," Angie said. She was our resident saint. "It was his illness. According to what everyone said, he loved his mom and they got along. But he was having a psychotic break; he didn't know what he was doing."

"But he needed help *before* he got dangerous," Rita said. "That's why I always carry this with me." She held up her key chain with a small can of pepper spray on it. That pink canister was going to be her first responder to any possible violent behavior by her son that could put her in danger. Rita was a realist. She loved her son dearly, but she also knew he didn't take his meds regularly and wasn't always in control of himself. Truth was, none of us knew for sure how far our sons' anger might go someday, and we parents could find ourselves facing it, point blank.

By the next evening, the rains descended—finally. Some of the showers were soft; you could feel the earth soaking up as much water as it could, the sunburnt grass a parched sponge. Other times, the rain came in sheets. I could see streams running down my yard into a small creek along the road. During the rainfall's peak intensity, the whole street flowed like a river. Even the morning afterward, on my way to the office, I could hear the sound of rushing water in what was now a roadside creek. As I passed by the culvert that carried it away across a nearby field, I thought about how humans are such skillful engineers within the physical world. We can plan for storms from nature; we know how to build infrastructure all around us to divert torrential waters. But where are the culverts built to handle the storm surges that can occur in someone's mind, especially if the person has a psychiatric disorder?

When Dylan came by on his bike to mow the grass the following weekend, the lawn had turned green almost overnight from the sudden rains. I noticed right off that there was an extra bounce in his step that day. It was Friday, so after he finished, I asked if he'd gotten paid at work. "Yes!" he said, beaming. He went on to say it wasn't in cash this time. He'd received an actual paycheck with money taken out for taxes and social security. For Dylan this made all the difference: it meant he was actually on a payroll now. Wow! It had been a couple of years since he'd laid eyes on a printed paycheck with his name on it. He underscored the marvel of it by stating that he'd actually gotten more than usual because it was a check for two weeks of work.

"Good, you see, you were making that amount all the time. You just had to wait to get officially paid," I told him. We were both relieved.

"I know," he said. "I have to get rid of this fear I have. Even the fear of taking a job as a bricklayer's assistant because I see it as the first step toward being a bricklayer's assistant forever. Like that's going to be my lot in life."

"I don't think you'll have to worry about that," I said, sounding confident. We jumped from bricks to stepping-stones. How you have to hop from one stone to another sometimes, just to see where you can go next.

"Guess I just have to put my fears aside and trust that it's going to work out," Dylan concluded. "Even that girl at AA: what she said, well, at first it made me mad. Of course, I felt bad. But then later after I thought about it, what Amanda said made sense, and it sounds like a good idea for her. So we're friends; we still talk. It's OK."

Before he took off, he agreed to put his week's allowance as well as $120 of his pay into savings. He decided to entrust it to me, because otherwise the whole wad could get spent in one weekend. Guess he didn't trust himself.

He was halfway down the driveway when I suddenly remembered. "Wait a minute, so when's our appointment with Darlene Winchester?" I asked.

"Oh, it's on Friday morning, at 10:00. That good for you?" he asked.

"Sure, I'll be there," I confirmed. "Maybe she'll help us discuss a plan."

On the appointed day, Dylan and I met with Ms. Winchester at Drug Court. Once again, we found ourselves seated around her desk in lamplight.

"How's your health now?" Darlene asked him.

"Much better. I had a bad cold, but that cough medicine really helped, even if it did have a tiny bit of alcohol in it."

Darlene smiled and nodded. She'd had to approve it beforehand.

"But before we get started here, I have a question for you," Dylan continued.

"I'm wondering if you can let me have some time off from the AA meetings."

"What? No, I don't think so," she said, looking puzzled. "What's up?"

"Just for a week. There's been some rumors about me going around," he said. "People are talking and now I feel like I have to go to a meeting every single night, just to make sure people aren't saying things about me behind my back. First, one person had a relapse, then another. It's been a kind of chain reaction going on and now there's this whole hotbed of gossip. It's getting toxic!"

Darlene took it all in calmly, rolling her eyes. "Well, you know, that's how people are; they *love* drama."

At some point during the exchange, Dylan said that even his sponsor Arlo was among the gossipmongers, which Darlene found hard to believe.

"I know," Dylan said. "I can't even take it personally. They say things behind my back, but then the next minute, they love me. They're supportive, too."

"Well, you can't worry about what people say," Darlene told him. "Go to meetings at another time, another place. Go to the one on Saturday morning. That's a good one, right? You have to go to the five per week required now. Just pick and choose which times and places are better for you. That's it."

I was fascinated by how well Darlene was able to fend off Dylan's anxieties. The type of situations that were so tense between him and me seemed effortless for her. Of course, she wasn't the mom. Plus, she had a circuit judge to back her up. Next, about two seconds later, I felt an uneasy tremor rising up inside about these vague allusions to relapses. And whose relapse, exactly? Was Dylan involved? But then why didn't I hear about it?

But there wasn't time to sort it all out. Or maybe I should have intervened: "Stop! Hey, what's going on here? Please explain this to me." Instead, the conversation charged ahead, as it always did with Dylan. Ever since he could walk and talk, I've been running to catch up. Within seconds, we were all embroiled in an animated conversation about how, since Dylan was going to earn his hardship license soon, could he come up with a plan so that he could eventually get a vehicle? Dylan took the floor, which he's good at. He said it had been a long time since he'd had a vehicle; he admits that the two cars he'd owned in the past had been basically thrown away through his own careless behaviors. Now, though, he'd been toeing the line in Drug Court for ten months. He felt he was ready to own another vehicle and not repeat the same mistakes as before.

"I've learned since I've been sober that you just have to tough it out through the hard times. When you make a mistake, it can take years to make up for it. You can't feel sorry for yourself; you can't compare yourself to someone else who seems to be better off. But if you start doing what's right for you, then things start going better, and you don't care if you're coming from behind. You're on your way and that's all that matters. I feel like I'm ready to move to the next level."

For me, hearing these words was like a Mojave Desert hiker catching the soft trickle of spring water somewhere close. I latched on eagerly to these acknowledgments that now Dylan could talk about a mature change of perspective. The implication? I should trust him. He was on his way.

After recognition of what Dylan had accomplished during his time in Drug Court, we started discussing the particulars of a plan. I suggested that Dylan and I could split the amount for a down payment with him putting in money from his earnings. Then for the rest, he could take out a loan. I was willing to co-sign but not to pay his part of the monthly payment for the loan. Darlene stayed out of the particulars; she only cautioned him against taking on too much.

"Don't take on a payment of more than $50 per week, or $200 a month," she advised. That was, in fact, the amount he had talked about with me the last time we were on this topic. I also said that if he didn't pay, I would want to renege on the deal, because he wouldn't be holding up his end of the bargain. I didn't want to get stuck with payments other than what I agreed upfront to pay. Dylan nodded readily in agreement. Having thought about this ever since he brought it up a week ago, we discussed the positives of this move: #1, he could build up his confidence in his ability to make payments, and #2, he could build up his credit. Dylan was obsessed with credit, that much I knew. Let's just say living the simple life was not his credo.

So with all this money talk, I was taken off-guard when, toward the end of our appointment together, Ms. Winchester brought up a day when Dylan said how good he felt after I had told him that I just wanted him to be happy. He didn't have to be rich or famous, just supporting himself and being responsible. It came out in this context—that, according to Darlene, Dylan did not want to disappoint me or let me down. I was moved by this (and almost surprised), because I didn't think Dylan thought too much about my approval or not. Maybe because when the two of us were together, he was always fighting off too much closeness, too much parental control. I never thought Dylan would misinterpret my actions as a desire to control him or have power over him.

After finances, there were still a few practical matters to sort out. Dylan asked about particulars: how would he get around to make the inquiries, look at cars and go to banks? I agreed to help him with transportation. I said afternoons were good for me; mornings, he worked and so did I. He nodded. "Sounds like an agreement, sounds like a plan." He told me he just wanted to test that out, "because sometimes I have a certain expectation but then when I call you, Mom, I find out you have a completely different expectation, so then we start getting irritated with each other." No kidding. In the end, we both agreed we were glad we could have this three-way conversation with Darlene present because discussions about money were always tense.

The hour was gone in what seemed like minutes. Before we left, Darlene came around her desk for the ritual hug. She hugged

Dylan and then me. She told us how much she enjoyed this job, and I thanked her for everything she was doing.

I was feeling good, too. But later, just for a moment, I felt a strange undercurrent: did Dylan already do something to let me down? Is that why this topic came up? Or was that just a general fear he was talking about? And during the night, about 3:00 a.m., I woke up and found myself thinking about that troublesome allusion to relapses. And why the reaction at AA? But if it was Dylan who had a relapse, then he would get sanctions. He would have to go back to jail for a time, I reasoned. Still, Darlene didn't seem too worried. Not at all. Nobody said anything about jail. On the contrary, she was encouraging this deal about the plan to get a vehicle.

After getting up to check the time and drink some water, I went back to bed. Tossing and turning, I couldn't seem to get back quickly to sleep or resolve this dilemma. Was it true Dylan was making great progress in his self-awareness? Or was I starting to see the tip of some treacherous iceberg out there ahead in the fog? If only I could have complete reassurance that his two steps forward would stand. Could I trust him? That was the question. When I woke up in those dark hours before dawn, I just didn't know for sure. Maybe things would look clearer by morning.

CHAPTER 22: ONE STEP BACK

The next morning, Saturday, I opened the sliding glass door onto the patio and stepped outside to test the air. To my surprise, I felt a refreshing coolness, enough to make me think about having breakfast under the tulip poplar. I noticed a strange quiet, too. The cicadas hadn't even warmed up enough to start their pulsing, mid-summer music yet.

Later, coffee mug parked carefully on a book next to the radio, I looked at my purple wave petunias. They were doing amazingly well, considering the heat they'd been subjected to lately. A strange bird song floated in from close by—it sounded like a woodland bird, one that didn't usually make an appearance in my yard. Not long after, I spotted a black and orange towhee flitting through the trees. He was a beautiful, long-tailed bird with a sliding up-note whistle, followed by a series of trills. The bird instantly reminded me of my mom. She had an ear for bird songs and almost always got them right. It was her voice that came into my ear now; her gaze came too, searching for the vanished towhee. I got up to fill the birdbath.

Back at my table under the tree, ruminations rumbled around in my head. I was inclined to be optimistic, even after only four hours of sleep. The topic: how to get Dylan driving again without being taken for a ride. Wait a minute, was it even time for him to be driving again? I could already hear both Mike and John shouting in unison from their separate domains: "NO, NO, NO! Have you lost your mind? No more vehicles!" But they weren't here now, and they weren't there with Dylan and Darlene at the meeting yesterday either. Nor were they called upon to be chauffeurs. Besides, they were both mavericks, so their opinions had to be taken with a lot of salt. I decided to draw up a list of pros and cons, to see which one was longer. That would surely yield objective results, wouldn't it?

Cons:
- Previous traffic tickets and irresponsible driving history.
- DUI charges with increasing alcohol use.
- Previous poor planning with regard to car maintenance.
- Family plan is for him to wait until he finishes college to get another car.
- Dylan wants to build his credit, but credit economy can be a slippery slope. Better to save up before shelling out.
- If Dylan ends up not being able to make regular payments on a car, it will just reinforce his feelings of failure: "I can't make it in this world."

Pros:
- Dylan's in a recovery program now. The other craziness happened BEFORE the recovery program, before Dylan even admitted he had a self-medication problem and that it was serious, life-threatening.
- If I say "No, because you screwed up before," that could mean to him "I don't think you should have any more chances to screw up." And he'll resent me forever.

- Most, if not all the other guys in Drug Court have access to vehicles—or are working toward that goal—if they are legally able to. The prevailing belief they buy into: guys without vehicles are total LOSERS.
- Since Dylan is in Drug Court now, which has an excellent accountability and support structure, this could be the time to take chances. Get him started on the path of planning and payments, so that he learns how to do it. If he can't, it's better to find that out sooner rather than later.
- Building credit can be useful for later life goals, like purchasing a house.
- If Dylan has his own transportation, no more phone calls to yours truly at weird, random times when he can't get anyone else to give him a ride.

Having made the lists, I read through all the "Cons" and could see that it was extremely risky, not to say crazy, to help Dylan drive again anytime within this decade. If he were anyone else's kid, I would say unequivocally, "No, he's not mature enough; you're wasting your money. Wait until he works his way closer to this goal." For the record, I *can* be rational. However, I also believe that there does come a time in the course of human events when you have to let rationality step aside in favor of other, more compelling arguments.

So, contrary to sound judgment, I was leaning toward the "Pro" column, largely because of arguments 1, 2, and 4. Along these lines, something Dylan said at our latest meeting with Ms. Winchester stuck in my mind. At one point he said, "I've been afraid of success, and I've been afraid of failure. But that doesn't leave me anywhere to go." If Dylan was doing what he needed to do to succeed in the recovery program, then maybe he deserved the benefit of the doubt. He had to work within a structure now; there were consequences.

This could be an open test of his ability to follow through toward a goal. So maybe it was worth the risk. Then, too, I had to admit: the last item on the "Pro" list did carry a certain convincing weight with me—probably more than it should have. Besides, I sure didn't want him to drive MY car! So much for objectivity.

One hot July evening about four days later, I got hit with a curve ball. It all started with a phone call from Dylan: he needed a ride to the AA meeting and no one else was available. When I picked him up, he had a dark look on his face. He told me he was really angry with himself. Said he'd had a bad day, but he needed to go to AA anyway—no, especially now. "I have a lot of self-hatred," he said; then a few moments later, "I can never be happy." I wasn't sure how to react, so I didn't say much. "Well, maybe you'll hear something tonight at AA that will help you," I offered.

"That's what I do every day, just look for one more thing to keep me going."

Respecting his wishes, I dropped him off at the meeting but at a distance, so he could walk the rest of the way to the building. He said he'd be fine, he'd get a ride home.

Back at my place later, I put off my worries by setting off for the community garden to see how the melons were ripening. I checked the cantaloupes, but my special favorite in the garden was an heirloom "Moon and Stars" watermelon that I'd been keeping an eye on. "Wait until the small tendril near the melon stem dries up," a farmer told me. "That's the sign of ripeness." Well, this evening was the time. I disengaged it from the stem and took the sleek melon into my hands, marveling at its weight. The light flurry of markings on its dark green skin really did look like stars at night.

At the same time, I couldn't help but be disturbed by what my son had just said. Something was definitely going on, and it wasn't good. Better to get this out in the open, I thought. After toting the prized melon back home, I decided to text Dylan later after the meeting to see if he wanted to have some watermelon with me. That way, we could talk. He didn't answer right away, but later called me back. I asked how things had gone at AA; it seemed that the meeting had helped. I asked if he had talked there about his situation: "Yeah, a little." At my house, he seemed in a better frame of mind. I showed him the watermelon I had just harvested. We admired its beauty, and I offered to cut us both a piece. "No thanks, Mom," he replied. So I just sliced one for myself and waited to see what would happen next.

Seated at the table, he folded his arms in front of himself, looked stoic.

"I have something to tell you," he said. I braced myself.

What came out wasn't a smooth narrative. He'd had a relapse a while ago. Apparently, it had happened when he was with Jeremy, the guy at the tattoo parlor and a new guy in Drug Court. They had been drinking. "It just happened," Dylan said. "We were hanging out, and then we just looked at each other and he said, 'Let's get high.' We both wanted to, so that was it." Dylan said he enjoyed the alcohol at first, but the aftermath was bad; he felt anxious and, of course, guilty. Dylan had already served a weekend in jail as a penalty for this transgression, which I hadn't known about. So, my suspicions had been right, after all.

But that wasn't the worst of it. Following that incident, Dylan said he relapsed AGAIN the past weekend, Saturday. It was with the same guy, Jeremy, only this time they'd gone to the casino across state lines because Jeremy knew how to make easy cash playing blackjack. There'd been drinks there, too, and who knows what else. Now Dylan was afraid the results were going to show up in the drug test, and he was going to have a worse penalty—and more shame. Gut-level sickening news. I took a breath and kept my mouth shut. Clearly, he was trying to figure himself out. Why had he done this?

Dylan knew the consequences were going to be rough—probably a whole week in jail. I figured he was wondering why he had taken the chance, especially the second time. To me, it seemed that this Jeremy—whoever he was—represented his dark side, the shady addict side. Maybe now Dylan realized how close he might come to losing his diversion. I repeated things that Dylan had said about his situation a few years ago in Cleveland when things started slipping. That was after several good, clean months following his graduation from the program in Jamaica. I pointed out that he starting hanging out with the wrong people then, too. "Don't hate yourself; hate the decision you made because it was harmful."

Dylan was worried about what Darlene would think. He said he'd tried to tell her but hadn't gotten hold of her yet.

"Yes, admit it before you get caught. You don't want to be sneaky on top of everything else."

"Yeah, I don't want to be like Connor. He finally got kicked out of Drug Court because nobody believed him anymore," Dylan said.

Ah, Connor, the ex-housemate with the steady gaze, recently caught lying. I thought about his mom, too, what she must be feeling. I had seen her in town, but we'd never spoken. After a pause, I asked Dylan if there were persons in AA that he could call for help if he felt he was going the wrong way.

"Yeah, I got some numbers tonight; they're in my wallet."

We talked about the strange timing of this dramatic slip-up, how it mirrored the risky behaviors of a year ago, last summer. And he still had two months to go before doing his first twelve months in Drug Court. Could he make it?

While we were talking, a call came in from his AA sponsor.

"Hey Arlo, I'm just here talking to my mom now. Yeah, man, I'll talk to you tomorrow."

I encouraged him to take advantage of his support group; he couldn't do this alone. When he was about to go, I gave him a hug, told him he had a whole circle of support around him, people who cared about him, wanted him to do well. He had to be back before curfew at 10:00, so I drove him home. One last thing: as we were pulling up to his apartment, he told me that he hoped that his actions didn't make me too upset; he didn't want to ruin my life with his actions. That was the first time he had said something like that.

"No, I'm not worried about you," I told him. "You have to worry about yourself. What you do, Dylan, won't prevent me from having a good life."

"OK, Mom, because if I thought my actions were ruining *your* life, that guilt on top of my own guilt would just make my situation worse, not better."

I told him I understood (another lie), and we said our goodbyes.

Back home, I sat on my couch in a daze. The picture of events was getting clearer, but my feelings about it weren't clear at all. On the one hand, Dylan had finally confessed his relapses to me that very evening. I knew Dylan had kept silent about this for well over a week now—at least with me. Was that because he was ashamed and tried to deal with it on his own? Or was it because he was afraid it would prevent my helping him get a vehicle? I felt a slow burn coming on: should I be angrier about the concealment, or be relieved now that he opened up and finally told me the truth?

My mind went over the timeframe. OK, so Dylan had had his first drinking scene with Jeremy prior to our meeting with Darlene Winchester. She knew about it, and Dylan must have already taken his sanction, a weekend in jail. I knew nothing. Then, as it turned out, hadn't the second relapse occurred the evening *after* our brilliant, soulful talk with Darlene just last Friday afternoon? The irony of that prickled under my skin. It couldn't be, but it almost seemed that Darlene was in collusion with Dylan. Why didn't they both tell me about the original relapse? Or was Darlene expecting him to do it on his own? Knowing her policies, I figured she wouldn't intervene in something she felt was his responsibility to make a decision about.

True enough, I was angry again. Why did Dylan seem to take these wrong turns after speaking so convincingly, and with such insight, about his own psychological situation the day before? Did our meeting together make him over-confident? I felt scorched by the slap to my own naïve mother-trust ways. Sometimes, my son acted like the type who would walk right next to the top of a high cliff, as if tempting fate to take him over the edge. It was maddening as hell! And why was he always drawn to these hard-luck, high-risk guys like Jeremy in the first place? Didn't he already know that being with Jeremy would bring him trouble?

Yet another irony: this was the tattoo artist who had done Dylan's recovery tattoo, the one that read, "To thine own self be true." Yet I saw why my son felt bonded to him—not just because of the tattoo. It was because he knew Jeremy bore the same invisible mark of Saturn on his forehead, too. The sign of the hard-luck, misfit persona Dylan had taken on as a teen. It rankled me to think that these two guys understood each other to the core in a way I never would. Their psyches clicked into place like two molecules looking to exchange electrons.

So what about my role here? Had I been too accommodating through all this? Maybe I was wrong about always trying to be the wise, steady Rock. Maybe I should have yelled a few times or kicked over a chair. Well, at least I would ask more questions next time. Moments later, I decided to deliver another message to Dylan. "I hope you will graduate from Drug Court," I texted sternly. "I think that is even more important than graduating from college."

Not long after came his reply: "I agree. I will do it. Good night."

CHAPTER 23: HOW FAR IS IT STILL?

A few days later, in the late afternoon, I fielded another call from Dylan. I knew immediately from the bright tones in his voice that he was doing much better than the last time we'd talked. He told me he'd been to see Dr. Peltay, a minor miracle since the lone town psychiatrist was always booked solid for months. A last minute opening came up so Dylan was able to get in. After the appointment, he requested a lift to the pharmacy to fill his prescription. On our way, Dylan admitted "a little bit of denial" in his previous consultations with the physician, who had now prescribed Lamictal for him. Dylan had good associations with that medication, as he'd had his best quarter at UC taking it.

OK, so he was admitting he *did* need a mood stabilizer. This was significant. I remember that he'd said to me repeatedly over the last few months, "I really don't think I have mood swings." Well, he would tend *not* to if he were taking the proper medication. Unfortunately, the good results often became the excuse to go off the medication that brought them. He'd also mentioned at least once that Darlene Winchester didn't think much about the diagnosis of bipolar. But then most people didn't know much about it, didn't want to know. Trouble was, if you happened to be in a smooth period of your bipolar, then you could have an invisible illness that the world didn't notice. Not only that, but you could go further and convince yourself you didn't *really* have the dreaded illness. Sooner or later, that tends to be a big mistake.

"This last episode, though, really scared me," Dylan said. "The slump I was in just went on and on. When I get down like that I can't think straight. Everything seems bad, like it's never going to change. I can't seem to get out of it, no matter what I do."

I remembered that when he first started going to AA, he rebelled against the idea of "I am helpless and can't do this by myself," but now maybe he's starting to accept that in his darkest moments—not all the time—that is exactly how he feels. "Weak, totally defenseless," he said.

According to him, it wasn't all biochemical, either. There were plenty of real-life causes to be depressed, too. Things could go wrong, like the budding romance with the young woman at AA. "My expectations were unrealistic," he admitted. "You can't have unrealistic expectations like that." Next, his former housemate Connor had gotten kicked out of Drug Court for being dishonest, and of course, Jeremy was right behind him, after his drug test results came back. Dylan himself had gone through first one screw-up with drinking, then another. It was almost like a snowball effect. He knew now there would be sanctions; he just hoped they wouldn't be too bad. I asked him about how his boss would react. "I think he'll try to work with me, as long as I'm not gone for too long," he said. Then, after a pause, he said, "You know, I made these mistakes but I have to remember overall, I've done well. I mean, these last couple of weeks, at least I went to work; I kept up with things. I kept it together for the most part."

We both remembered times at the University of Cincinnati when he'd go through serious dips like this. He'd close himself off from friends, disappear into his apartment, not even opening the door to go to class—even though up until then he'd been doing well. He didn't tell anyone about it, either. It was as if he'd turned into another person, a total recluse with no energy. We parents would only hear about it afterward, when he came out of it. Other times, he could go into an anxious, hypomanic state. That was as bad—lots of energy, but all going haywire. He could get irritated over the smallest trifles, too. That could be a dead giveaway. At those times, he'd raise his voice, make big gestures, scare people, all the while barely realizing what effect he was having until someone pointed it out to him, or else scurried away. They say people with bipolar need someone close and trusted enough to be able to cue them when things start to drift toward the edge. Sometimes, they don't even know it's happening.

"Dylan, you really need to stay on your meds, especially the mood stabilizer. If it makes you feel sluggish, ask the doctor to lower your dose—but keep taking it," I told him.

"Yeah, you're probably right. Well, I'm starting Lamictal today."

I've always tried to understand how it happened that Dylan could have solid plans for his life, then suddenly make decisions that went completely in the opposite direction. How could the same brain, the same mind, be so out of synch with itself? I read David Eagleman's book *Incognito: The Secret Lives of the Brain* and learned that decision-making in the mind is not purely cognitive at all, but in fact involves different specialized parts of our complex neuro-circuitry interacting with each other. So the way the mind works actually involves different actors, different forces, each one receiving inputs in his/her own sensory language. With all this input data, each subunit then argues more or less strongly for a particular mode of action to respond to life situations. It sounds downright political, doesn't it? The neuroscientist likens this phenomenon to President

Lincoln's Cabinet members, often at odds with each other—so much so that historian Doris Kearns Goodwin called them a "team of rivals." Lincoln preferred this arrangement because, as President, he could listen to the crossfire of different viewpoints, then choose the best course of action after weighing the possibilities, gaining some insight into the likely consequences of one scenario or another. This is essentially what any group leader has to do, whether CEO or President or, as in the case of a human brain, the prefrontal cortex (PFC). Eagleman gives many examples of how different subunits of the brain each present their most compelling arguments, with the executive PFC intervening, comparing, and often negotiating to get the best deal between them all. And, of course, sometimes the PFC has to just say *no*.

From what I've observed, it seems like this: usually a bipolar brain's executive function can step in and solve the problem in an acceptable way. However, given that some of the message systems aren't always working so well, it happens that the PFC isn't always at the top of its game. And that's apt to occur at a moment when a sudden overload of wayward impulses and differences of opinion need to be to settled among the team of rivals. What if the PFC gets confused by all the data? Or can't maintain rational controls over unruly subjects? Then what? Well, it's not going to be a good day at company headquarters.

To conceptualize a "team of rivals" scenario that might take place in my son's bipolar brain, I imagine something along the lines of a *New Yorker*-style cartoon, one featuring a corporate boardroom meeting. The two factions are seated around a seminar table, where the emotional, limbic system members are seated on one side and the more practical, analytical cerebral cortex planners are on the other. Both memory archivists are there: the Hippocampus, with long poetic locks and his gold-leafed journal, and also the Amygdala, who looks quite a bit shaggier, more like he just got out of bed. As we know, in any boardroom cartoon—no matter how fraught or absurd the meeting may turn out to be—the CEO will remain calm and in control. Not always the case in real life for a PFC. Definitely not for a bipolar brain having to manage the pressure of internal events. And if you've got internal noise going on, how will you be able to listen clearly and make good decisions about things happening in the external world?

When executive function goes awry.

In my imaginary live-action version, Dylan's PFC appears today as a harried, nerdy CEO right in the middle of a tense drama. He's wearing a nice suit, but his glasses are getting foggy from sweat, his tie's askew. He's running his hands through ruffled hair, trying to calm down a bully Amygdala who's up from his chair and yelling loudly. The Amygdala—he's a muscular jock type of guy—has appointed himself ringleader of the entire limbic system today: "No, this is too much talk. We got too much stress around here. We need some relief. We gotta take action NOW!" This is not surprising, coming from him. Either he's terrified and wants to head for the hills, or he's on overload and wants to head for the nearest tavern. Not only that, but he has only a stimulus-response memory, so if he isn't listening to the Hippocampus and the PFC, he doesn't know anything about weighing consequences or doing risk analysis. Right now, he's making so much noise that the strategic planners are shocked into silence.

Meanwhile, the PFC isn't feeling so well at the moment. Only this morning, the accountant turned over some bad news—bills to settle and not enough revenue to do it. Both of them feel a migraine headache coming on. Problems, problems, problems. Against his better judgment, the PFC says he has to leave the office and lets the Amygdala—along with the whole limbic system gang—have their way. An ill-advised series of motions gets made. Disaster ensues. The young man visits the nearest casino with an out-of-recovery addict instead of attending his AA meeting.

Another possible scenario: this one occurs when the PFC is feeling underpowered and somewhat disoriented. Meanwhile, the *nucleus accumbens* (the brain's pleasure/reward center) is restless and militating for action. So he pipes up in a heavy Bronx accent: "Hey, I remember feeling really good when we bought some new clothes. Yeah, what we really need now is to go out on a little shopping spree: shoes, clothes, upgrade on the cell phone, new auto parts to jazz up the car a bit." The limbic system crowd is loving it, especially the Amygdala. Things have been so dull lately. "Yeah, or how about a trip to Vegas to win some cash and round up some girls?" In no time, the whole Pleasure Unit is ready to amp up on overtime. Whoa! It just so happens that now the brain circuits are all on fire, every voice clamoring for action, no matter how ill-advised. Ideas, desires, motivations are racing around like Formula Ones at the Indy 500. The Prefrontal Cortex is buried in noisy commotion; he can't even get the attention of the rowdy assembly! It's as if the mind is driving a vehicle with a Ferrari engine but only Ford brakes. Result: the executive function has been pre-empted again. Not surprisingly, disaster ensues once more: accounts overdrawn, DUIs, arguments, fights, somebody in jail, etc. None of the family members around the person with this kind of hijacked brain can figure it out. "What?! I can't believe it!" they say. "Why did he do *that*? He seemed so calm yesterday. In fact, we had the best conversation, and he was making solid plans for the future."

Well, that's just it; yesterday, things were different in the Dome of Reason. Nothing was triggering the Amygdala, so he wasn't running his anxiety loops and pressuring for action. And yesterday, the pleasure/reward center at the *nucleus accumbens* was doing just fine with the work-out routine at the gym and a nice grilled chicken sandwich. But not today. That's why the meds are important, as is a therapy like Cognitive Behavioral Therapy (CBT). If impulses are going to be stronger than usual, then the cortical controls have to be jacked up, too. The Ferrari engine needs Ferrari brakes, or there's going to be a crash.

I can imagine all this, but I can barely imagine what it must feel like to actually *live* with these 180-degree re-orientations, especially if they happen unpredictably. No wonder Dr. Kay Jamison prefers the older term "manic-depression" to the bland term "mood disorder." The earlier term conveys a sense of the psychic centrifuge a person can be subjected to. If I had this illness, would I learn to read the signs of my instrument panel in enough time *before* my craft started to tailspin? And even if I could, wouldn't I need training in how to come out of it so I could land safely, the way pilots have to do?

Just as we were leaving the drive-through of the pharmacy, precious packet of mood stabilizer in Dylan's hand, the two of us saw an amazing apparition. It was a wide, long behemoth of a car making a turn into the road just a few yards ahead of us. Yes, the topic of vehicles was right there in front of us again. No doubt, this one had once been a sleek beauty in its day, but now, with its debonair, 60s-era fins looking a bit worn, its paint job in need of repair, the low-down, lumbering bulk of it made us both burst out laughing. What a beast! Watching its pale blue mass turn into street traffic was like watching an aging hippo ease into a broad river somewhere in Tanzania, something you might see on the Discovery channel.

"Hey, Dylan, there's a car for you. Maybe that one wouldn't cost so much." He laughed again at my joke.

"Yeah, well, if I don't finish Drug Court, if I go the wrong way, that's the car I'm going to be driving."

I smiled but caught the side implication: if I go the right way, I want to drive something way better. By now, most of his native optimism was back. He said he'd had to remind himself that for most of the past year, he'd been staying on track. He had slipped off badly but was back on it now.

"Well, I hope this incident isn't going to set me back in terms of getting a car," he went on. "I don't even know yet what the sanctions are going to be."

"Me either," I said. "We'll see."

Dylan soon found out about his sanction at Drug Court: go to jail for seven days. He would report for lock-up the next day at noon. "Might as well get it over with now," he told me. He was glad he'd called Darlene to make the first move to come clean. She'd told him she saw the results of the drug test where his had come back dirty, and she wondered what was going on—especially a second time so close on the first one. They talked for a while. Dylan's voice sounded tired, ragged around the edges, but he was resigned. He knew what he had to do.

"With Darlene, we talked about how if I had to make a mistake like this, it's better that it happen now and not later. If I got all the way through the program and into after-care, and then started drinking again when I wasn't being drug-tested as often, then I'd really be in trouble. I wouldn't get the checking, the help to get back on track."

"I know," I told him. "Sometimes when we talked about the future, it sounded like you planned to stay on your path for two years and then after that, you weren't sure if you would go back to drinking or not."

"Oh no, I'm not. This is something I had to go through. My intentions were good, but my actions weren't, so now I have to take the consequences. It doesn't look pretty, but hopefully, this will lead to something that looks way better later on. Darlene said that when I come out, I can talk about it with the group."

On another note, he said he'd called his boss to tell him he wouldn't be able to work with the crew for a week. The boss said they were still waiting on a brick shipment and wouldn't be pouring concrete on a new site until next week. So Dylan could go back to work when he got out. He felt lucky: he'd lose the income but not the job. We talked a bit about jail. I said at least he could read and occupy his time. He said yes, in fact, he was going to bring a book with him to read, a book he had started but hadn't been keeping up with. It was called *Recovery, the Sacred Art: the Twelve Steps as Spiritual Practice.*

"Well, maybe it's time to do that," I said. "Time to slow down and pay attention to your spiritual life."

"Yes," he said, "I'm exactly where I need to be. I'll go to jail for seven days, and when I get out, I'll pick up my life again."

"And you'll be stronger. Well, I'll be thinking about you."

"But don't worry too much about me," he said.

What, me worry?

Given the circumstances, I decided to pack my bags and visit John for a week. Now that it was August, he was back home again. In a short while, the semester would be starting up with a full round of classes for both of us, and this might be the only chance I would have to get away to see him. I could already imagine myself on the open road, heading east, my cares lightening. Of course, what I really wanted was a clear resolution to the problem—Dylan's problem, which felt like my problem. Clear answers.

I could already hear John's voice on the topic of cars and driving. "Why do you feel you need to give him a ride around a small town?" he would ask. "Why can't that guy use his bike or walk? It would take him ten or fifteen minutes." But I looked at the situation differently. Since my schedule was freer now, I figured it was a good thing for Dylan to spend more time under my influence rather than someone else's—like Jeremy's.

Being a cabbie wasn't glamorous, but it did offer conversational time with my son that I wouldn't get otherwise. Besides, I'd been reading Buzz Bissinger's book, *Father's Day*, about a dad taking a long road trip with his son Zach to reconnect. The son is autistic and he's turning twenty-four, the same age as Dylan. Zach has an adult life ahead of him, and the dad has to turn a few emotional corners before accepting that it won't be the one he once imagined for him. "Zach's life will take on a shape of its own," he finally admits. That summer, the way I saw it, my son and I were making our own kind of intermittent road trip, the one through the first year of Drug Court. And so we frequently found ourselves sitting side by side, crossing a different but vaguely similar terrain. After we got to where we thought we were going, what shape would my own son's life take?

But for now, an unexpected reprieve. OK, I'll take it. Like when you're climbing a steep mountain trail and you keep asking passersby, "How far is it still to the top?" Better not to ask. Better to just take a break. Look around and take in the cloudscapes, the views. Breathe for a while.

CHAPTER 24: A GARDEN IN THE FOREST

Once a King and Queen lived with a young prince in a small castle on the edge of a woods. The King and Queen, though they governed their affairs largely in common, had differences that came between them. One day the King left the castle to seek his fortune elsewhere. The Queen stayed at the castle with the young prince, and they were very close. But soon, the Queen took on many responsibilities in the world. The young prince, as he grew older, became restless and unruly. Eventually, the King came back to the castle to reclaim his son, and the two rode off on their travels to a distant place.

Now, the Queen fell into great dismay. To avoid being alone, she took on even greater responsibilities during the week, and then fled to the big city on weekends to seek refuge and amusement. She met friends and made another life. While she was gone, a small forest began growing around the castle. The trees grew taller and more numerous; vines with heart-shaped leaves crept closer and closer, beginning to cover the doors and windows of her abode. One day, the Queen woke up in her castle, as if from a long sleep, to look around her. "The forest is approaching!" she exclaimed. "Soon, branches will be growing through the walls, and vines will be growing through the open windows of my chambers." She pondered the situation to look for a solution. "Where will I find a woodsman to help me?" she wondered.

By mid-August, I was beginning to wonder whether the landscape company would ever arrive to create the garden I had consulted them about earlier that summer. Now that I was making import-ant transitions in my personal life, and with Dylan's health and college career apparently back on track, I'd finally decided to put some order back into my front yard, where a small forest was fast encroaching on a neglected planting bed. I anticipated taking up gardening again, one of my favorite pastimes. First, however, I would need some assistance. The main landscaper had told me in May that it might take a while for their crew to arrive. When I called again in August, he told me the extreme July heat that year had set them back, and they had a long list of clients before me who wanted work done before late fall. I just needed to be patient; they would get to me eventually.

Besides, the landscaper had visited my yard; he knew about the overgrown state of the front planting bed. Whole trees had grown up seemingly overnight due to distracted-gardener syndrome. Not to mention the proliferating clumps of ornamental grasses with their plumes, which did not observe the rules of staying in their desig-nated places as part of the décor but cast their roots and seeds out in all directions. Then there were the long, trailing vines of Virginia creeper that wrapped around trees, shrubs, and anything else in their paths, making a person think twice about walking too close to them. Lastly, some tall, thorny weeds with prickly leaves added some unusual textures to the mix.

Though a longtime lover of trees, grasses, and vines, I learned the hard way when I came to Kentucky that a homeowner's best friends could end up being a chainsaw and an herbicide sprayer. Either that or you just mowed the entire yard weekly to keep the vegetation at bay. Creeping vines from a derelict planting bed could be an enormous problem. At first, their tendency to climb up the brick exterior of the house and wrap their curling tendrils around doorframes and windows charmed me. The vines would give my abode the aspect of an old English country cottage, decked with ivy. However, I soon found out these picturesque vines could be downright pernicious, infiltrating narrow spaces between windowpane and frame, anchoring themselves in place by inserting brush-like attachments. From there, they could grow, expand, and eventually break the seal of any window. Fortunately, I discovered this destructive tendency while pruning wreaths of them away from the house one day, thereby saving my precious windows from ruin in the nick of time.

Of course, the vines in my yard weren't growing into the window frames to be intentionally malicious. They were just quietly positioning themselves to search for more light to make more leaves. That was their growth plan. They were opportunistic entrepreneurs: expanding their inventory, reaching out for new markets, growing faster by the mile than even Dollar General. These green, photosynthetic conquistadors weren't friends to trees, either. Instead, vines used their same brushy attachments on the bark of tall pines to boost themselves up toward the airy, sunlit canopy, meanwhile smothering the tree's foliage with their own luxuriant verdure. Learning their sneaky ways, I knew it was imperative to give all groundcovers a good haircut at least twice during the summer—just to keep the house, the tool shed, or any other surrounding structures safe from their wiles.

The landscaper's professional gaze scanned the forbidding sight in my front yard, and he told me the obvious. Before any new garden could be installed, all the offending trees, tangle, and under-brush would have to be removed. When we discussed the price of the design installation, he told me I could save on my end if I could get my own crew together to do the prior cleanup work. That way, his crew could focus on preparing the soil and planting the garden itself. I nodded, but inside I was groaning. Where was I going to find workers to tackle this job? And since it was getting so late in the season, what if the landscaper never made it to my name on the list before next year?

That's when Dylan asked me, "So, Mom, do you have any work for me in your yard like you did last year?" He'd just been released from what he called his "recovery retreat" at the local jail, the week-long sanction imposed by Drug Court. He explained that while he'd been there, the masonry crew foreman had hired another guy to take his place for the current job, so—while waiting for the next one to come up—he was looking for work. "Didn't I do a good job for you before, helping to clear all that brush away in the backyard by the fence?" he added. That had been a major task for him and a buddy over a year ago; they'd used a chainsaw to cut down myriad privets that had grown thickly at the very back of the property, along with a few other uninvited guest trees around the house. Afterwards they cleared all the fallen wood by taking it to the curb. Things had shaped up nicely, and Dylan's share of the earnings had gone toward the purchase of his moped.

So now, yes, here I was again, needing serious yard work done, and he was available to do it for pay. I wanted the garden to move forward; it was a timely match. After short discussion, we arrived at a price per hour: $15. Dylan could see there would be plenty of hours; this would be a project to tide him over until the masonry crew hired him back for the fall. As for me, I already knew most people would not do this kind of hard, physical labor, or they would rent heavy equipment—a small dozer, for example. But Dylan viewed it as workout time. Now all those protein supplements and bench presses would pay off. We agreed I would keep a tab of his hours, and we would confirm them each day he worked.

In August, the planting bed was full of tall, withered grasses along with assorted trees. Earlier in the summer, Dylan's sponsor Arlo had come over to spray the grasses in anticipation of their removal. The drought of this particular summer had hastened their demise, but now they would have to be dug out of the dry clay soil. Several trees would have to be cut down as well: the protruding ironwood stump that lived up to its name in sheer toughness and the "dwarf" black pine, which grew tall enough now to completely block the view from my front window. Then there was the small clump of persimmon trees that dropped their waxy, gooey fruits every fall in heaping quantities in just those areas near the front walkway where any visitor would be sure to step on them. Even John, a confirmed defender of trees, wanted the persimmons to go, after innumerable shoe cleanings. Once the orange, squishy mess hardened on the bottoms of his running shoes, it was as troublesome to remove as well-baked chewing gum. Besides, two more persimmon trees down by the street could easily carry on the tradition all by themselves. And then there were the ubiquitous privets that cropped up underfoot and were soon waist-high. All had to go, all except for the tall hemlock tree on the northeastern corner of the mound; it was a sentinel guarding the house. Way back when the house was first built, this tree—a live Christmas hemlock—was the first one we'd planted in the front, and it had had to dig its roots down into some horrendous clay soil, some of it so gray it looked like something out of a cement truck. That the tree survived to grow into its present lofty form was nothing less than miraculous. For all I knew, those deep, penetrating roots helped to produce the soil that everything else around them could grow in.

For the persimmons, I knew by now to hire a company to

remove them, because of the sheer volume of wood to be cut and the stumps to be ground down below ground. Professionals had the equipment to do this job in half a day. That done, Dylan could move on with the rest. To remove the smaller superfluous trees that had moved in later, we rented a chainsaw again, this time for an afternoon. So for the first day of work on the project, Dylan spent several hours cutting them down, then sawing the wood into logs and branches small enough to be hauled away.

The second day that Dylan was able to work on the feral planting bed happened to be the Saturday before classes started at the college. Over the phone, he told me he was still transitioning off an anti-depressant he didn't like. The previous night, he hadn't gotten to sleep until 4 a.m. Hearing this, I could only shake my head. There was always some issue with the meds he was prescribed; either they didn't work as expected, or they worked for a while and then stopped working, or there were unpleasant side effects. Today, though, once he arrived, energy drink in hand, he said he was feeling better and ready to go. He told me he'd been gearing up for the new semester: got his books, a planner, was getting organized. Standing with him outside, I decided to work outdoors, too. After the gray rains of the previous day, this particular Saturday was clear, sunny, and refreshingly cool—only in the low 80s. Perfect for yard work.

While I weeded and trimmed around my backyard roses, Dylan weeded the front dirt mound and then tackled one of the larger grass clumps. There would be plenty of those to dig out, including ones near the hemlock. They were all escaped ornamentals that had cleverly found ways to reinvent prairie life right in my front yard. Next, he took on the ironwood tree stump. It was one thing to take down a tree with a saw, but we knew the entire stump had to removed to prevent it re-growing from below. As he dug a hole around it, Dylan could see several live roots that had to be cut clean through to release it. Some were as big around as my arm. He took great swings with the heavy-duty mattock we had just purchased. It took a while, but eventually he covered the bottom of the wheelbarrow with short pieces of the severed root limbs.

He called to show them to me; we could see there was live, white wood under the bark. The root chunks took on strange animal shapes as they lay randomly strewn against the weathered metal. The tree stump was a marvel; we had to admire it. Though part of it seemed dead as a doornail—in fact, was rotting—another part of its root system was still live and green. As Dylan remarked, if we hadn't taken the trouble to get it all out, these roots would still be sending out small, leafy shoots, some of which we had already seen, ones that would eventually sabotage any new landscape plantings.

During one of his breaks, we walked out to the street on one side of the yard and then walked over to a neighbor's house to observe the space starting to open up from another angle. You had to get some distance to see the possibilities. Dylan stood next to me, feet splayed in a painterly pose, eyeing it over his thumb, like a young Monet. The proposed canvas offered a good wide space, anchored on one corner by the tall hemlock tree. The only trick was to somehow mentally erase all the unwanted vegetation within it, then imagine something else. At one point in its history, this had been a mounded planting bed. But now, the undulating front curve of the bed was blurred by intruding lawn. Then, too, after well over a decade, the raised effect was not as noticeable, either. Both of these features needed to be accentuated. That would mean digging a narrow, clean trench all along the front and side of the garden to provide a smooth line, then later on, adding topsoil to bring the whole mound higher and give it more of a feminine contour.

As we talked about what needed to be done to rehab the garden, Dylan said he didn't see any reason why he couldn't do the whole job, not just the clearing phase. He could do the installation as well. Hadn't he seen his dad construct garden landscapes for clients in several different states ever since he was a little kid? He under-stood how you started from a clean space, then put in any major structural elements—like boulders. After that, you prepared the soil for plantings. He knew about making a drawing, about how the garden itself could be viewed as a three-dimensional painting. He had the know-how and the strength to do the construction, while I had most of the tools he needed in the shed. Only, he would have to do the work in phases, since classes would be starting. He assured me he'd still have times in the afternoon when he could work and, of course, on weekends. After the clearing phase, he would re-dig the outline. Then, if the nursery would bring in topsoil, he was pretty sure he could borrow a tiller from Arlo. With that, he would work a mixture of compost and peat moss into the soil. Finally, he could put in the plants and cover the remaining soil. It would be a step-by-step process. I liked the idea, as it meant the garden could be done sooner rather than later. Dylan was motivated, and this would be an excellent project for us to work on together.

As for the actual garden, I needed to figure out what plants to put into the space once it was cleared. I conveyed to Dylan what some of the possibilities were: small bushes and shrubs, maybe one specimen tree that would stay relatively small. After my experience with false dwarves growing into giants, I was intent on keeping the scale to the miniature side. I also wanted the garden itself to be min-imalist, like a Japanese garden. As we walked along the rough, lumpy bed, now looking more like an Arizona desert with a few crater-sized holes in it, we both tried to imagine what would achieve this effect. Also important was a touch of color; I wanted roses. Without the per-simmon trees, there would be much more sun on the west, and roses love sun. Dylan, who has a much better spatial sense than I, immedi-ately liked the idea of planting some around the curved walkway to replace the tall, plumed grass clumps that had gotten out of control. Perfect. Then, we both liked the idea of placing an ornamental tree right in the center of the garden, which corresponded to the space between the front windows. We agreed the tree should have a horizontal growth pattern to fill the space gracefully.

In the afternoon, we went to the nursery to get some mulch, see about topsoil, and look at plants. As we strolled among the greenery, we found what we were looking for: Japanese maples, blue pacifica junipers, some other low-growing evergreen types. When a sales assistant approached us, we took turns asking questions about the plants: how tall would they get, how wide, what kind of environment did they like? We especially investigated the Japanese maples from all angles. Dylan and I agreed that one nice specimen would harmonize with the house and hold its own near the giant hemlock. We found a small tree with an interesting shape we liked. The nurseryman assured me it would not get too tall, and that in any case, it would be slow-growing. "We'll take it," I said. The assistant put a tag around the slim trunk.

Back at the work site, Dylan said he was sure there was still one big root down there somewhere that was holding in the ironwood stump. It was living up to its name, that's for sure. Digging once more all around it, only more deeply, he eventually found the stump's anchor. "Look at this," he called out. The root was twice as large as the others he had already severed with the mattock, the ones that were lying in pieces in the wheelbarrow. The stump wasn't going anywhere as long as that one powerful root, as big as the tree trunk itself, held it in place from below. Once it was finally cut through, the whole stump rocked loose and could be removed in chunks, like the others. Next the hole had to be filled in again with all the dirt that had been pushed aside. One last item for the workday: Dylan used an electric trimmer we found in the toolshed to cut the remaining tall grasses between the hemlock and the stone path. He placed the golden clippings over the rest of the bare earth, along with the other grass remains. To me, it looked like an Indian ritual, maybe an offering.

"It's just a good way to aerate the soil," he told me. "Plus, the nutrients from the plants go back in." I always marveled at how much horticultural knowledge my son possessed. But maybe that shouldn't be such a surprise, since he grew up among gardeners.

On another day, after Dylan had been working hard on the project, I remarked to him, "You know, you see yourself as so different from your dad, but you do have certain things in common. You both have an artistic sense; you like physical work outdoors; you enjoy working with plants, and you're a perfectionist."

"I know," Dylan replied. "That's what scares me. Me, being like Dad."

"What's scary about it?"

"Dad's too sensitive. He's all about touchy-feely. He could use his design ability to make money and be successful—but he doesn't. He doesn't want to push himself; he holds back. He makes excuses."

"Well, I think your dad's living just the way he wants to," I countered. "He always told me he wasn't willing to give up all his time and energy to be 'successful' by someone else's standards. It was a choice."

"Yeah, well, it's not my choice," Dylan said.

For Dylan, the garden project was a stepping stone to his foremost objective, and I knew he would be in no way distracted from the plan to get his license back and somehow obtain a vehicle. For him, doing that meant he would be on the Road to Success. So even before the idea came up of him working on the garden, even before he was released from his seven-day sanction at jail, I felt I had to visit Darlene Winchester at her office to ask a few more questions. Mostly I wanted her advice— post-relapse, post-sanction, that is. I knew her main concern was for her clients, but as parent and chief financial backer, I needed more input. When I arrived, she was busy moving aside piles of folders, probably Drug Court case files. Seeing me at the door, she put aside her paperwork and directed me to my now-familiar seat by the lamp-lit desk.

"Thanks for agreeing to see me on such short notice," I said. "So, now what?" I asked, looking her in the eye. "When we were both here a short while ago, Dylan was talking about a plan to get a car. Now, after the relapse, and with him taking the sanction in jail, do you still think this is a good idea?"

She put her fingers together, looked thoughtful.

"Well, has he told you about what happened?"

"Yes, at least some of it. He told me some bad things were going on when I took him to an AA meeting, then he talked more afterward about a second relapse. With Jeremy."

"So do you feel he's been honest with you?"

I hesitated.

"Well, yes . . . eventually. I know he was holding back at first, maybe because he didn't want to lose my support for getting a car. But he told me what happened the second time right away. He said he was trying to call you about it, too."

"Yes, I remember." She folded her arms on the desk. "OK, here's how I see it, " she said, leaning forward, with me hanging on every word. "If he hadn't told you anything, if he hadn't been honest with you, then I'd say no help with the car. But if you think he's been open about it, then I'd say to go ahead."

She paused, and I exhaled slowly. She went on, "Me, I'm always looking for teachable moments for my clients, and I think this has been one for Dylan."

To elaborate, Darlene stressed how important it was for people in Drug Court, if they were serious about getting free of their addiction, that any relapse occur—if it was going to happen—within the structure of the program. That way, they could be guided through their feelings before, during, and after the relapse. They could analyze how it happened: What were the factors at play? How could this be prevented another time? How do they feel about being high? About being sober?

She summed it up by saying, "We want the person to be pushed by the relapse incident to find out: what is going on with you to make this happen?"

As before, I felt reassured by her words. For me, there would be no risk-free decision, but with eyes open, I could make a choice. I nodded, thanked her, and we shook hands before I left her office.

In fact, as the weeks went by, I noticed this post-relapse self-interrogation by Dylan was occurring. Though not an official member of the Drug Court group, I sometimes had a front-row seat on the sidelines. To me, it all felt like part of that road trip my son and I were on. I say this because our talks would frequently occur while the two of us were seated side by side in my car. After I'd taken him somewhere, before I dropped him off, he'd slowly unearth his thoughts with me. Some of what Dylan revealed from the past frankly horrified me. I realized how little I really knew about what had been going on behind the scenes. Once, when I took him back to his apartment, he told me more about how his connection to Jeremy recalled aspects of his risk-taking life back in Cincinnati. Jeremy was somehow tied in with an old buddy back there, Nick. As often happened with my son, the story would start with a fragment. Then, after a pause, his words came in a steady stream, a torrent, a rush of memory and emotion.

"It took a long time to admit that I'm an addict. At first, I was in denial. I also denied what I was feeling during my time in Cincinnati. Especially that year when I dropped out of school to work on my own. I had plenty of things going then. I used to think that was my high point in life, at least, so far. I had a lot of money sometimes—that is, when I wasn't scrounging for my next dime. I'd be sure then that Caitlin knew I had a lot of money. We'd go out to the clubs; we'd have the best new clothes, and we'd order Grey

Goose. We'd drop hundreds of dollars a night. I thought that was the high life. Baby, I've arrived! But then—and somehow I hid this from myself for a long time—I started to realize that was bullshit. Those 'golden times' really lasted only a few hours. The whole rest of the time was hell: the fear when me and my roommate Gabe made the pick-ups, the shame, the shady characters, the constant anxiety. We really only had a few moments of glory. The rest of the time we were miserable. Take Nick, for example."

"Nick? Wait, was he the high-rolling club guy you used to talk about sometimes, especially that first summer?"

"Yeah, Nick was a guy who seemed to be a real player at the clubs—and later on, we had the most amazing conversations on all kinds of topics. Only I found out he kept most of his stuff—his clothes, his shoes—in a trash bag! I mean, he was ready to run at any moment. He totally depended on his girlfriend for a place to live—otherwise, the guy would've been homeless! He didn't have a regular job; his life was mainly on the street. But what's strange is that up until recently, I would often think back on the 'glory days' of my life in Cincinnati. I called them that way because it was a time when I felt important, powerful, like I was in control. That's what I told myself then. But I wasn't. I was just in deep denial."

He shook his head and stayed silent for a while.

"I didn't get arrested in Cincinnati for what I had done. They had shootings and armed robberies to deal with. The police weren't worried about pot being sold, or even cocaine, unless it was obvious. We were below the radar. But, eventually, it did all come down on me: Life, God, the Universe—whatever spiritual force you want to call it—punished me. Everything crashed down. I couldn't continue what I was doing. I had to leave all that behind. I've had to slowly try to build myself up since then."

In listening to this, it felt like I was sitting next to a total stranger. It's not as if I'd held onto the blind belief that my son was some kind of saint, but I didn't exactly see him as a criminal, either. I mean, he had charges, but I thought of him as someone who was just irresponsible, thoughtless—frustrated, too. Someone who'd temporarily lost his way. But now the stories he told me gave me a different slant on it, as if my son had felt like a desperate ghetto kid who'd chosen to go underground because he didn't think he could ever do things the right way, the usual way, the way other people with more means did them. That's the part of his identity that I never really understood because it seemed so alien to me. I remember how he used to tell me (whenever I launched into one of my indignant mom sermons), "You don't know. You're not like me. Only God can judge me." That last one was a quote straight from Tupac. It's taken me a while to revise my thoughts.

"They say that if you tell someone, you're more likely to leave that life behind," Dylan continued. "I know now that I could slip back into that life. It started to happen just last month with Jeremy. You know, I liked him. We got along. His dad owned a local business, a movie and game rental shop with a tanning salon. He'd traveled to places like Aspen, Colorado with his family—places I knew about, so we had things in common; we could talk. He was in Drug Court, too, and for a while, he was doing fine. Since I didn't have a car, he ended up being my main ride. He was a poker player, used to make hundreds or a thousand a game playing poker. He used all his smarts, and he would read people, so he knew the ones he could beat and take their money. But he had his hard-luck story too. He'd been a hard user of drugs. It all started when his grandma got cancer and was prescribed strong pain control medicines, like OxyContin. These opioids were around the house, and Jeremy tried them. When he got addicted, he had to spend a lot of money to support his habit. He even started stealing from his own share of the family business, robbing himself to pay off the drug dealers."

I wondered later how his family found out, if they'd had to turn in their own addicted son for theft or if he got arrested somewhere. Probably the latter.

"When Jeremy got into Drug Court, he stayed clean for weeks. But then, he was feeling down, like he wanted to get high again. I was at a real low point; I did, too. Once, when he started drinking and reaching for his pills, I told him, 'Come clean, tell them you're having a relapse, so you can get help and stay in.' But Jeremy, he somehow thought that he couldn't mess up at all. He didn't understand how it worked in the program, how he could slip but still get back in. Or maybe he just didn't care after a while, after the addiction became too powerful. He just went into total free fall. Can you believe that?"

I shook my head, and there was silence.

An image came into my mind. I saw a young man climbing up a sheer rock face. Somebody was inching up a granite wall like Half Dome at Yosemite, and he may or may not have any ropes on him. He may just be using his hands and feet—and every muscle in his body—to go upward, one handhold, one foothold at a time.

"Well, then what happened to him?" I asked.

"Oh, he's way out of Drug Court now. When I had to do my sanction time in jail, I heard Jeremy was locked up in there somewhere, in another cell—only for longer. I never saw him after that incident."

I had a sense of the young rock climber falling off the cliff. How would he be able to crawl back up again? If he didn't change, he could die young. Or maybe he'd live for years and keep doing the same painful things over and over, go through the same addiction cycles. What would help him?

Dylan's revelations were painful to hear, but—following Darlene Winchester's statements—I knew it all had to come out. Like they say, you have to bring what's hidden out into the clear light of day if you want to heal. Maybe it was like those tree stump roots; they had to come out, too, in order to free up space for a new plant. Otherwise, they would just keep sending up more shoots to interfere. My hope now was this: if Dylan could learn to observe himself more closely, if he could understand his own motivations, then maybe he could catch himself faster from falling into destructive behaviors. Eventually, maybe he'd be less likely to put himself into a precarious situation in the first place. He'd be less drawn to take a detour.

You know, in movies, there's always one dramatic moment when everything changes for the protagonist. From that one moment, the character either rises to the heights or falls into the depths. But in real life, there can be many incremental moments, and you don't always realize which way they're going at the time. The path isn't clear ahead. For a recovering addict, just getting through a day without resorting to drugs is a triumph, while giving in to the urge to use again can lead to disaster. And who knows what the factors are that allow someone to know the difference, to care about it, to seize the possible right hold on the rock face in that moment and take it?

As for what Darlene Winchester said, it seems to me there would always have to be way more than just one teachable moment for a person. To me, the way we each learn different lessons about life, about ourselves—even side by side within the same family—this seems to be one of the greatest mysteries of all time.

Not long after this, Dylan told me about a talk he'd had with Darlene after he got out of jail in early August.

"When I was a teenager, because I didn't feel that I fit in, I started hanging out with the troublemakers."

"So what were your best times, the times when you felt you belonged?" Darlene asked him.

"Not when I was doing what I was doing in Cincinnati. I remember times when I was young and in school; maybe a teacher would come over and talk to me so I would feel special, or it could have been when I was with a church group doing fun things, or maybe taking trips with Dad. It wasn't so much being with Dad, but with his friends, like up in Maine or in Arizona or someplace like that. We would have such good times! Those times made me realize how good life could be."

In the remaining weeks of August and September, in between classes, rains, meetings, and responsibilities, the garden took shape. Dylan and I collaborated on what needed to be delivered when. We made a couple more visits to the nursery to select plants, soil, and mulch. By late September, I could see a small Japanese maple with star-shaped red leaves standing atop a gently sloping mound. It stood amid patches of low pacifica junipers that would one day fill the space to look like a blue-green sea. The tall, wide hemlock looked more nestled in, more at peace, less besieged by grasses. The whole garden was neatly defined, with a curving line and narrow trench along its borders. A thick carpet of fragrant cedar bark chips covered the soil, preventing weeds and retaining moisture. The summer heat was gone now, and the root systems of the new plants could grow for at least two more months before winter. Along the curved walkway to the right, Dylan planted four small drift roses that would eventually expand to twice their current size, each of them filled with miniature red blooms. The next May, these would make a fine contrast to the surrounding evergreens, a celebration to behold each day. And to the left of the walkway, I could maintain a small herb garden for the kitchen, starting next spring: rosemary, basil, sage, even a few strawberry plants with their decorative, sea-shell leaves.

And who would have believed what this whole area looked like a few short months earlier? Of course, I told Dylan how wonderful it all was. About that, we were in complete agreement. Even John was amazed when he saw the transformation. After this, I vowed to be a better gardener. Every week of the next growing season, I would scan the area for suspect intruders and pluck them out when they were tiny. Eventually, the new plants would spread and grow vigorously enough to discourage implantations from outside. However, even then I'd have to be vigilant. An unintentional forest could happen again if I didn't watch out. And I did not ever want to resort to a chainsaw or herbicide again—at least not for another ten years.

The Queen knew all along that the sturdy woodsman was really her son, the Prince. So that when she saw how steadfast he was in clearing the woods and cutting back the vines, she was proud. And when she witnessed the beautiful garden being created in place of the wilderness, her satisfaction was all the greater, knowing this was the handiwork of her own son, and there was harmony between them. What she really wanted for both of them was greater understanding, mutual respect, and affection.

Every day the Queen walked outside, she marveled, especially when she saw the roses. She vowed to protect the garden for as long as she lived there. Never again would she allow the wild forest to come so close to the castle.

CHAPTER 25: FIREFLIES AND STARS

When my son was very young, maybe five, he went through a phase in the springtime in which, just before we all went to school or work, on his way to the car he would suddenly run around in the yard or in the open field next door and pick dandelions. He would run up to me and give me his bouquet. I'd tell him how beautiful they were. Then he'd laugh, get in the car, and we would all be on our way.

Like boys everywhere, Dylan loved catching all kinds of wild creatures: tadpoles, frogs, toads, large insects, crawfish. But in the summer, a favorite pastime was capturing fireflies. Once he drew me into the house shortly before nightfall. He stopped me right inside the screen door of our porch. "We can't turn on the lights yet," he said. "OK, now close your eyes," he said. "You can't peek." I kept them shut, but I was getting nervous. It was hard enough to keep up with this child even with my eyes wide open. Who knows what he had in his pocket or up his sleeve this time? "OK, now you can open them," he commanded. When I did, at first I didn't see anything. It was pretty dark, after all. Then I started to see a small glow of light nearby, then another near my son's head. Dylan said, "Look up there," and I looked up to see another glow of light, then another and another right near the high rafters of our living room. They were fireflies, and he'd just released them from a jar he'd concealed to carry them in. We laughed to see them; they were joyous and magical. He knew I loved the tiny, flying light bulbs that flashed at night among the trees in the early days of summer. The area around our house in the woods was a flickering light show most early summer evenings.

This reminds me of a story I once heard. It was about a mom in Ireland who had just moved with her children from Dublin to a remote place in the southwestern county of Kerry. One evening, she sent her young son out to get some twigs for the fireplace because it was fall and getting colder. Soon, he came back running to tell her, "Mom, Mom, quick, quick, quick, come out here!" And she went out, expecting a catastrophe. And when they went out into the pitch-black night, he shouted "Mom, Mom, look! Look at the stars!" He knew his mom loved the stars; she was an amateur astronomer who knew the names of constellations. And when she looked up, she was amazed: so many rivers and currents and swirls of stars against the inky darkness. She couldn't even find the familiar constellations she knew so well. She had never seen a night sky like that one before.

That mother's name is Julie Ormonde. As her children grew up, she started a campaign to get formal recognition of Kerry, Ireland, as a "Dark Sky Reserve." Of course, part of what makes the Dingle Peninsula such a good candidate is its proximity to the vast expanse of the north Atlantic. But another part of Kerry's qualification comes as an unexpected legacy of poverty: the Irish farm families of the region subsisting on potatoes, the potato blights of the nineteenth century, then the terrible famines, the flight away across the sea, the land abandoned. This previously forlorn space has become, in our own century, a magnificent portal for visiting astronomers to observe the outer worlds.

I love this story, and I'd like to think of my own son as my dark-sky child. That's because he's pointed out the stars to me in the same way, all the mysterious wonder of stars and fireflies that we forget to notice as we become adults and so full of cares. And it's also because I sometimes need to remember to look up and see all the light in my son, too, even those times when the dark seems deepest.

CHAPTER 26: WHEELS

With everything going on, Dylan still hadn't forgotten about his plan to get his license back and obtain a vehicle. He needed wheels to get around, and so he was ready to jump through any hoops necessary. He was just finishing his series of DUI classes, some of which had included terrifyingly graphic film clips of fatal collisions for the students to consider. Even Dylan was taken aback.

"Our instructor told us it's frequently the people who think they can drink the most and be the least affected by it who end up being the ones *most* impaired. They don't even notice that their reactions are off the mark; often the alcohol just gives them more confidence and they drive faster," Dylan remarked. "They did interviews of drunk drivers who survived after a crash, and that's what they said."

Listening to Dylan, I hoped fervently it was all sinking in. Completing the course over the summer, after a year of not driving and not drinking, meant that soon he could apply through the courts to get his license back. He said he was ready.

Meanwhile, I'd agreed to take him around to investigate vehicles to see what was available. He'd already spotted a car right here in town. It was a trade-in, a 2006 Infiniti G35 with sixty thousand miles on it for $13,500. He wanted to go see it with me; I could test drive it for him.

"Wait a minute," I said. "We have to check into financing first. We need to go to the bank before we look at cars." Time to put up a speed bump. "How about we make an appointment with the loan officer for next Tuesday afternoon?" We set the date.

"Hey, we can still look at the Infiniti today," Dylan said, never slow to jump on an opportunity at hand. "We've got time, and this is a real deal."

It was a bright sunny Saturday, perfect for admiring interesting cars, so why not? When we got to the lot, the amazing car in question had already been sold, but the dealer happened to have another Infiniti G35 sitting on the corner. That one was a beauty, but it cost about $15,500 and had 104,000 miles on it. Still, it was a car in gorgeous condition: flawless exterior, elegant interior with leather seats, adjustable amenities. On the test drive, it handled beautifully, almost like the BMW I'd tried out a couple of summers ago—just on a lark, with Dylan. Back on that other Saturday, he was trying to convince me that I should get a more upscale vehicle as befit my station in life, maybe a Beamer or at least a hip Mini Cooper. I agreed to test drive some models for fun, though in the end, I kept my modest hatchback.

"Yep, this G35 is a driver's car, like a BMW but more affordable," Dylan confirmed. "And you can get a really good deal if you buy a nice used one. Usually people who have these are car lovers and they take good care of them."

So persuasive. Maybe he could be a car salesman someday?

"You could get a simpler, more affordable car for now, then trade up for something better later on when you get a regular job," I countered.

Without a pause, he replied, "Oh, I am going to do that; but I want the nicest car I can get for now, at a good price. I mean if I'm going to be making payments for several years on a car, I want it to be something I really like."

He made it clear he wasn't limiting himself to Infinitis but wanted a car with features: maybe leather seats, for example, because when he worked out, those would be much more comfortable and easier to clean. Before I could reply, the dealer returned to ask us how it went. Dylan asked for the Carfax sheet, and we saw this car scored a 91.

"This is good, but let's keep looking around," I said. "Remember, there'll be more to see in Parksville." In retrospect, I likely would have saved much time and energy had we checked out the G35 further and, if it passed muster, purchased it on the spot. Ah, but then, the teacher part of me realizes we would have missed the bigger "learning experience."

By the time we went to People's First Credit Union on Tuesday, Dylan had already found another vehicle online that interested him, a 2008 Honda Accord XL. This was his concession to practicality. He'd texted me to take a look at it, sending me the link. He knew that one would probably sell quickly, but the dealer there in Memphis had other comparable cars. *Memphis?!*

"When I get my license, I can see us going there. I could test drive some cars, pick one, have a mechanic check it out," he said optimistically.

I wasn't too keen on going that far away; we'd find something closer, I was sure of it. But at least he could use the Accord XL as an example to show the loan officer. Dylan laid out the case he was making. Ms. Clark showed Dylan how she checked out his credit score. Eyeing the figures, she stated that he wouldn't qualify for a loan without a steady, substantial paycheck, which, as a part-time worker and student, he didn't have. A loan would only be possible if yours truly co-signed. In Mom we trust. Not to mention, if they used my credit rating, not his, then the loan would have the most affordable interest rate. People's First wasn't about to take too many risks; this was the newly sensible attitude after the subprime mortgage crash of 2008. Dylan was getting a lesson in credit, and so was I. No way around it: if Dylan didn't keep up the payments, I would be the poor schlub holding the bag.

Dylan sounded confident through all this, even as I was second-guessing. After our talk with Ms. Clark, Dylan felt he could easily do a payment of $50 a week, even with just the part-time work Arlo had passed along to him over the last year. He looked up what his insurance payments would be: hefty, given his age, gender, and driving record. Ah yes, his driving record. Ms. Clark had been adamant he would need full coverage for the loan to go through. It was clear Dylan and I had two completely different attitudes toward acceptable risk—and toward money. Just by sitting there at the bank with my son and the loan officer, imagining my pen poised over the multiple documents yet to sign, I was already way over my risk threshold. In my mind's eye, I caught sight of John, Mike, and Linda all riding by together in a long, ancient Oldsmobile, the kind with chrome and fins. They rolled down the windows and waved to me. "Good luck!" they shouted. Then the pack of them drove off in a haze of exhaust.

When I asked him later, Dylan talked about how the different guys in Drug Court were handling the transportation situation. Some were making car payments and building credit; others went the way of getting an old beater.

"Will, he's the king of the beaters; he just keeps an old car, throws everything on the floor, doesn't want the extra expense of a nicer vehicle," Dylan told me. "Now, his buddy, Tyler, he's a ladies' man, so of course, he's going to have an attractive car." I should have inserted, "Oh, and how does he pay for his car?" In fact, the two of us had several conversations about money, and there were two main attitudes presented. You could either save and then spend frugally like his dad, who—amazingly—always had money in his account. Or you could learn to use credit and play it skillfully to move up, a strategy Dylan loved to expound on. "Yeah, be a part of the modern world," he remarked. Only that was riskier, and you still had to stay within your means. I wasn't sure Dylan fully understood the part about risk. For him, there was no contest whatsoever between the two options: saving money to buy later or buying on credit now.

So I was thinking "good buy for less," and he was thinking "best bang for the buck." Was buying a vehicle about practical transportation or was it about lifestyle, savvy, self-image? During the used-car search, I couldn't help but notice that we moved from an Infiniti to a Honda Accord XL to, eventually, some kind of truck. Especially after Dylan's sanction time in jail, he came around to the idea that a truck would be much more useful. He cited his time with his former housemate.

"The problem with Connor," he told me, "is that even though he had a truck, he wasn't enterprising enough, didn't feel comfortable with tools. I'd get jobs on Craigslist, but then Connor would back out on me. Me, I grew up with my dad's tools. I saw him using them all the time. So now, if I had a truck, I'm pretty confident I could get a wider variety of side jobs."

Before classes started, we had to go to Parksville anyway to pick up Dylan's computer, in for repairs. We could just swing by some dealers to look at what they had. I suggested a Ford pick-up, like a Ranger. One of my students drove one, and I thought it would be low-maintenance perfect.

"No, that's too small," Dylan said. Besides, we didn't see any used Rangers. Their owners were probably busy driving them into the sunset until they fell apart. Instead we looked at an old Chevy Silverado, the only used truck on the lot within our budget. Appearing upbeat, Dylan asked questions, checked under the hood. We took it for a test drive. As a passenger, he wasn't impressed.

"This truck is OK size-wise, but it's got too many miles on

it. Not only that but the gas mileage is really low—fifteen miles per gallon; it'll need gas constantly. It won't have good resale value either. I want a better deal than that."

Wait a minute, good resale value?

Dylan had a lot of requirements for this proposed vehicle. It not only had to be a mode of transport, but it had to perform. It had to be fuel efficient; it had to have resale value. It not only had to get you to a job, but also generate jobs through its sheer capabilities. Little did I know then that the truck would have to do even more than that.

After visiting a couple of dealers, we took a break and went to lunch. Despite the fact that I was clearly playing the role of fall guy, I enjoyed these relaxed times talking with Dylan. Our conversations were all part of the road trip we were on that summer, part of our adventure. In between bites of his sandwich, Dylan kept me apprised of truck stats from his smartphone: gas mileage, horsepower, Blue Book values over time. Then, eyeing me munching my Greek salad, he took it upon himself to give me dietary advice. He warned me I might not be getting enough testosterone eating so many vegetables; even women needed to attain the right levels to keep up their vitality.

"Look, if you only eat plants, you probably need to supplement your diet with zinc. You can get that from pumpkin seeds or pecans to keep your hormones balanced."

"Hum, well maybe I'll put some pumpkin seeds on my next shopping list," I conceded. Before long, he turned to the topic of his workouts.

"I can now bench press just under what LeBron James did: 250 pounds, ten reps."

I'm sure he could tell my eyes were glazing over—after they rolled.

"If I keep this up, I can try out for professional football."

Now, he knew he was going to get a rise out of me. "What? And be a physical wreck at age forty? You have to learn to use your brain to make a living!"

He laughed at my elder common sense.

"Mom, you need to live a little on the wild side." We both laughed at that one.

"Well, if I lived as wild as you, we'd both be living in boxes under a bridge."

How did my son come to be such a high roller? It can't be his parents' influence. His dad is a confirmed tightwad who fully subscribes to his own father's 1930s depression attitude toward money: you had to hold on to whatever you had because it was damn hard to come by. As for me, I wasn't exactly a skinflint, but I had learned the value of not spending down to the last dollar. Grad school poverty taught me to keep back a stash for rainy days. There was always that next unexpected expense to be ready for. As for a car, I didn't get one until I had a real job with a real paycheck—and even then, it was a hand-me-down from the family. That was fine with me.

Then, too, Mike and Linda lived in a modest 1950s-style house with simple furniture from the same era. They mostly cooked at home and tended to curate their clothing by brand from thrift shops, all of it stored in a couple of small closets and two chests of drawers. They each drove cars that were at least twelve years old and counting. They traveled every year, but it was always for work, always a tax-deductible expense. And then there was John, Dylan's other parental role model. He'd driven an old, red Beetle for years, stuffed to the roof with sports gear until he decided to get something larger but just as stingy with the fuel. His house was nice but old and rambling, full of heirlooms from long-lost relatives. As for clothes, he still wore tee shirts and sweaters he kept from twenty years ago. So the fact is that none of us could be held up as role models for Dylan's extravagance.

How did my son, surrounded by all these models of money management, become a high-rolling spendthrift? Well, it could be

the influence of Grandpa—my dad, not Mike's. My dad worked hard
to get out of poverty, but once he had money, he found plenty of ways
to spend it: travel, new furniture, nice things. Luckily, credit was
tight back then, and my mom kept control in the bankroll department. "We have to pay off the mortgage first, before you retire," she
would say. Fortunately, he listened to her, but I bet my dad's the
culprit. He must have passed a few spendthrift proclivities to his
grandson on the sly. Ah, but then there were the cousins on Mike's
side, especially Harris and his wife Chloe; they were high-earning
professionals, and they could be big spenders, too. At family dinners,
Harris always loved to talk about his latest investment coup.

It was part of Dylan's personality to want to identify more
with that free-spending side of the family than with his parents,
as if he'd grown up with this unspoken but firmly entrenched attitude: "Look guys, as seedy and tweedy as you all are, I'm going to
be different. I'm going to be greedy. I'm going to be a millionaire!"
Dylan always wanted the best he could get. As a little kid, he was
always ready to trade up for a better bike. When he was into BMX,
he roamed the aisles of the bike shop often. If anything went wrong,
he'd take his bike in for repairs, then see if he could get me to spring
for a better bike part: wheel hubs, brakes, tires, whatever caught his
eye. Once, he had to get just the right blue and yellow banana seat
for his low-riding BMX. He had to save toward getting it, too. And
then one day he left his bike parked and locked at the schoolyard,
planning to get it later, only to find that the prized seat had been
stolen right off the post. He cried for the longest time. Later on,
after his own actions caused him to lose the Camry in Cincinnati,
he consoled himself by getting a special Kona dirt-jumping bike, one
with built-in springs that could propel amazing jumps over the hilly
course he constructed in Mike and Linda's back yard.

As for managing money, Dylan had the best intentions to be
smart about it, build credit, act like an investor. But truth to tell, he

was too much in the moment, acted too much on impulse—more like my dad, but further on the spending spectrum. The eternal question for the family: how much of this spendthrifting is due to his bipolar disorder? We may not have been asking that quite yet. But according to just about every book on the subject, bipolar and big spending go together like golden retrievers and flying Frisbees. When mania or hypomania kicks in, a person will spend down to their last cent and quickly max out any credit or debit cards in their possession, all through sheer exuberance. Standard advice to those in the know is this: when you see your retriever giving chase, CLOSE all accounts and HIDE any cards immediately until further notice! But stubborn me, at this point I was still convinced my careful coaching could surely lead Dylan to take the long view.

All that being said, I did set boundaries. Earlier, the four of us parents and step-parents had been on the same page: it was wiser not to help Dylan get another car until he graduated from college. Now, however, I had moved into a different position because I was closer to the action, closer to how things were developing day by day. But if it was easier for me to skirt around Mike and Linda's advice, it was less so with John's. He was my reality checker.

So here was my strategy: I would contribute half of the down payment if Dylan saved up his half. He already had a big chunk from the proceeds of his bricklaying job and the garden work. Next, Dylan would take out a loan for the remaining $11,000 over six years for $200/month. If he could finish Drug Court and graduate, that should be possible. I would have to co-sign, but he would be the one to pay. Essentially, he would take a cut in his allowance. It meant he would get $50 less per week, but it also meant that I wasn't paying more. He would still have enough for food but not enough for gas; he'd have to work for that. He'd also have to set money aside for the auto insurance—he knew how much that would be. That deal, if I was going to help him finance a vehicle, seemed to be the best one I could swing. Overall, I took solace in the belief that I was following the playbook of then-current Federal Reserve Chairman, Ben Bernanke. I considered my monetary aid a "stimulus package," on the condition that my support would "taper off" once Dylan completed his degree and was able to earn his own living.

Through it all, it was imperative that Dylan continue to do well in college and in Drug Court. If he failed to fulfill his duties or he had any serious driving infractions, the deal would be off. Then I'd re-possess the vehicle and sell it. The stakes had to be high to get Dylan's attention—that much I knew.

We all have our accounting systems, and they encompass way more than money. Even though Dylan saw himself as being majorly disadvantaged in one key way—having Bipolar II, which gave him an endless array of problems to solve—in other ways, he was privileged. He was able to attend college and work toward his degree while being supported with an allowance, which wasn't exactly the case for most students. He was also fortunate to have received the option of a court-ordered diversion, unlike many facing felony charges who get incarcerated for years. We talked about this, but I'm not convinced he could fully appreciate his good fortune yet. Maybe because his internal issues seemed to override these advantages. Or maybe he did realize it but was always comparing what he had with what he thought he deserved—that old entitlement grudge.

I let Dylan do all the research for a vehicle, but he had to stay within the parameters of what we'd discussed. I don't know how skilled his research was for his college classes, but when it came to this particular project, his investigational acumen was phenomenal. He was motivated. He used Carfax, sites like carsdirect.com, and the Blue Book to find what he deemed "a good deal." Finally, he located a 2010 Dodge Ram at a dealership in Atlanta, selling for $17,000. Despite being still fairly new, it already had 90,000 miles on it. Even so, it was under the mileage limit set for the loan, though Ms. Clark at People's First did fuss over it. "The price should be lower," she said. Undaunted, Dylan was able to produce the vehicle's estimated resale value from the Blue Book. Besides, everyone knew that Dodge Rams held their value well over time. Even the testy loan officer had to agree with that.

Then there was the issue of how to make sure the vehicle would live up to the dealer's claims. Dylan located an online service that could check it out; they would e-mail comments and even photos to clients after an examination and test drive—for a fee, of course. It cost, but not as much as going to Atlanta and back. The report, when it arrived, was promising. Eventually, contracts were duly signed and money transferred. Where we found the energy to do all this while fall classes were already in full swing, I can't say. It must have been the adrenaline.

Finally, the big day arrived. We'd arranged for the truck to be delivered from Atlanta to my house. On the designated morning, a text message came in, then two phone calls, one from the driver, the other from Dylan. The truck was on its way and would be in town at about 9:15. Before long, a huge trailer with a bright red truck mounted on top rolled past my front windows. The driver had missed my house and sailed right on past! After an orienting phone call, he rolled back, and going out to the street, I found myself gazing at a spectacular muscle truck in all its glory. I waved and called out to a neighbor, obviously bewildered as the trailer had backed into his driveway in order to turn around. Seconds after the driver parked in front of my house, Dylan arrived on his bike. The rest of the sequence passed as if in a dream. Of course, we'd seen plenty of pictures, read all the specs and details online, but to actually see the object of desire in the morning light was beyond imagining.

The driver and his assistant got out and greeted us. Then the driver climbed into the Ram to start the engine. A smooth rumble began, and he slowly, slowly backed the truck down the ramp. Next, he had us check the truck over and sign the delivery papers. The driver mentioned that while crossing one of the narrow bridges in the area, the side mirror on the driver's side of his rig had suffered a nick by another passing vehicle. He shook his head—another one for the insurance company. But it looked like the Dodge Ram was fine. I hugged Dylan.

"This is a big moment," I told him.

"Yeah, I know."

"If you hadn't worked hard and saved your money, it wouldn't have happened." I'd actually told him this several times over the last two months. "Just remember, it's important that you stay on your path," I continued. He nodded. For a few moments, we both stood there, transfixed.

Then, as the rig drove off to another job, Dylan started up the truck and went to do his errands. He drove slowly down the street, and I knew he was excited; he hadn't driven a vehicle for a long while. Later that same day, he told me the truck was exactly what he thought it would be—even better. It drove like new and handled smoothly. He'd put in $25 worth of gas and the gauge had gone way up; he felt it was going to be conservative with fuel. Someone at the evening AA meeting had told him a truck like that could go beyond 200,000 miles with no problem; his own was up to 177,000. So far, Dylan didn't seem to be puffing up too much. He was just another muscle guy with a muscle truck, and that was fine.

Dylan said he worked for Arlo on Wednesday afternoon after classes and earned $100. He needed part of that to pay off a debt for the DUI classes. And now he would need to save for fuel. That would keep him busy.

For days and weeks after the arrival of the Dodge Ram, a strange phenomenon occurred. I started seeing huge, red trucks everywhere. They cropped up on every street corner, in every parking lot. They were at the bank, on campus, at the supermarket; in town and out of town, rolling on every highway, moving in all directions. Not only that, but my neighbor across the street magically acquired a huge, red truck too, parked in plain view right on his driveway. The case was contagious—or maybe a conspiracy.

There was another phenomenon ushered in by the truck. I got wind of this one Sunday afternoon a couple of weeks later. Dylan wanted to meet up with me at home so that I could reimburse him for the bags of pine bark mulch and a soaker hose he'd bought for the garden taking shape in my front yard. He'd bring the receipts to show. Glancing out the door when the truck rolled up, I noticed a young woman was with him up in the cab. There seemed to be some brief discussion before Dylan got out, receipts in hand. Not used to seeing him with any women now for a year, though often hearing about them as classmates on projects, I asked him about the dark-haired girl.

"Oh, she's helping me with a project. Well, gotta go now. Have a lot to do. See ya later!"

I wondered if I'd see her again. Better hope she was calmer than the last one! I knew about his volatile relationship with Caitlin, whom he'd met the first day of his freshman year. Though charming, she turned out to be possessive, with a red-hot temper. Once she threw a wooden rolling pin at his bedroom window on a drive-by and broke a pane of glass. And who knows how many arguments and changed phone numbers occurred over many months?

"Well, you know," I told him one day, "with women, it's like looking for the right car. Just like in the Smokey Robinson and the Miracles song, "Shop Around." That's what *his* mom told *him*, and it still stands true in my book."

"Well, I've met plenty of girls," he told me. "It happens that one will say to me, 'I'm attracted to you, but I don't think I could put up with you.'"

"Oh, yeah? That's happened often?"

"Many times, many times," he answered, shaking his head. But not, I think, in total despair.

I've reflected since then that the proposed vehicle of that summer had slowly and inevitably morphed from being a mode of transport to being a mirror reflection of Dylan himself. The 2010 Dodge Ram was a rough and ready truck. Bold, powerful, it could take on heavy loads and still move fast, still rumble. It may have been high-maintenance, but it was high-performance, too. That was exactly how Dylan wanted to see himself, and the way he wanted to be seen in the world—as if he could be invincible. The Ram wasn't just a vehicle. It was a talisman, a totem, a techno spirit animal. It had a job to do: give him the strength to achieve his dreams.

Whatever else the truck may have represented, for both of us it marked a turning point. We were still in the middle of changes. There was still another year of Drug Court to go, and still at least another year of college before any degree could be conferred. Nothing was certain. But shortly after Dylan started up the Ram's engine, I began to realize that the unique road trip I'd been on with Dylan for about a year was officially over. He had his own wheels now. More than that, he was *at* the wheel; he was the driver. We still met up and talked, but it was clear that Dylan wanted to manage his own affairs. From now on, he would be more under his own recognizance, taking on more responsibilities.

Was he ready for this? Was I? I'm sure we both asked ourselves this question all through the truck acquisition process. But to him—to both of us—it became the inevitable next step. For the rest, we would just have to find out what would happen the way most everybody does, by trying it.

CHAPTER 27: WHEN

When do parents and adult children start to look at each other as separate persons, instead of as aspects of their own personalities, destinies, and desires? When can each one see that the other is truly another individual, that their qualities and faults are their own, not anything powerful enough to tie you up forever or hold you back from becoming the person you are meant to be?

It's true that the bond between parent and child can be long and complicated. For a while, at the beginning or at the end of your journeys, one will be the protector of the other. If both live long enough, these roles can change completely, will reverse. The once-child may become the strong caretaker, the decision maker for her parent. We know this could happen.

Yet in between these early and late care-takings, there can be an open field of possibility, a space for two unique persons to encounter each other. The bond strong but almost weightless.

My question is this: when will a parent and her adult child start to see each other as fellow travelers on the rocky, curvy road of life? A place where you get hurt, where there is so much to learn?

Does it ever really happen? And if so, how long does it take?

Will they both still be alive when it happens?

CHAPTER 28: MOM, WHERE ARE YOU?

Please, Mom, let's get together. My sixty-year-old self would like to speak to your sixty-year-old self. Yes, finally, I caught up to you. Listen, we could sit down and talk together just like we used to—only now it will be as friends exactly the same age. Let's agree to meet at your house, the one on Dogwood Court. I'll bring us some cake, and we can make coffee. I hope we can be together out on the patio.

We could talk about our marriages, our sons. Good God, how are those for topics? Bring Kleenexes—ha! I know you always had a ton of those stuffed in your jacket pockets for all occasions. We can compare notes. Be forewarned, though: I'll have lots of questions for you. You can tell me how you made it through the long days of uncertainty. How you managed to stay calm when you woke up suddenly in the night, then remembered the latest crisis looming up. Did you get up and walk outside? How did you get through those days?

I'll ask how you managed to be so brave—first, about things physical, like the operations you had. The emotional ordeals, too. You knew that there are times when you just have to force the issue, like when you foresaw a threat to your marriage. You staged a choice for your husband. One morning while he was at work, you packed your suitcase. Then you left a note for him on the table: "Meet me at the beach condo if you want us to stay together. I can't accept you slipping away from me like this. If you want to talk, you know where to find me." Who would believe that such an easy-going woman, with your ready smile, your cheerful laugh, could be so bold? So uncompromising in your emotional life? Mom, it felt good when you and Dad told me about all this. To say we had gotten beyond secrets.

Then there was your son, Mark. How did you find your way through all those painful times? What on earth steadied your nerve back then? Like when you saw the scotch in the bottle was going down faster than usual. Or when he was sick with delirium tremens, and he begged you for a drink and you said no. Instead, you put a cold cloth on his forehead and kept vigil. Yes, I know you prayed a lot—that much you told me before. Well, me too, Mom. Me, too.

Strange, the whole time I was growing up, we were both convinced I was so different from you. By the time I was twenty, even before, I was sure my life was going to take a completely different direction from yours. It did, in fact. So who would guess we would live through some of the very same challenges, you and I? Who would guess that I would come to regard you as my model for strength? Yes, I know, no one could have told me that when I was younger. I wouldn't have believed it for an instant. Well, now we can just be there for each other. You won't have to protect me anymore. Mostly, we'll listen to each other.

Our talk won't be only about serious things. We both learned there can be a storm brewing somewhere even on the most cloudless of days. But that won't stop us from enjoying our blue skies when they come. I hope you'll tell me again how much you love birds. How you learned to take care of them in the winter by making sure they had seeds and berries after a snowfall. I try to follow your example, and I think of you when I do. I think of how you loved working in your garden, even when we were in Pasadena, when the "ground rules" were completely different!

Tell me the story again about how you tried to grow Minnesota flowers in a subtropical zone. What a disaster! Do you remember the night you had us all outside in the back yard with flashlights, collecting snails in plastic bags? You and Dad, my little brother, Mark, and me. We must have seen hundreds of snails chowing down on all the tiny green leaves of the flowers you had just planted that afternoon. I didn't think you would ever recover from the sight. Neither did Dad. While you were trying to save the tiny plants, he was lecturing to us about ecological niches, trying to convince you that Pasadena probably just wasn't the right place for petunias. And that was right around the time of the first moonwalk, too: July 20, 1969. Apollo 11. Remember that night? We watched the whole spectacle on TV. How unreal it all seemed! So now Neil Armstrong's historic boot prints in moon dust are inextricably linked to my memory of us snail-hunting together under the moonlight.

CHAPTER 29: NAMI III

Laura's Story, Part II

About nine months after my first encounter with Joan's daughter, Laura, the NAMI group invited her back for another visit to see how she was doing. By this time, funding had been cut at the Safe Harbor Center at Chesterfield; they lost their director, who had taken another job. Before leaving, however, the director had given Laura special counseling training so that she could step into an advisory role. She was becoming a peer support specialist for the group she had belonged to now for about three years.

This time, rather than sitting among us NAMI parents, Laura took her place at the head of the table as our main presenter and spoke to us about her new job. She admitted she still had ups and downs, still some bad days. But now, the bad days tended to be due to external events rather than internal dysfunction. For a person living with a mental illness, this can be a positive development. As an example, she told us about a recent bureaucratic snafu. One of her prescriptions suddenly stopped being renewed because of a decision made by the insurance provider. We knew Laura was feisty; she would get the paperwork filled out and fight for what she needed. She eventually prevailed, though she joked that it took a few months off her lifespan to do it. She didn't mention anything about Zach, the boyfriend, but it appeared that he was gradually coming around to understand her situation better—after she left. The romantic part of her life remained uncertain.

No matter, Laura looked composed and on top of it, like any other professional woman taking her place in the world. She told us she felt calmer and more anchored now than she had been for decades. The reason: she was able to see how far she had come, knew better how to keep herself balanced. She had a safe place to live. She had a team to help her keep on the path: a case manager, a therapist, a psychiatrist. For the rest, she had valuable work to do, and she knew she could be good at it. She showed us materials she used with her Safe Harbor Center participants—told us about their lives, how she planned activities for them, how well she knew each one, how they problem-solved together. As advisor, she took things as they came; peers trusted her because they knew she had weathered some of the same storms they had.

"I tell them that if they're coming to the Harbor, then I'm going to be their captain. My dad was in the Navy, so I can do that," she said, laughing. I remarked on how much more at ease she seemed this evening. This was my first time to encounter Laura when she was at her best.

"I know not everybody in the group is going to react the same way," she went on. "We're all individuals. Some of my people will come regularly for discussions, for example, but some of them won't. I just figure if someone comes to an activity, then I want to be sure they get something from it. They're welcome to come and participate as much as they want."

She admitted it was harder to reach the men at the Center. She regretted that one of the male counselors who had worked there left after the budget was cut. That was a big loss for everyone, but especially the guys.

"It just seems like the men want a man to be their counselor," she said. "People who already feel so different, like they're on the outs from everybody else, they want to get their mentoring from someone who's walked in their shoes, knows what it's like from *their* perspective. So sometimes, I'll admit, I have more luck with the women. They can relate to me."

We already knew from what Rita told us about her son's time at Safe Harbor Center that it hadn't worked out for him. Maybe Brett couldn't identify. Or maybe he wasn't well enough to understand how the counseling and group support could help him. Before he arrived, it certainly hadn't helped his mental health situation to be out roaming around without any kind of treatment for so long.

"When Brett gets really bad, really delusional and hears voices, he just wants to go to Western State Hospital," Rita said. "He's had so many bad experiences out there in the world. It's as if Western is the only place he feels safe. But we're still looking for a good residential center for him somewhere." They had already tried so many.

On this particular evening, there were about ten young nursing students in attendance, listening intently, along with a few others majoring in social work. Though our core group didn't have the same degree of privacy when students were there, we were glad they could hear all this. We had each introduced ourselves earlier, and we learned that a couple of the students had siblings or other family members with mental illness. One student volunteered that she'd been diagnosed with bipolar herself, was taking medication, and had received counseling. Even at her young age, it had been a long road, but she was doing much better. She asked Laura questions and spoke compellingly about the need for better types of treatment. A student with a personal or family connection to one of these illnesses was especially motivated. I noticed, too, from previous discussions, that some members of the younger generation were far braver about these issues than we had been, at least until now. They were open, ready for change. They would be among those to make it happen.

After the talk, we asked more questions, and Laura affirmed that her work at the Center was by far the most fulfilling she had ever done.

"All I can say is, if you students should be interested in pursuing this as a career, it will be a very demanding one, but I would definitely encourage you if any of you feel the calling. It is stressful, though, I won't lie to you about that. To be honest, I'm not even sure how much longer I can do it. But for however long, I'll continue and do the best I can." Her warmth and sincerity touched us all, and we gave her a round of applause when she concluded.

After the meeting, we stayed for a while, talking, energized. It was as if the whole bunch of us, of completely different ages and life circumstances, were bound together in solidarity. I wondered if Dylan would ever agree to come to a meeting like this. I'd mentioned it to him once; he was reluctant.

I knew Dylan held a hidden fear that he wouldn't be able to fit in, especially not later on, not into a career, not into the life he wanted to have. That night, I felt the need to tell him: Look, don't give up. Don't think the world won't make room for you. Sure, some doors may close in your face; you may have to give up some of your dreams—all that is true. But you can come up with different dreams, new ones. Not everyone is going to run when they find out who you really are. Keep working, keep walking. Just when you think it can't happen, the world will shift and make a place for you.

CHAPTER 30:
VISIONS IN THE SLIPSTREAM

Of course, my dearest wish was to see my son graduate—from Drug Court and from college. These were the double portals through which he had to pass in order to have any kind of regular middle-class life—that's how I saw it. That's what I believed. By the summer of 2013, both were coming into view, but both were still a ways off. Though Dylan thought at first he might be able to finish his degree by December, he later learned that not all his credits from UC would fulfill certain requirements because they'd been based on the quarter system. So, fitting everything in without overloads, it looked like May of 2014 might be the soonest he could earn a diploma. As for Drug Court, Dylan assured me (despite my growing skepticism) that graduations *did* actually occur. All of the current participants attended the ceremonies, too, Dylan said, and they took place only in December and May, the same months as the college graduations. I sighed.

By now, I was getting used to backing off, being in the wings. You'd think I'd also get used to the recovery mantra: one day at a time. But this didn't come easy for me, being a hardcore goal setter.

In fact, until recently, I'd been an administrator whose job entailed creating goals for our small college contingent, and together we'd set timetables for their achievement. However, since we were being judged on our performance, we learned pretty fast not to set goals we weren't at least ninety percent certain we could reach. Needless to say, things can be different in the personal realm.

"Hum . . . any news about when you might graduate from Drug Court?" I would ask Dylan after another May graduation date came and went.

"Well, I was told that I was high risk," he said matter-of-factly. "I have to keep going and wait to graduate DC until I'm ready to finish my college degree, so I'll have both together."

I could definitely see the wisdom of Drug Court's decision to keep him in. I was pretty sure that if Dylan actually finished college, it would be largely because of the structure Drug Court provided. High risk, yes; no argument there. Just this past December there had been another sobriety slip-up. This time, the circumstances were completely different. Dylan hadn't been at a low point; he'd been riding high. It happened that some of his classmates were going out to celebrate the success of a project they'd been working on for weeks. His group's in-class presentation had played well; then someone suggested they all go to a neighborhood bar. Dylan said that under the jubilation of the moment, he'd let down his defenses and instead of ordering a soda, went with beer. Under the rules of Drug Court, he'd admitted what had happened. Now he'd be spending another week in jail, scheduled right after final exams. He would check himself in again, just like at a hotel. This time he didn't feel he'd done anything wrong. It wasn't fair.

"Well, it's not fair, but the world isn't fair," I told him. "Sometimes you just have to know what the rules are for you—not anyone else." Then, to try to cheer him up, I said, "Look, it's just a temporary setback. Just learn from it and keep going." But we both knew he couldn't afford any more slip-ups. His screw-up account at Drug Court was just about maxed out.

So now, by June, we found ourselves entering another summer. Sometimes, it felt like doing the last five miles of a marathon race. Time to take a sip of water and fall deep into a trance-like rhythm of just running and breathing. "We'll all get where we're going eventually," I told myself, trying to fend off the need to cross a finish line out there. In fact, I often wonder if the obsessive goal setting in our midst doesn't interfere with the process of living. Fine, make the goals, then put the list in your back pocket. After all, unlike a race course, there are too many times when the real-life territory ahead doesn't even exist on our maps yet. We have to get there first, then look for a map later—maybe make it up for ourselves as we go along.

It was around this time that a unique opportunity came my way. One of my undergrad college friends put out a call for a possible reunion. She suggested a weekend in mid-June, while she was back visiting in Indiana where her father still lived. By now our group was scattered across the country, but in a relatively short while about five of us signed up. We could stay at Jen's house in Richmond, since she had plenty of space. I'd only been in touch sporadically through the years—mostly on visits to conference cities—but now the prospect of reconnecting was too tempting to pass up. It must have been my age, the times. I was curious to reestablish contact with these women; we'd shared a significant period of our young lives. When we took up residence our freshman year at Todd Hall on the Bloomington campus of Indiana University, we were on the threshold of our adult lives: growing out from under our childhood families, seeking new relationships, making career choices. And all this personal drama was right at the beginning of the 1970s—a time of war, protest, change, and opportunity.

Now many of us were on another threshold: leaving our professions behind, taking on new responsibilities as our parents faced old age, seeing our kids and step-kids go off on their own. How were we doing? How did my former college mates imagine their future lives unfolding from this vantage point? I packed my bags, bringing a few photos of my nearest and dearest with me, as we all agreed to do. Like in grade school, we would have a time for show and tell. We would try our best to catch up on each other's lives. Intriguing, fun, and perplexing.

It made sense to launch my reunion trip to Indiana from John's home in the eastern hill country. When the weekend approached, John encouraged me to be open with my friends about what was going on for me, especially with Dylan. "Look, these are people you can share with. I'm sure they've had plenty of adventures and misadventures, too. Who hasn't had major challenges to deal with by age sixty?" True. I resolved to be brave.

The Friday morning of my trip, John and I trundled my last bag down the steps of the porch and into my car. Whenever one of us left, the other always waved goodbye and waited until the car was gone from view. It was the same today. John rehearsed with me how to take Route 32 to the northwest from Blue Valley. I'd been on it before and loved how this small road curved through woods and meadows, eventually climbing high up to a ridge where you could see for miles around. On a June morning, everything looked so fresh and green along the way: pastures with scattered barns and houses, grazing cattle with names like black Angus and white Charolais, dispersed like beads on velvet, all under blue skies that looked like they could go on forever. It was heaven, rolling free over the hills like that, listening to young Sasha Colette's voice billowing out from the speakers like a strong wave, then pulling back to let the sinuous violin weave in and out around the cowboy dance steps of the electric guitar. The song playing was "Goodbye Buffalo" from her album with The Magnolias, *Ridin' Away*. And when her voice came back again it was to sing about the desire to roam far into the wide-open spaces, leaving all troubles behind, and it felt exactly right for me on that day. After Flemingsburg, you can pick up Route 11, which goes almost straight north, until you come to the AA Route 9, a parkway heading west and north again, following at a distance the curve of the Ohio River all the way to Cincinnati.

I admit I was looking forward to going through Cincinnati again despite—or maybe because of—all the memories I held of that city. I hadn't been there in four years, not since Dylan transferred out of UC. This time I would be going through it solo. When I reached the city from the southeast, I felt a twinge of regret not to be approaching the way I usually did, through Florence and then Covington by the edge of the river, seeing the city from a hilltop, then going over the bridge. So many times I had come in that way, and I always felt the same anticipation. Especially going up that last big slope, slowly, slowly in all that traffic and then, at the top, the Ferris wheel exhilaration of gliding down into the fray, seeing the whole magnificent metropolis spread below on either side, pieces of it tucked into the surrounding hillsides. Back then, I would be excited to meet up with Dylan and see how he was adjusting to college life in the big city.

Maybe it was the influence of the upcoming reunion and traveling back to the past, but on that day I was intent on plunging right into the vortex. Rolling with a multi-lane tide of vehicles, I held my breath because I understood that I would be entering another time zone of my life—already four to seven years distant. As I began flowing under bold green exit signs, each one became a gateway to another memory. Early on came the Hopple Street exit, the one closest to where Dylan lived near the University of Cincinnati. From there, we could visit the Gaslight District with its interesting shops and eateries. Or we could go for walks in one of the nearby parks.

I still had a whole roadmap of those neighborhoods in my head. There were scenes, too, of us strolling about—sometimes just the two of us, but usually three with John there—and Dylan talking a mile a minute like he always did about this and that, with us asking a question or making comments. He sure loved showing off his new city, loved the dynamism of it, the constant movement.

Soon came the Smith-Edwards exit: flashback to an evening together at our favorite Italian restaurant there, the one with the darkened rooms and nostalgic photographs of another era. John was with me, and on this evening we were celebrating Dylan's birthday in full family-style culinary extravagance, joking and laughing as each gargantuan dish was set down before us, right down to the tiramisu for three. As the freeway snaked left and right around the hills, with me gliding along in the middle lane, I thought of another place: the nice, old neighborhood at Hyde Park we'd go to sometimes because it was interesting and had a magnificent grocery store. I flashed back to the produce department: me buying primo foods for Dylan the last year he was there, after the robbery incident in 2008. Dylan liked that store because, as he put it, the upscale middle-class setting reminded him of his journey forward, that even though he was a cash-strapped student, he was still upward bound. So many things happened during those three years back then! Who wouldn't be looking for some oases of everyday normalcy, especially in that last year at the University of Cincinnati?

More twists and turns of the highway, more flash photos coming back to my mind: Dylan's dorm, then his series of apartments. Scenes from different visits we two sets of parents had made, separately or together, played like a shadow movie across the physical evidence of the road I was on now. We'd been all over town with one thing or another. Visits during those three years could be casual, friendly adventures, true. But toward the end of that time, they were more like salvage missions.

Another scene came back, the memory of a district where Mike, Linda, John, and I had convened once. Together, we hunted down an office so that Dylan could pay a traffic ticket and make some progress on his driving record, which by then was only one speeding ticket away from suspension, as I recall. We drove through an amazing neighborhood on our way to find the office. It was an older, black community where people on a nice day would be outside, hanging out, laughing, and hustling. Talk, hustle, and rustle: that's what Dylan loved about the city because he was just that kind of rough and ready person deep down. He loved the ambiance there but, being a white guy from a small town, he didn't exactly fit in. He didn't exactly fit into the college campus scene either. Social life was great, but then there were all those troublesome assignments, the endless schedule of demands. They weren't nearly as easy to navigate as the streets.

Where, exactly, would he ever fit in?

So many adventures and misadventures! Another scene flashed: in a courtroom somewhere in downtown Cincinnati, Dylan facing another traffic violation. Back then, it seemed we were more worried about it than he was. Good God, how many traffic tickets there were! And later, hadn't Dylan vaguely alluded to spending a night in jail up there? How many infractions and summonses and trips to the courtroom and the DMV to get reinstated had there been? Wasn't Dylan always trying to get reinstated somewhere?

Would my son ever be reinstated?

I tried to steady my breath, my hands clutching the wheel. By now, the velocity of memories hit me as hard as the G-forces around every curve. All the while pushing to keep up with the stream of traffic, I flashed back to the other side of the river. June, 2008: another rescue mission. It was after his second year in the city, the year Dylan was out of school, working on his own with his buddy Gabe at a string of temp jobs provided by an agency. Toward the spring he landed one he felt good about, the logistics job at a warehouse near the Cincinnati airport in northern Kentucky. Back then, he used to fly along in this city traffic every day back and forth across the bridge. He was in the maelstrom, being a regular working-class guy trying to hold it together. By then, Gabe could barely pay the rent; his family was insisting he move back home. "But hey, the job I have now is good," Dylan said. "The boss likes me. I'm learning new skills." He was sure he would move up soon. There was always optimism; there were always stories.

One Friday he crossed the city on his lunch break to pick up his check to cash from the temp agency. He had to be back in time to start the afternoon shift, had to floor it to move fast. That's when the cop pulled him over. "Were you aware you were speeding? Sorry, your record is over the point limit now, buddy. We have to impound your car." This predicament gave us the opening we parents had been looking for. We could deliver our ultimatum: "If we come there to help, you have to sell the car and go back to school." He took our offer. John met us up there, too. Seems like during those years we would all step back for a while and then—when disaster struck—we'd convene, explain, make agreements, set up a reimbursement plan, put things back on track again. Until the next time. Then we would feel better, and we would say, "Let's hope this is the lesson he'll finally get."

Is there a lesson out there that he'll finally get? When will this happen?

Why in the world had Mike and Linda and I all thought back then, before any of this started, that Dylan could make it at a big-city campus like this? Didn't he need a more protected environment? Would that have saved him from all the craziness that happened here?

I recalled going with Dylan to visit a small liberal arts college. On the idyllic campus with real ivy growing up the brick buildings, we strolled through a beautiful small quad with giant oaks. Dylan met with an advisor and also a clear-eyed professor who, I'm quite sure, correctly identified him as a wayward youth on the way to meet adulthood at some as-yet undisclosed location. "No, Mom," he told me later, "I'm not like those other Goody Two-Shoes students you see around here. I can't be like them. This place is too small for me." Yep, that's Dylan for you. He always saw himself as an action hero in a place like Gotham City. Bigger than life.

Are you learning now? Who is learning?

Amid fast-moving traffic, it was time to get left quick or risk getting stuck in a logjam further on. I powered through the torrent, taking note of the BMWs, the Lexuses—I've been trained by riding with Dylan to do this. Suddenly, a silver Jaguar convertible glided ahead of me, the driver's short hair bristling in the wind, as if the wind itself were part of an electric current pulling everyone forward to some unknown destiny.

Before long, the sign for Blue Ash exit. Yes, Blue Ash, there among the corporate campuses, that's where the meditation teacher had an office. I took Dylan there several times. A young woman of Indian descent welcomed us: instruction, a mantra, then a ceremony with white cloth, blessings, flowers. "How are you feeling now, Dylan? How did it go?" So many teachers, so many lessons. This could be the answer, I thought back then. This will help him be more mindful, less in conflict with himself. Will this be the key that opens the door?

But wait, I need meditation lessons, too! Don't you see how hard all this is on me?

Yes, we were problem-solvers in my family, but all I really wanted was some kind of peace of mind. For all of us. That goal seemed so simple, and yet so impossible to achieve, the very thing I was least likely to find in the same sentence with my son, Dylan—as if the only time I could truly relax when thinking about Dylan was if he were in some protected zone, in a special community somewhere.

Not jail, exactly, no. But maybe a monastery, or maybe a retreat like Gampo Abbey in Nova Scotia, studying with Pema Chödrön for six years.

Is there not a place somewhere away from this rushing river to find a little peace? If even sages need retreats, then how about us lost folks and sinners? Don't we need them, too?

At that moment, I was still in the midst of a multi-lane traffic stream going at full speed that seemed it would never end. I hung on to the wheel, memories blazing. Who knows where all these cars were going? Yet each one was commandeered by a driver who had a special destination in mind. Each of us would end up somewhere different, but for now we were all here, in this intense stream, this unstoppable flow. While you were in it, you felt it could go on forever. Only the green sign markers reminded me I was still on course.

Before long, making the long arc west, I saw a sign for Fairfield. Yes, Fairfield Mount Mercy Hospital! Another flashback: September 2008. I casually answered the phone early one evening, as I always did back then, because I never knew what was going to happen. Anything could happen. This time, a nurse from Mount Mercy was on the other end, asking for me. Her soft voice seemed hesitant, reluctant to inflict harm. My gut clenched. *What is wrong?* She told me my son was in the emergency room up there; his shoulder had been dislocated; there was blood on his forehead. He was in pain; he was faint. No, he couldn't talk to me. It seemed he might have been shot. All of a sudden, I couldn't breathe, I had to sit down. *No, this can't be happening . . . this can't be real . . shot? In the head? My God! . . .* She told me they would take care of him and she would call again later with more information. There was nothing more I could do. It was all so far away; I was helpless, in shock. I could only wait.

I felt total numbness until almost an hour later, when another phone call came in from the ER. It was Dylan's voice; he could speak. Relief. He could tell me he was going to be OK. He told me the physician at Mercy Hospital set his shoulder, too; his arm was in a sling. He wasn't feeling queasy anymore, just weak. They were going to release him in a short while. That was right after the assault, the time Dylan fought a guy off to keep his money, but the other man had a gun and fired it as they wrestled on the ground. The bullet went right by Dylan's head, grazing his scalp. When the doctor cleaned up the blood, that's what they found. Nothing a surgical staple or two couldn't fix. But I didn't know that for the hour I was waiting in total turmoil, waiting to know if he would even survive.

Dylan claimed all this was a life-changer. No more trusting Nick. No more of the "shady life." *What shady life? What is he talking about? Was Dylan involved in some kind of hustle?* I asked, but I didn't get any straight answers. Ha, Mom will be the last one to suspect anything. Even then, did he know that somehow I'd believe him, believe in his better angels, no matter what?

I hear his voice again. "Mom, I have to go now. I'm going to report this to the police. They're here now. I'll talk to you later. Don't worry. A friend will drive me home." Click.

Maybe Dylan thought he was a cat with nine lives. So which one was he on now, #6? Or was it already #7? Maybe he actually thought he was the Houdini of escape artists. Lock him into a chest and throw him into the sea. He was always sure he could get out, no matter what. But at least Houdini trained for his stunts. Dylan didn't train for his; somehow he'd make a plan and then think that the laws of gravity wouldn't apply to him. He was high on schemes and dreams, low on risk analysis. And meanwhile, I'd be looking for the key, the way to crack open the lock on that mysterious vault of his mind so he would change.

Following the assault, I had gone up to the city to help him get ready for the fall term. John met me partway and we went together. With Dylan looking like a pirate, wearing a sling for his arm and patch on his head, we went to the new IKEA store in West Chester, just north off this same highway. We bought a desk, a chair, and a lamp so he could have what he needed to get back into civilized student life. He said he didn't want to leave the city—not even after such a violent event. He wanted to go back to school. He could do it with help. I was only too happy to inject a dose of normalcy into his life, which always seemed on the verge of spinning out of control. Dylan said he was leaving all that behind, all the bad stuff. He wanted to keep trying. He was like some crazy kind of valiant warrior. Did I attach myself too tightly to his dreams because I felt guilty that he hadn't had a better childhood? A better adolescence? That he'd been sent away when he needed help, and none of us understood what was wrong? Yes, that could be in there, too. The whole stewpot of it.

Was I really helping you then? Am I helping you now? How can I be sure?

Where is the exit I need out of here? I felt I was on the verge of breaking down; it was too much. Why on earth did I think I could go through this city and still hold together? But the traffic was like being in the middle of a tidal wave. I couldn't think fast enough or react smoothly enough to get out of the surge. I could only look ahead and hope to see an exit for the route I needed to take, Route 27 for Indiana. It had to be close. I steadied myself: just breathe and watch.

Finally, there it was, coming up on the right. I rose on the off-ramp, finally out of the maelstrom, easing up on the gas pedal. At the stoplight, I looked around for a place to turn off the road. I spotted a small shopping center nearby, next to an empty field. Turning into all this sudden calm, my car came to an unceremonious halt, as if I'd been flung out of some distant spiral galaxy—my space capsule just fell out of the sky and landed there. I couldn't even get out of my flame-charred tin can yet, though. My eyes brimmed; I couldn't hold back the tears anymore. I crossed my arms over the wheel and just cried.

By the time I stopped, I had no idea how much time had passed. I was still shaken, but there was a release, too. The raspy sound of my breathing mingled with the tumult of thrashing winds in my chest, in my mind. Gradually, it was all slowing down. Like a thousand demon birds had just let go and flown away to their mysterious lairs.

Let's get out of here.

My eyes still burning, I half-crawled out of the car. I had to stretch, move. My whole body ached as if I'd aged by twenty years. "Look at what you've come through," I said to myself. "What we've all come through." I felt twisted and stiff as heavy rope on a cargo ship.

And yet I wouldn't have believed I could take in so much pain, so much disappointment and heartbreak, and still be alive, still be here. My mind flashed back to that tree in Jamaica I saw once, the one in St. Elizabeth Parish near the ocean, the one that's been through hurricanes but is still standing. Coming near, you see it's three feet thick, with a gnarled trunk that gives the impression of being bolted into the earth like a live corkscrew, its twisted roots bracing and coiling themselves to resist the next devastating wall of water from sky or sea.

So now I wonder: how could my family have gone through all this and survived? So much of who I was, or thought I was, had been built around making good plans, seeing them through. So how could I deal with my son, who seemed to be the exact opposite of me? How could I make plans for that? These coiling roads I'd been through: how many painful lessons had been taught in this place? Had I learned any of them? What if all the goal setting and careful planning now, just like then, weren't going to work? What if Dylan had his own ideas, his own timetable for what he was going to learn and when? And from whom? Then what?

Somehow, real life was always escaping from my management concept, and so was my peace of mind.

No, I saw now: I could plan to my heart's content, but there was no way I could ensure what I considered a good outcome. There was no assurance of that. None. What if the learning curve here took a few more loops up and down? What if the life-story dance steps were always going to be two steps forward, one step back—or maybe three steps sideways?

I swung my arms high over my head, twisted back and forth, breathed in, surveyed the open field. I was still searching, still feeling my way through this. In no way was I ready to get on the road again, even if I wanted to keep on my journey. I decided to take a walk, even in this unlikely place. I remembered a conversation I had with Dylan about things. I'd said to him, "Well, you know, maybe you'd do better to just make peace with your anxiety, make peace with the bipolar—just accept it." And he'd replied, "Make peace with it? No way!" Wasn't his method of dealing with the situation to keep it all at bay, try to medicate it away, use chemistry against chemistry so he could keep up the image he wanted to maintain for himself? So now was he learning a different way? Or was he just using Drug Court as a special kind of obstacle course to get through now until later on, when he would be under less scrutiny?

What if the plane I'm in takes a nosedive? What if Dylan doesn't graduate from Drug Court after all? Gets sentenced, has to serve time in jail? Then what?

Truth to tell, I couldn't take my own advice. I wouldn't be able to accept this situation until I had one hundred percent certainty that things were going to turn out fine—as in, no more storms. Security, that's what I wanted. The solid rock of security. Ha! I shook my head. I could already hear Rita's quiet voice coming from right next to me at our monthly NAMI meeting: "Good luck with that," she'd say. She'd been there, too—all of us had. Might as well tell the St. Elizabeth tree, "Don't worry! There will never, ever be another storm on this beach." Good luck with that.

When my stroll took me past a deli, I suddenly realized I hadn't eaten for a long time. Walking out with a cold roast beef sandwich and an iced tea, I headed for the edge of the open field. I still craved space, even if it meant eating my sandwich standing up. Eventually I sat down on the field side edge of the sidewalk and took a few sips of tea. Its cold bitterness was bracing, and I realized how thirsty I was. I bit into the sandwich; it was better than I thought it would be, probably because I was starving. Well, at least there were a few comforts in this world you could count on.

By the time I finished my sandwich, dusted the crumbs off my cargo pants, and went back to sipping my cold tea, I started to feel better. I looked back over the torrential interstate I'd just left, the one that had swept me through the mythic landscape of a thousand traumas. I realized that the city in all its sprawling splendor was that particular way for me—it was today and had been for a while now. But apart from me, the city had its own rhythms, its own patterns. Today was just another day, with many different lives unfolding within its streets and byways. Even at this very moment, someone else was probably getting a traffic ticket, a car impounded, meeting an alluring new girlfriend or boyfriend, meeting up with a smooth, fast-talking acquaintance. And even among the rush of events, there would still be quiet moments, too: lovers meeting to take a walk in the park, a dad playing ball with his young son, a college student setting up a hammock between two trees to read a book. Who could count how many projects were afoot in this place? The sheer puzzle of it all was far beyond the scope of whatever I had imagined lay out there when I crossed the bridge and saw the metropolis as a landscape I was entering for the first time.

So can I just accept my place now on the edge of all this, just take it in, then let it go?

Somehow I needed to be able to appreciate the successes and the good times—and these were very good—without blindly counting on them to go on forever, because I knew everything could turn over in an instant. I needed to be prepared to handle a recurrence, a crisis, a relapse, even an arrest, without falling apart myself. I had to have empathy and love for my son, yes, but I had to set boundaries, too. I had to figure out when I could trust him and when I couldn't, and to know that sometimes the best thing to do would be nothing, straight up. That, or just ask a question. It was his job to unlock his own doors, find his own keys. Life experience would be his teacher, as it had been mine.

I started to feel as if some kind of heavy weight was lifting from me, that godawful responsibility of being a parent. Not completely—that would be far too much to assert—but there was a shift, a space opening up. The bond between my son and me was still there, but I was holding on with less tension, less expectation. Call me ridiculous, call me backward, but I can tell you the fact of it was surprising. Let's say I was starting to see myself as just one little boat in this mysterious stream passing through, and my son was another, over there. And everyone else had their own boat, too, and they were just moving along, doing what they thought they needed to. I wasn't going to have any special powers just because I was a mom. Forget all that secret mission stuff, all that "Mission: Impossible" bravura. I'd played my part on that stage, for sure, and I had made my share of mistakes. But now . . . ? I wanted to forgive myself, forgive my son, and let go.

Come to think of it, even the new young priest at St. Alban's Episcopal recognized the limits to what he could do, and he was half my age. "Look, I can do forgiveness. I can preach love and understanding; I know I can do that," he told me once, flashing his winning smile, standing tall in his long, white robe. "But as for saving people? I'm afraid that's a little above my pay grade." He shook his head. "I have to defer to a higher authority on that one."

I glanced at the sky—slightly overcast, but with intermittent sun—then toward the road ahead. I knew I would have cornfields and a number of small towns to pass through before late afternoon. I had to get going again soon. Enough of the past for one day. Breathe. Take in all that's good. I took out my cell phone.

"John, I made it through Cincinnati. There were so many memories! It was an ordeal; it was like the Fourteen Stations of the Cross at St. Alban's before Easter."

Being a hereditary Episcopalian, he knew exactly what I was talking about.

"So, are you still standing? Are you OK?"

"It was tough, but I'm all right now. I'll make it. I even found my exit here for the way north—a bit harrowing in the traffic, but I found it. I can tell you more later. Right now, I'm just glad the hard part of the drive is behind me."

"Good, well, enjoy the country roads. Take your time. Don't forget to eat some lunch. Maybe you'll find some fresh corn up there at a roadside stand. There should be some this time of year."

"Yes, it'll be nice. I still have plenty of daylight left to get to Jen's house. I'll let you know when I get there. Miss you. Bye!"

I put my phone away and took one last look around, taking the measure of the place. Then I got into my car again and turned in the direction I'd be taking up the road.

CHAPTER 31:
LOOKING OUT THERE TOGETHER

There's a photo of my dad and me that I keep in a special folder. I knew it was from a while back, but I had forgotten the exact period. When I turned over the photo, I could barely read a blurry date: February, 1985. It went back further than I thought, when I was in my early thirties, before Dylan was born. And it wasn't the North Carolina beach in summer. Instead, judging by the sunset, I must have gone with my parents to the Gulf Coast of Florida. That was unusual for us. Suddenly, I realized that this trip must have been taken during my family's first Christmas after my brother's death. Staying at home would have been too painful for my parents; I remember they decided it would be best for us all to go to a new place that year.

My mom loved the beach. She had taken the photo. The three of us were walking on the sand together, and you can see how the sky is orange with a glowing sun about to drift down past the waves on the horizon. A trail of light is reflected on the surface of the water, reaching all the way to the shore. Of course, the lighting was so amazing that I would say to my dad, who happened to have his ever-ready Olympus camera slung on his shoulder, "Let's take a photo of this!" My mom did the honors.

Of course, the resulting picture is not what most people would call a successful photograph. No photographer could admire this into-the-light, dark-on-one-side photo of two people walking along a beach where you can't really see their faces very well. No flash. It doesn't matter. Actually, you can make out that we're both wearing sunglasses; I'm wearing some kind of a striped t-shirt, and my dad is smoking his pipe. Maybe I would prefer to see our faces more clearly, too. And yet I love the photo and cherish it, just as I cherish the moment of quiet intimacy, wonder, and reverie all of us felt that evening. We were trekking up the strand, as far as we could see, way up to the rocky shelf that jutted out into the sea, with waves breaking over it and strange barnacles growing on the sides of the boulders. We'd climb up on top of them for a while, look out to catch sight of any passing boats, then we would turn back and retrace our steps, stopping to admire the antics of seagulls flying in to catch whatever the surf brought in for dinner. During our stay, the sunset walk together was our beach ritual.

The photograph, as well as the strangeness of darkness in the foreground and light coming toward us from the distance, reminds me of a talk I would have alone with my dad in my parents' house back in North Carolina. This was quite a few years later, after I started to open up to my parents about all the problems Mike and I were having with Dylan when he was about sixteen years old. One evening, after my mom went to bed, the two of us talked again about what to do. No one in the family was at all sure of what could be done. Still, we had to make some decision, and we discussed trying the special school, the program we were about to invest in. We knew there were no assurances, but it seemed a worthy attempt at an intervention that could have a positive impact. I remember my dad stretching his legs out from his recliner chair, as he would so often do, then fixing his gaze off into the distance. He probably already had a hint about my mom's illness, how it would slowly erase the memory of the woman he loved and had shared his life with since he was twenty years old. He didn't talk about that, though—not at that time.

And he was probably thinking about Mark, too, about how he hadn't been able to help his son, but maybe he could help his grandson. I remember my dad talked about how we were all in this together, how we were all looking out into the shadows, the mystery of a future that was so uncertain, but we would do the best we could.

That's what John thinks, too. That some problems in life are so deep, so intractable that you just can't solve them. Still, you do the best you can. And we are, we have been, all this time. Just like that day we were walking on the beach. Somewhere between the darkness on one side of us and the glowing light shining on the other.

ACKNOWLEDGMENTS

This book would not be in its present form if it hadn't been for many persons who contributed their time and talents to help bring it all together.

Many thanks to Brooke Warner's entrepreneurial skills and the strong editing, coaching, and design team she has put together at She Writes Press. It's been wonderful to have such support through a complicated process.

I'm happy that artist James Secor of Montpelier, Vermont agreed to work with me to provide the portraits and drawings that accompany the text. More of his artwork can be found at *www. jamessecor.com*. Thank you to Angela Palm, author of *Riverine*, who applied her copyediting skills to the manuscript and kept me on track with my verb tenses and many other writerly matters. Great appreciation expressed to Susannah Felts, co-founder of the Porch Writers' Collective in Nashville, for agreeing to give a read-through with suggestions. She taught a course in creative non-fiction that helped me re-tool in the early stages of writing, and since then the Porch has provided a steady stream of informative, inspirational workshops for local writers like me.

I'm very grateful that individual members of NAMI gave their consent to sharing their family stories (with names changed) beyond our support group. Surely, there are more of us than we know.

Heartfelt thanks to the Green River Writers Group of Louisville for their welcoming spirit and astute critiques. As various chapters rolled through at our camp-like retreats, so did the useful questions, tips, and suggestions from the alert assembly. Couldn't ask for a more generous bunch of writers and readers!

A very special thank you to my early full-draft readers, whose comments contributed so much, each in their own way, to making this a better book: Ernie O'Dell, Meg Brown, Ann Marie Montgomery, Brenda Benson, Jim Benson, Brenda Harrington, and Reika Ebert. And many thanks to poet Jean Tucker, whose stamina often went beyond my own as her sharp eye and editing pencil cut through many a vine of wayward prose.

I thank the members of my family (both alive and those no longer living) for their love, support, wisdom, lessons, and inspiration—even when I wasn't always ready to receive their gifts. *Shalom* and love to all of you.

And I especially thank John—mostly for staying with me. He has been my first and principal reader/commentator all along. He's also been principal advisor, therapist, and pit crew foreman. In all these capacities, he not only helped me to keep writing about the experiences recounted in this book, but—more importantly—to live through them.

REFERENCES

Akiskal, Hagop. "Developmental Pathways to Bipolarity: Are Juvenile Onset Depressions Pre-Bipolar?" *Journal of the American Academy of Child and Adolescent Psychiatry* 34:6 (1995): 754-763.

Akiskal, Hagop. "The Evolving Bipolar Spectrum: Prototypes I, II, III, and IV." *Psychiatric Clinics of North America* 22:3 (1999): 517-534.

Barks, Coleman. *A Year with Rumi.* New York: HarperCollins, 2006.

Bissinger, Buzz. *Father's Day.* New York: Houghton Mifflin Harcourt, 2012.

Brown, Brené. *Rising Strong.* New York: Speigel and Grau, 2015.

Carroll, Lewis. *Alice's Adventures in Wonderland (1865)* and *Through the Looking Glass (1871).* New York: Alfred A. Knopf, 1992.

Chopra, Deepak. *Perfect Health*. New York: Harmony/Crown Publications, 1991.

Cloud, David. "On Life Support: Public Health in the Age of Mass Incarceration." Vera Institute of Justice, Nov. 2014. www.vera.org/publications.

Eagleman, David. *Incognito: The Secret Lives of the Brain*. New York: Pantheon, 2011.

Gravity. Directed by Alfonso Cuarón, 2013. (Burbank, CA: Warner Home Video, DVD.)

James, Doris J. and Lauren E. Glaze. "Mental Health Problems of Prison and Jail Inmates." *Bureau of Justice Statistics Special Report*, Sept. 2006.

Jamison, Kay Redfield. *An Unquiet Mind*. New York: Alfred A. Knopf, 1995.

Kerman, Piper. *Orange is the New Black*. New York: Spiegel and Grau, 2010.

LeDoux, Joseph. *The Emotional Brain: The Mysterious Underpinnings of Emotional Life*. New York: Simon and Schuster, 1996.

MacDonald, Ann (ed.). "How addiction hijacks the brain." *Harvard Mental Health Letter* 28:1 (2011): 1-3.

Peck, M. Scott. *The Road Less Traveled*. New York: Simon and Schuster, 1978.

Sacks, Oliver. *On the Move.* New York: Alfred A. Knopf, 2015.

Shapiro, Rami. *Recovery, the Sacred Art: The Twelve Steps as Spiritual Practice.* Woodstock, VT: SkyLight Paths, 2009.

Skowyra, Kathleen R. and Joseph J. Cocozza, Ph.D. "Blueprint for Change: A Comprehensive Model for the Identification and Treatment of Youth With Mental Health Needs in Contact with the Juvenile Justice System." The National Center for Mental Health and Juvenile Justice, 2007.

Tupac Uncensored and Uncut: The Lost Prison Tapes. Directed by Ken Peters (2009), based on interview with Tupac Shakur in 1995. (New York: Cinedigm, 2011, DVD.)

FOR FURTHER READING

Chödrön, Pema. *When Things Fall Apart: Heart Advice for Difficult Times.* Boulder: Shambhala, 2016 (1997). An American Buddhist trained in the Tibetan tradition teaches practices of non-judgmental awareness and compassion for self and others that many find relevant to their lives today.

Fast, Julie A. and John Preston. *Take Charge of Bipolar Disorder: A 4-Step Plan for You and Your Loved Ones to Manage the Illness and Create Lasting Stability.* New York: Grand Central Life & Style/ Hachette, 2006. Written by a knowledgeable team, this is a useful workbook to treat and train for a life with bipolar. Includes individual stories and clear explanations of bipolar behaviors along with space to write out your own observations/goals. I especially appreciate the text boxes addressed to family and friends on specific ways to help your loved one.

Fawcett, Jan, M.D., Bernard Golden, Ph.D. and Nancy Rosenfeld. *New Hope for People with Bipolar Disorder.* New York: Random House, 2006, 2007. This book gives a solid overview of the illness, treatments, medications, therapies, lifestyle adaptations.

Federman, Russ, Ph.D. and J. Anderson Thomson, Jr., M.D. *Facing Bipolar: The Young Adult's Guide to Dealing with Bipolar Disorder*. Oakland, CA: New Harbinger, 2010. Written by a university mental health counselor, this book offers advice for persons in their twenties learning to grapple with the challenges of an autonomous, bipolar-under-treatment life.

Forney, Ellen. *Rock Steady: Brilliant Advice from My Bipolar Life*. Seattle, WA: Fantagraphics Books, 2018. A cartoonist shows the complexity of staying stable through personal experience, advice, and coping tools gleaned over fourteen years of balance adjustments. Funny drawings and bold layout will appeal to your arty, tactile, kinetic side.

Greene, Esq., J. D., and Olivia Allen. "Disrupting School-Justice Pathways for Youth with Behavioral Health Needs," *National Council of Juvenile and Family Court Judges*, 2017. This is one of the studies available from the National Center for Mental Health and Juvenile Justice at https://www.ncmjhjj/resources. It shows how setting up a School Responder Model (SRM) can help schools, families, and courts work together to get at-risk kids into behavioral health treatment before they get arrested.

Kennedy, Patrick J. and Stephen Fried. *A Common Struggle: A Personal Journey Through the Past and Future of Mental Illness and Addiction*. New York: Blue Rider/Penguin Random House, 2015. This personal testimony comes from within the Kennedy family, and is followed by the author's recommendations for evidence-based policy changes to improve outcomes for people with mental health disorders.

Lederman, Judith S. and Candida Fisk, M.D. *The Ups and Downs of Raising a Bipolar Child: A Survival Guide for Parents*. New York: Simon and Schuster, 2003.

Long, Liza. *The Price of Silence: A Mom's Perspective on Mental Illness*. New York: Hudson/Penguin, 2014. A courageous mom talks about her family's difficulties and makes the case to show why these issues matter to everyone. Long is also the author of "I am Adam Lanza's mother," an article published after Sandy Hook Elementary shooting.

Lowe, Chelsea and Bruce M. Cohen, M.D., Ph.D. *Living with Someone Who's Living with Bipolar Disorder*. San Francisco, CA: Jossey-Bass/Wiley, 2010. This is another good book for family, friends, partners, or co-workers of people living with bipolar.

Miklowitz, David J., Ph.D. *The Bipolar Disorder Survival Guide*. 3rd ed. New York: Guilford, 2019. This comprehensive classic by a respected physician in the field remains the main map of Bipolarland that later guides follow.

Miklowitz, David J., Ph.D. and Elizabeth L. George, Ph.D. *The Bipolar Teen: What You Can Do to Help Your Child and Your Family*. New York: Guilford, 2007.

Papolos, Demetri, M.D. and Janice Papolos. *The Bipolar Child*. 3rd ed. New York: Broadway, 2006. Ths guide, for parents navigating the confusing complexities of this disorder in children and adolescents, offers useful advice and resources for life at home, at school, and with doctors and health insurance providers. It also contains important guidance in preparing an IEP (Individualized Education Program) for your child at your local school, and is accompanied by a website: https://bipolarchild.com.

Pierce-Baker, Charlotte. *This Fragile Life: A Mother's Story of a Bipolar Son*. Chicago: Lawrence Hill Books, 2012. This is a riveting account of how two professional parents coped with young adult-onset bipolar, addiction, jail, trauma, and the costly search for treatment. The book includes a useful list of resources.

Pozatek, Krissy. *The Parallel Process: Growing Alongside your Adolescent or Young Adult Child in Treatment*. New York: Lantern Books, 2011. A therapist's guide that shows parents how they can let go of old patterns and grow new ones, even as their kids struggle with responsibility and self-awareness in treatment.

Sheff, David. *Beautiful Boy: A Father's Journey through His Son's Addiction*. New York: Houghton Mifflin, 2008. This book chronicles a father's close relationship with the son of his first marriage, Nic, even as the teen falls down a rabbit hole of meth addiction and treatment cycles that impact Sheff's new family, as well as Nic's mom. Guilt, remorse, rebuilding, boundaries: they all come up in this story.

Sheff, Nic. *Tweak: Growing Up on Methamphetamines*. New York: Atheneum, 2008. This through-the-looking-glass, parallel memoir (by the son of the author of the above book) tells how he became addicted and why he preferred self-medication to taking prescribed pharmaceuticals, and describes his struggles/ruses in treatment programs. The television screenwriter has continued to be open about his life with bipolar and his efforts to maintain recovery, in articles published online at https://www.thefix.com and elsewhere.

USEFUL RESOURCES

Active Minds
https://activeminds.org
Nonprofit organization of college students dedicated to raising
awareness of mental health issues on campus and beyond.

Al-Anon [for family]
https://al-anon.org

Alcoholics Anonymous
https://www.aa.org

Bp Magazine
https://www.bphope.com
Printed and online magazine with useful articles to help someone
live with, or next to, the complexities of bipolar disorder. Articles
often stem from someone's personal experience walking the walk.
Takes a problem-solving, creative, colorful, upbeat approach.

Brain and Behavior Research Foundation (BBRF)

https://www.bbrfoundation.org

Provides competitive research grants to neuroscientists seeking to better understand and treat brain circuitry disorders like schizophrenia, bipolar, severe depression, autism, etc. Families and donors are educated about scientists' work through online newsletters, webinars, and conferences.

Bring Change 2 Mind

https://bringchange2mind.org

Co-founded by Glenn Close after her sister Jessie was diagnosed with bipolar after many troubled years. Encourages open conversation about a variety of mental health issues to promote understanding and improve lives.

Child Mind Institute

https://childmind.org

National non-profit dedicated to transforming the lives of children who struggle with mental health and learning disorders. An excellent resource for families, teachers, and policymakers.

Depression Bipolar Support Alliance (DBSA)

https://www.dbsalliance.org

Major organization to promote understanding and empowerment of those living with these illnesses. Hosts support groups, trains peer mentors, and provides community for those in need.

Juvenile Bipolar Research Foundation

https://www.jbrf.org

Provides wide-ranging information enabling families and clinicians to work together to provide better outcomes for children and adolescents. Gives guidance for finding alternative education possibilities or residential treatment if needed.

Mental Health America
www.mentalhealthamerica.net
Community-based non-profit dedicated to promoting the mental health of all Americans. Known for its "B4Stage4" philosophy: create awareness and treat mental health conditions long before they reach crisis level.

Mental Health Recovery
https://mentalhealthrecovery.com
Features Mary Ellen Copeland's template for setting up a Wellness Recovery Action Plan (WRAP), a tool that can help persons at risk and their loved ones be able to recover more quickly and safely from a mental health crisis.

Narcotics Anonymous
https://www.na.org

National Alliance on Mental Illness (NAMI)
www.nami.org
Largest grass-roots organization set up to educate, support, and advocate for those living with mental illnesses as well as their families. Offers peer support groups. A good place to start finding other local resources available.

National Center for Mental Health and Juvenile Justice
https://www.ncmhjj
Agency founded in 2001 that aims to improve outcomes for youth with mental health, substance abuse, or trauma-related conditions who have come into contact with the juvenile justice system. Offers research, training, and strategic planning for schools and court systems, so they can work together with families to help kids in crisis get the care they need to continue in school and stay out of jail.

Oxford House
www.oxfordhouse.org
Self-run, self-supported recovery houses for adults who have addiction issues. Founded in 1975 and listed on the National Registry of Evidence-Based Programs and Practices, Oxford Houses offer housing, community, and accountability for adults in transition from detox/jail/prison to a life of recovery on the outside.

Substance Abuse and Mental Health Services (SAMHSA)
www.samhsa.gov
Government agency created to make this critical aspect of health care more widely accessible. Consult website to find critical hotlines, information, and the behavioral health centers supported by SAMHSA located nearest to you.

Treatment Advocacy Center
https://www.treatmentadvocacycenter.org
Source of legal and policy information for families of adults who are most severely impacted by mental illness and who refuse treatment. Helps to legislate Assisted Outpatient Treatment (AOT) and to advise local Mental Health Courts.

Vera Institute of Justice
https://www.vera.org
Nonprofit organization committed to securing equal justice for all, ending mass incarceration, and strengthening families and communities. Produces thought-provoking criminal justice research studies and promotes pathways to reform.

ABOUT THE AUTHOR

J anice Morgan formerly taught courses in French language, liter-
ature, and cultural history as a college teacher in rural Kentucky.
During that career, she wrote about social issues in French cinema,
publishing in *The French Review*, *Cinema Journal*, and the *Quarterly
Review of Film and Video*. Based on her family's experiences, she
now advocates for better mental health awareness, substance abuse
recovery, and criminal justice reform.

Author photo © John Secor

SELECTED TITLES FROM SHE WRITES PRESS

She Writes Press is an independent publishing company founded to serve women writers everywhere. Visit us at www.shewritespress.com.

Blinded by Hope: One Mother's Journey Through Her Son's Bipolar Illness and Addiction by Meg McGuire. $16.95, 978-1-63152-125-6. A fiercely candid memoir about one mother's roller coaster ride through doubt and denial as she attempts to save her son from substance abuse and bipolar illness.

Off the Rails: One Family's Journey Through Teen Addiction by Susan Burrowes. $16.95, 978-1-63152-467-7. An inspiring story of family love, determination, and the last-resort intervention that helped one troubled young woman find sobriety after a terrifying and harrowing journey.

Saving Bobby: Heroes and Heroin in One Small Community by Renee R. Hodges. $16.95, 978-1631523755. A raw, honest, deeply moving memoir about the difficulties of managing recovery from opioids—the number one killer of American kids age 18–25—told from the perspective of the addict's aunt, who took him in and dedicated herself to helping her nephew save himself.

Searching for Normal: The Story of a Girl Gone Too Soon by Karen Meadows. $16.95, 978-1-63152-137-9. Karen Meadows intertwines her own story with excerpts from her daughter Sadie's journals to describes their roller coaster ride through Sadie's depression and a maze of inadequate mental health treatment and services—one that ended with Sadie's suicide at age eighteen.

Loving Lindsey: Raising a Daughter with Special Needs by Linda Atwell. $16.95, 978-1631522802. A mother's memoir about the complicated relationship between herself and her strong-willed daughter, Lindsey—a high-functioning young adult with intellectual disabilities.

Scattering Ashes: A Memoir of Letting Go by Joan Rough. $16.95, 978-1-63152-095-2. A daughter's chronicle of what happens when she invites her alcoholic and emotionally abusive mother to move in with her in hopes of helping her through the final stages of life—and her dream of mending their tattered relationship fails miserably.